199_ EDITION

The Zondervan Minister's Tax & Financial Guide

Daniel D. Busby, CPA

ZondervanPublishingHouse
Grand Rapids, Michigan

A Division of HarperCollinsPublishers

1997 MINISTER'S TAX AND FINANCIAL GUIDE

THE ZONDERVAN MINISTER'S TAX AND FINANCIAL GUIDE: 1997 EDITION

Copyright © 1996 by Daniel D. Busby

For information, write to:
Zondervan Publishing House
Grand Rapids, Michigan 49530

Publisher's note: This guide is published in recognition of the need for clarification of the income tax laws for ministers. Every effort has been made to publish a timely, accurate, and authoritative guide. The publisher, author, and the reviewers do not assume any legal responsibility for the accuracy of the text or any other contents.

Taxpayers are cautioned that this book is sold with the understanding that the publisher is not engaged in rendering legal, accounting, or other professional service. You should seek the professional advice of a tax accountant, lawyer, or preparer for specific tax questions.

References to IRS forms and tax rates are derived from preliminary proofs of the 1996 forms or 1995 forms and some adaptation for changes may be necessary. These materials should be used solely as a guide in filling out your 1996 tax return. To obtain the final forms, schedules, and tables for filing your return, contact the IRS or a public library.

ISBN 0-310-21060-7

All rights reserved. No part of this publication may be reproduced, stored in a retrieval system, or transmitted in any form or by any means—electronic, mechanical, photocopy, recording, or any other—except for brief quotations in printed reviews, with the prior permission of the publisher.

Printed in the United States of America

96 97 98 99 /DH/ 10 9 8 7 6 5 4 3 2 1

Contents...

■ 1996 New Developments 1

■ Form 1040 Line by Line 13

■ 1 Taxes for Ministers 19

- Ministers serving local churches 20
- Evangelists and missionaries 21
- Members of religious orders 22
- Ministers in denominational service, administrative, and teaching positions 24
- Individuals not qualifying for ministerial tax treatment 26
- Social security status of ministers 27
- Income tax status of ministers 27
- Forms and schedules for the minister 30
- Importance of the employee vs. self-employed decision 31
- Recommended filing status 32

■ 2 Compensation and Financial Planning 33

- How much should a minister be paid? 34
- Can pay be too high? 35
- Plan your compensation 35
- Avoid recharacterization of income 38
- Use fringe benefits wisely 39
- Use accountable expense reimbursements 40
- Money and the minister's family 41

3 The Pay Package 45

- Should you delay paying tax on a portion of your salary? 45
- How much income can you defer? 46
- Can churches discriminate when providing fringe benefits? 46
- Tax Treatment of compensation, fringe benefits, and reimbursements 47
- Table of compensation, fringe benefits, and reimbursements 64

4 Home Sweet Home 67

- Types of housing arrangements 69
- Structuring the housing allowance 71
- Reporting the housing allowance to the minister 74
- Accounting for the housing allowance 75
- Other housing allowance issues 77
- Housing allowance worksheets 80

5 Business Expenses 83

- Accountable and nonaccountable expense reimbursement plans 83
- Documenting and reporting business expenses 86
- Travel and transportation expenses 87
- Auto expense deductions 90
- Other business and professional expenses 95
- Allocation of business expenses 99

6 Social Security Tax 101

- Computing the self-employment tax 102
- Both spouses are ministers 103
- Self-employment tax deductions 105
- Use of voluntary withholding agreement to pay social security taxes ... 105
- Opting out of social security 106

- Working after you retire 109
- Canada Pension Plan 110

7 Paying Your Taxes 111

- Tax withholding 111
- Estimated tax 112
- Excess social security withheld (FICA) 114
- Earned income tax credit 114
- Extension of time to file 114
- Extension of time to pay 116
- Filing an amended tax return 117

Sample Returns 123

- Example No. 1
  Minister-employee for income tax purposes
  (accountable plan) 125

- Example No. 2
  Minister-employee for income tax purposes
  (nonaccountable plan) 135

- Example No. 3
  Minister as self-employed for income tax purposes 148

Citations 158

Index 166

Important Tax Dates for 1997 170

INTRODUCTION

Yes, you can understand the tax rules for ministers! It's easier than ever with this year's edition of the Guide.

Taxes can be a very unpleasant aspect of your personal finance. You don't have time or the interest to master thousands of pages of complex tax laws and regulations. But you want a basic understanding of the tax strategies available to ministers.

This book is the one for you—written in plain English, clearly explained—advice you can act on. And there are icons in the margins to direct your attention to the most important provisions in the book.

Tip   This marks strategy recommendations for saving your tax dollars.

Planning Idea   This alerts you to ideas for tax or compensation planning steps that can save you taxes in future years.

Key Issue   These are the most basic provisions in the tax law that impact ministers.

Remember   This is a friendly reminder of information to review that you'll definitely want to remember.

Action Steps   This highlights easy-to-follow steps to structure your tax planning.

Caution   This marks subjects that you should carefully study to achieve the best tax treatment.

Warning!   This alerts you to some of the most serious tax mistakes made by ministers.

Cross Reference   This is a reminder that more material on a topic appears in the companion guide, the *Zondervan Church and Nonprofit Tax and Financial Guide.*

1996 New Developments

Congress did not pass a major tax bill in 1996. However, certain legislative provisions were signed into law that will significantly affect many ministers. This chapter also includes court decisions, IRS rulings, and regulations of importance to ministers.

Greene Tax Court case focuses on employee vs. self-employed status of a minister/missionary

Richard G. and Anne C. Greene petitioned the U.S. tax court asking the court to overturn a determination made by the Commissioner of Internal Revenue that Rev. Greene was an employee of the Department of Foreign Missions (DFM), General Counsel of the Assemblies of God, for the 1993 tax year.

Rev. Greene took the position that the General Counsel of the Assemblies of God did not exert the degree of control that would normally exist in an employer/employee relationship. The DFM did not invest in Rev. Greene's work facilities, provided Rev. Greene with no employee benefits, and did not have the right to terminate Rev. Greene as a missionary. While both the DFM and Rev. Greene hoped for a permanent relationship, Rev. Greene was free to resign his position at any time. Further, Rev. Greene had the possibility of losing money in his attempts to obtain adequate funding for his missionary work, which was admittedly the type of work which the DFM was formed to support. Also, neither the DFM nor Rev. Greene believed they were creating an employer/employee relationship. Rather, both parties operated under the belief that Rev. Greene was self-employed.

In the IRS court brief, the IRS took the position that Rev. Greene was an employee and cited the Weber case which found Rev. Weber (a United Methodist Minister) to be an employee of a local church. They cited the Assemblies of God church's right to control the means and details of a DFM-endorsed missionary's work beginning with the missionary's initial involvement with the church as a minister and continuing through the eventual service in a mission field.

The ruling in this case is not expected until early in 1997. The DFM treats all its missionaries as self-employed for income tax purposes. Therefore, this ruling could have a significant impact on hundreds of missionaries.

IRS reduces recordkeeping requirements for business receipts

The receipt threshold for lodging expenditures and any other expenditure of $25 or more was increased from $25 to $75 effective for expenditures incurred on or after October 1, 1995. Churches and nonprofit organizations may still require receipts for expenditures of less than $75 based on administrative discretion.

Spouse travel and club dues treated as income

The IRS has announced that the payment of club dues and spouse travel expenses by an employer may constitute income to the employee recipient. 1993 tax legislation provided that no deduction was allowed for most club dues and spouse travel expenses. However, the provisions had little practical impact on churches and other nonprofit organizations because deductibility is not an issue.

In regulations issued in 1996, the IRS dealt with the issue of when the non-deductible expenses must be treated as income to the recipient and thus reported to the IRS Form W-2 at year-end. While dues paid to country clubs, social clubs, and airline and hotel clubs are non-deductible to a church or nonprofit, they are taxable to the employee on whose behalf the payments are made to the extent that the employee uses the club for personal purposes.

For example, if a church or nonprofit pays for a staff member to belong to the Northwest Airlines Club, the payment qualifies as a non-taxable working condition fringe benefit to the staff member only if the club is used 100% of the time for business. If, however, the employee uses the club 25% for personal use, e.g., on family vacations, 25% of the cost must be reported on Form W-2.

In the case of employer-paid expenses for the travel of a spouse, dependent, or guest of a staff member, the payment will qualify as a non-taxable working condition fringe benefit only if the expenses would otherwise be a deductible business expense and if the employee adequately substantiates the expenses.

What is the bottom line for churches and nonprofits? If an employee's club memberships or spouse/dependent/guest travel are paid or reimbursed by the employer, be sure proper records are kept and that the personal-use portion of the expenditures are reported to the IRS on Form W-2 or 1099 when applicable.

College is "integral agency" of church for self-employment tax purposes

The IRS recently ruled that a certain college is an integral agency of a church and that ministers who teach at the college are performing qualified ministerial services and are therefore subject to self-employment tax.

The church consisted of a confederation of churches under congregational government. For theological reasons, the church doesn't have a central governing body or term itself a "denomination." Its congregations form a close-knit federation with common doctrines and goals.

The congregations cooperate with one another to establish and maintain various "parachurch" institutions, including missionary organizations, charitable organizations, and colleges. The IRS concluded that the college is an integral agency of the church. Accordingly, ministers who teach at the college are treated as other qualified ministers for self-employment tax purposes.

Schedule C-EZ use is expanded

For 1996, more taxpayers will be eligible to use Schedule C-EZ. The form may be used if your self-employment gross income is $25,000 or less and your expenses are $2,500 or less (up from $2,000).

Wiring refunds to your bank

You are no longer required to file Form 8888 to have your tax refund wired to your bank. Lines have been added to Form 1040 for account and bank routing numbers.

Social security earnings limit increased

New legislation allows senior ministers to earn more money without losing their social security benefits.

For some time, ministers under age 70 who received social security benefits lost some of those benefits if their earned income exceeded certain levels. Ministers under age 65 who earn more than $8,280 in 1996 lose one dollar of benefits for each $2 of earned income above the limit. That is a 50% tax rate on those earnings imposed on top of the regular federal and state income taxes. In the new law this limit for social security recipients under age 65 is not changed, but the annual earnings limit does continue to be indexed for inflation each year.

Ministers aged 65 to 69 lose one dollar of benefits for every three dollars earned above the limit. The new law raises the earnings limit to $12,500 (up from the prior $11,520 limit) for 1996. It rises each year through the year 2002 (see the schedule in the box). Once you reach age 70, the earnings limit does not apply. You can earn all the money you want without having your social security benefits reduced.

The limit applies only to "earned income" — wages, salaries, bonuses, commissions, and so on. Investment income is considered unearned and does not affect your benefits.

New Social Security Earnings Limit
For Recipients ages 65 through 69

Year	Limit
1997	$13,500
1998	14,500
1999	15,500
2000	17,000
2001	25,000
2002	30,000

Social security taxable limit increases

The maximum amount of taxable and creditable annual earnings subject to the social security and self-employment income tax increased to $62,700 in 1996, up from $61,200 in 1995. There is no maximum wage base for Medicare.

1996 standard mileage rates

The optional standard mileage rates for employees, self-employed individuals, and other taxpayers to use in computing the deductible costs paid in 1996 in connection with the operation of a passenger automobile for business, charitable, medical, or moving expense purposes are as follows:

Type of Expense	1996 Rate (per mile)
Business	31 cents
Charitable	12 cents
Moving/Medical	10 cents

1996 depreciation deduction limits

The 1996 automobile deduction limits remain the same as for 1995. The annual limits on depreciation deductions for automobiles first placed in service in 1996 are as follows:

Tax Year	Amount
1st Tax Year	$3,060
2nd Tax Year	4,900
3rd Tax Year	2,950
Each Succeeding Year	1,775

Lessees of "luxury" cars for business will have imputed income on automobiles that cost more than $15,500 and are first leased in 1996. Thus, leased cars have a similar deduction limit as purchased cars.

You need not face the same IRS auditor in consecutive audits

At the taxpayer's request, an IRS examiner must be pulled from an audit if he or she has examined your return for any of the past three tax years, unless there has been an intervening audit by a different IRS examiner. This policy does not restrict agents from widening an audit to prior years.

As in the past, if the IRS has examined your return for the same items in either of the last two years and proposed no change, the IRS will call off the audit if asked.

New commuting fringe threshold for 1996

For 1996, a church can sell transit passes and tokens to ministers at discounts of up to $65 per month tax-free, up from $60 per month in 1995. Or, a church can just give cash in 1996 of up to $65 for passes and tokens tax-free. Also, if a church gives a minister a parking space near its premises, it is tax-free to the minister up to a value of $165 per month in 1996, up from $160 in 1995. It is also tax-free up to $165 per month if the minister rents a space near the church's premises and is reimbursed. The cost of a parking space located at the minister's residence is taxable to the minister regardless of its proximity to the employer's premises.

1996 tax rate and other changes

Here are a few of the key changes in the tax law for 1996:

✓ The refundable earned income credit increased in 1996. Low-income workers (earning up to $25,078) with one child are eligible to receive a maximum credit of $2,152. A maximum credit of $3,556 is available if income is under $28,495 with two or more children. With no children, the maximum credit is $323 (7.65% of first $4,220 earned), phasing out at $9,500.

✓ The amount of investment income children under age 14 can receive before it is taxed at their parents' maximum tax rate remains at $1,300 for 1996.

✓ The standard deduction and personal exemption amounts are adjusted as follows:

	1995	1996
Standard deduction:		
Married couples	$6,550	$6,700
Head of household	5,750	5,900
Single	3,900	4,000
Dependent children	650	650
Personal exemption	2,500	2,550

✓ The tax rates and brackets for 1996 are slightly larger because of the inflation adjustments. For example the married income tax brackets are as follows:

If taxable income is	The tax is
Not over $40,100	15% of taxable income
Over $40,100 but not over $96,900	$6,015 + 28% of excess over $40,100
Over $96,900 but not over $147,700	$21,919 + 31% of excess over $96,900
Over $147,700 but not over $263,750	$37,667 + 36% of excess over $147,700
Over $263,750	$79,455 + 39.6% of excess over $263,750

Elective deferral limit increased

The cost-of-living adjustment applicable to the exclusion for elective deferrals provides an increase from $9,240 to $9,500 for 1996.

More time allowed for payment before adding interest

Under the former rules, 10 calendar days were permitted for payment before the IRS added more interest. The 10 calendar days has been expanded to 21 calendar days. And the IRS will be able to forgive interest in more instances where there are audit delays.

Private delivery services approved

Effective with 1996 tax returns, private delivery services may be used the same as the U.S. mail as proof of timely submission of tax returns. You will have to wait for regulations to be issued, however, before you know which private delivery services are acceptable.

Retired minister's parsonage allowance tax-free for social security purposes

The IRS had issued guidelines that would include retirement benefits received from a church plan as earnings subject to self-employment social security tax purposes for retired ministers. The guidelines would have continued to exempt a retired minister's housing allowance, properly designated by a church pension board, for income tax purposes.

Based on 1996 legislation, and retroactive to January 1, 1995, a minister is not subject to social security tax on retirement benefits received from a church pension plan. Neither is the rental value of housing allowance, including utilities, furnished to a minister after retirement subject to self-employment taxes. This provision nullifies the attempt by the IRS to tax these amounts for social security purposes.

Savings Incentive Match Plans for Employees (SIMPLE plans)

Starting in 1997, churches with 100 or fewer employees who received at least $5,000 in compensation from the church in a preceding year may adopt a SIMPLE plan if they do not currently maintain another qualified plan. The plan allows employees to make elective contributions of up to $6,000 per year and requires churches to make matching contributions. Assets in the account are not taxed until they are distributed to an employee. SIMPLE plans are not subject to the nondiscrimination rules.

Self-employed ministers and chaplains eligibility for tax-sheltered annuities and church retirement plans clarified

Effective for 1997, ministers who are self-employed for income tax purposes may now participate in 403(b) tax-sheltered annuity programs. This change in the law applies to ministers employed by a church or by organizations other than nonprofits (such as chaplains). Prior to 1997, it was not clear if tax-deferred salary reductions could be made by ministers filing as self-employed for income tax purposes.

Another portion of the law provides that ministers who are self-employed for income tax purposes and ministers, such as chaplains, who are employed by organizations other than nonprofit entities may participate in church retirement plans.

Highly compensated definition changed for church pension plans

The simplification rules also provide that church pension plans subject to the pre-ERISA nondiscrimination rules will apply the same definition of highly compensated employees as other pension plans, rather than the pre-ERISA rule relating to employees who are officers and persons whose principal duties consist of supervising the work of other employees or highly compensated employees. Under the new law, highly compensated employees are defined as employees earning over $80,000 (indexed for inflation) and the highest paid officer rule is repealed.

Special missionary exemption created

Under former law, employer amounts paid towards an annuity contract were treated as an employee investment (creates tax basis making later distributions tax-free) if the amounts would have been excluded from income if paid directly to the employee. However, if the exclusion is based on the foreign earned income exclusion, no basis is created.

A special foreign missionary exemption takes effect January 1, 1997, that allows employer contributions to create tax basis if the amount would have been excludable as a foreign earned income exclusion if paid directly to the missionary. The law applies to contributions made by an employer for an individual who is performing services outside of the U.S. and who is either: (1) a duly ordained, commissioned, or licensed minister of a church, or (2) a layperson.

Compensation definition changed for tax-sheltered annuities

Increased amounts may be contributed to a defined contribution plan on behalf of nonhighly compensated employees effective January 1, 1998. The definition of compensation has been changed to include elective employee contributions to 403(b), 401(k), and cafeteria plans.

Educational assistance rules reinstated

The exclusion from gross income for employer-provided educational assistance (up to $5,250 per individual) was reinstated for 1995, 1996, and 1997. The exclusion is not available for expenses related to graduate-level courses beginning after June 30, 1996.

Equipment write-off increased

The one-time equipment write-off is increased from $17,500 to $18,000 for 1997. Annual increases will boost the write-off to $25,000 by 2003:

Year	Maximum Deduction
1997	$18,000
1998	18,500
1999	19,000
2000	20,000
2001/2002	24,000
2003 and later	25,000

401(k) plans now available to churches

Effective for 1997, 401(k) plans may be offered by churches and other nonprofits on the same basis as other employers. These plans may not discriminate in favor of highly compensated employees (see page 46-47).

Employer contributions to a 401(k) plan are generally tax deductible. An employee will owe tax on the amount of the employer contribution only if a cash payment is elected. An election to take a plan contribution defers the tax until funds are actually distributed, and the contribution will not be included in the employee's gross compensation.

Employees may defer up to $9,500 in 1997 (amount may be adjusted for inflation). The limit is reduced by the amount of contributions made on behalf of a taxpayer to a tax-sheltered annuity if the contributions are made under a salary reduction arrangement.

Four different types of contributions can be made to 401(k) plans: (1) elective employer contributions, (2) voluntary after-tax employee contributions, (3) matching employer plan contributions, and (4) nonelective employer contributions.

Tax-sheltered annuities flexibility added

Starting with 1996, participants in section 403(b) tax-sheltered annuity plans may enter into multiple salary reduction agreements. The frequency with which a salary reduction agreement may be entered, the compensation to which the agreement will apply, and the ability to revoke the agreement will be determined under the rules applicable to 401(k) plans.

IRA contributions rules changed

Starting in 1997, deductible IRA contributions of up to $2,000 may be made for each spouse (including, for example, a homemaker who doesn't work outside the home) if the combined compensation of both spouses is at least equal to the contributed amount. Under prior law, if one spouse had no compensation, a married couple was allowed a maximum annual deductible IRA contribution of $2,250.

Independent contractor rules adjusted

The 1996 Congress approved a temporary fix for the independent contractor/employee issue. They avoided facing head-on the contentious question of how to determine whether a worker is an employee or an independent contractor.

Section 530 of the Revenue Act of 1978 allows an employer that has consistently treated a worker as an independent contractor to continue to do so for employment tax (but not income tax) purposes, unless the employer has no reasonable basis for so doing. Originally intended to be temporary, section 530 has been extended again and again. The Small Business Job Protection Act made the provisions of section 530 permanent. The provisions do not apply to a worker unless the taxpayer and the worker sign a statement that provides that the worker will not be treated as an employee for employment tax purposes, along with some minor revisions to these rules.

Increased health insurance expense deduction for self-employed

Self-employeds can deduct more for health insurance — a gradual rise over several years from the current 30% to 80%. This deduction also applies to eligible long-term care insurance premiums (see next item). The increase is phased in as follows:

Year	Applicable Percentage
1997	40%
1998-2002	45%
2003	50%
2004	60%
2005	70%
2006 and later	80%

Clarification of the tax treatment of long-term care insurance premiums and benefits

Long-term care insurance contracts issued after 1996 generally are treated for income tax purposes in the same way as accident and health insurance contracts:

- ✓ **Employer-provided long-term care insurance.** Long-term care coverage provided by a church is tax-free to the minister. However, long-term care premiums are not excluded from a minister's income if provided through a cafeteria or other flexible spending arrangement.

- ✓ **Includable in medical spending accounts.** Long-term care insurance premiums also can be paid on a tax-favored basis through medical spending accounts.

- ✓ **Qualifying long-term care expenses.** Unreimbursed long-term care expenses are treated as medical expenses if the long-term care services are not provided by a relative, unless the relative is licensed to provide these services.

- ✓ **Annual limitations.** Premiums paid on qualified long-term care policies will qualify as medical expenses for itemized deduction purposes. The annual amount of premiums that qualify as medical expenses is limited, depending upon the insured's age:

Age of individual purchasing long-term care insurance (before year-end)	Limitation on premiums paid for such taxable year
Not more than age 40	$200
More than age 40 but not more than age 50	375
More than age 50 but not more than age 60	750
More than age 60 but not more than age 70	2,000
More than age 70	2,500

For 1997 and later years, the dollar limits are indexed for inflation.

Clarification of the tax treatment of accelerated death benefits under life insurance contracts for terminally and chronically ill individuals

The new law provides an exemption from income tax for accelerated death benefits received after 1996 from life insurance contracts on behalf of a terminally or chronically ill insured. It also excludes from income amounts received on the sale of a life insurance contract on a terminally or chronically ill insured to a so-called viatical settlement company. For chronically (but not terminally) ill individuals, the exclusion maximum is $175 per day, but only for per diem policies and not indemnity policies.

Penalty-free withdrawals for IRAs for certain medical expenses

Withdrawals up to 7.5% of adjusted gross income are not subject to the 10% tax on early withdrawals to pay medical expenses. In addition, the 10% tax does not apply to distributions for medical insurance if the individual has received unemployment compensation under federal or state law for at least 12 weeks.

Tax-favored medical savings accounts tested

A limited number of self-employed individuals and those who are covered only by a high-deductible or catastrophic health plan of a small employer may be able to maintain medical savings accounts (MSAs) during 1997 through 2000. They will be available to 750,000 workers, first come, first served. Contributions to an MSA up to a maximum of 65% of the deductible under the high deductible plan (75% for plans with spouse or dependents) will be deductible above the line, or income tax-free, and not subject to payroll tax if made by the taxpayer's employer.

Taxpayers with health insurance other than catastrophic coverage generally will not be able to have MSAs. Distributions from MSAs will be tax-free if used for unreimbursed qualified medical expenses of the taxpayer, spouse, and dependents.

Tax breaks for adoption expenses

In 1997, taxpayers who adopt an eligible adoptee will be able to claim a nonrefundable tax credit of up to $5,000 of qualified adoption expenses for each eligible adoptee. An eligible adoptee is one who has not attained age 18 at the time of adoption or who is physically or mentally incapable of caring for himself or herself. The limitation on the credit is increased to $6,000 for each special needs adoptee. A special needs adoptee is a child who (1) according to a state determination could not or should not be returned to the home of the birth parents and (2) on account of a specific factor or condition (such as ethnic background, age, medical condition, or physical, mental, or emotional handicap) could not reasonably be expected to be adopted unless adoption assistance is provided.

There is also a new exclusion for up to $5,000 of adoption expenses paid through a nondiscriminatory employer adoption assistance program, which can be received under a cafeteria plan. The limitation on the exclusion is increased to $6,000 for special needs adoptees. The dollar limit is a per child limit, not an annual limit.

Portability of health benefits provided

Group health plans will be required to expand the availability of coverage for plan years beginning after June 30, 1997. Some employees are big winners. Most gain nothing. Many will be worse off because their cost of coverage will go up. The law

✓ provides a limitation on preexisting conditions found in many plans,

✓ prohibits discrimination in eligibility or premiums based solely on an individual's health status, and

✓ allows employees to change jobs without the fear of losing coverage.

You are a winner if you have health problems, are currently insured, and take a new job with an organization that also provides a health plan. As long as you have had a policy for at least 12 months, your insurability is going to be guaranteed. You will get immediate coverage under your new employer's plan, including coverage for preexisting illnesses.

This protects individuals who are burdened with heavy medical expenses. Maybe you have a chronic ailment like diabetes; maybe you are pregnant, or your spouse is; maybe you're healthy, but your spouse or one of your children is not.

Today, such individuals are in a "job lock." If they change employers, their new employer might not cover those conditions right away. Under the new law, however, they will have to be covered. Group health plans will be changing their rules between July 1997 and June 1998.

The outlook is cloudier, however, for individuals who leave a group plan entirely. Maybe you are joining an organization that does not offer health insurance or you leave to start your own business. You will need individual health insurance, but you may not be able to find it if you are a high medical risk.

On paper, the new law solves your problem. You will be guaranteed access to two or more individual policies if you have been insured for the most recent 18 months under a group health plan. You will have to buy the insurance yourself. Any requirement that insurers take all comers, regardless of health, makes individual policies more expensive.

Five-year averaging option is phased out

Starting in 1999, there will be no more five-year averaging as an option to minimize taxes on lump-sum pension payouts. Made under the guise of tax simplification, it really constitutes revenue raising. It will ultimately raise the tax imposed on retirement benefits for anyone tapping into those benefits as a lump sum. This change will make IRA rollovers much more attractive. Ten-year averaging is still permitted, but only for people born before January 1, 1936.

FORM 1040 Line by Line

Form 1040

There are two short forms, the 33-line 1040A and the super-short, 10-line 1040EZ. Use the 78-line Form 1040 instead. It accommodates every minister, and there's no penalty for leaving some of the lines blank. Besides, going down the 1040 line by line may jog your memory about money you received or spent in 1996. (Line numbers noted refer to the 1040 and then to Schedule A.)

• **Filing status (lines 1 to 5). Line 2:** If your spouse died in 1996, you can still file jointly and take advantage of tax rates that would be lower than if you file as a single person or as a head of household.

Line 3: If you're married and live in one of the 42 separate-property states, compute your tax two ways—jointly and separately. Then, file the lower return.

Line 4: If you're single, you may qualify as head of household if you provided a home for someone else—like your parent. Filing as head of household rather than as a single person can save you a bundle on taxes.

Line 5: If your spouse died in 1994 or 1995 and you have a dependent child, you can also benefit from joint-return rates as a qualifying widow(er).

• **Exemptions (lines 6a to 6e).** Remember to include a social security number for any dependent who was at least one year old on December 31, 1996. If your tot does not have one, write "Applied for" and call social security at 800-772-1213 to get Form SS-5, Application for a Social Security Number.

• **Income (lines 7 to 22). Line 7:** If your church considered you an employee for income tax purposes, you should receive Form W-2 from the church. The total amount of your taxable wages is shown in box 1 of Form W-2; attach Copy B of your W-2 to your Form 1040. Include the data from other W-2s you or your spouse received on this line.

Line 8a: Include as taxable-interest income the total amount of what you earned on savings accounts, certificates of deposit, credit union accounts, corporate bonds and corporate bond mutual funds, U.S. treasuries and U.S. government mutual funds, and interest paid to you for a belated federal or state tax refund. If you haven't yet received any of the statements due you, call the issuer to get them. If you received more than $400 of taxable interest income in 1996, you must also complete Schedule B.

Line 8b: Here's where you note any tax-exempt interest from municipal bonds or municipal bond funds. Don't worry—that income is not taxable. But social security recipients must count all their tax-exempt interest when computing how much of their social security benefits will be taxable.

Line 9: Enter as dividend income only ordinary dividends, not capital-gains dividends paid by mutual funds, which are reported on Schedule D. Your Form 1099-DIV statements show the amount and type of ordinary dividends you received during 1996. If you received more than $400 in dividend income in 1996, you must also complete Schedule B. Remember: Earnings from a money-market mutual fund are considered dividend income, not interest income.

Line 10: If you received a refund of a state or local tax in 1996 that you deducted on Schedule A in a prior year, include the refund here.

Line 12: Enter the net income from all your Schedule C or C-EZs. If you are filing as an employee for income tax purposes, you will probably have some honoraria or fee income from speaking engagements, weddings, funerals, and so on. This income, less related expenses, should be reported on Schedule C or C-EZ.

Line 13: Enter capital-gain dividends here if you had no other capital gains or losses in 1996.

Line 15a: Report as IRA distributions even amounts you rolled over tax-free in 1996 from one IRA into another. On line 15b, you will report as taxable the amount of any IRA distributions that you did not roll over minus any return of nondeductible contributions.

Line 16a: It's likely that only a portion of the total pensions and annuities you received is taxable. Your Form 1099R will show the taxable amount, which you enter on line 16b. If you received pensions and annuities from a denominational-sponsored plan, you may be eligible to exclude a portion or all of these payments as a housing allowance.

Line 20a: No more than 85% of your social security benefits can be taxed for 1996 and none at all if your income is below $32,000 on a joint return, $25,000 for singles. If your income doesn't exceed the threshold, leave this line blank. If it does, use the worksheet on Form 1099-SSA to compute taxes on your benefits.

Line 21: Enter your excess housing allowance here. If your cash housing allowance designated and paid by the church exceeds the **lowest** of (1) reasonable compensation, (2) the fair rental value of the home furnished plus utilities, (3) the amount used to provide a home from current ministerial income, or (4) the amount properly designated by the church, enter the difference on line 21.

• **Adjustments to income (lines 23 to 30). Line 24:** If your church paid directly or reimbursed you for all your moving costs incurred in 1996, these amounts would not be included in your Form W-2 (if the church treats you as an employee for income tax purposes) or Form 1099-MISC (if the church considers you self-employed for income tax purposes). Therefore, you would have no moving expenses to deduct on line 24. However, if part or all of your moving costs were not reimbursed, deduct these expenses here.

Line 25: One-half of your social security tax is deductible for income tax purposes on line 25.

Line 26: If your church considers you self-employed for income tax purposes

FORM 1040, LINE-BY-LINE

and you pay your own health insurance (and the church does not reimburse you), you may deduct 30% of health insurance premiums you paid for yourself and your family on this line. The other 70% of the cost must be deducted with other medical expenses on Schedule A, to the extent the total exceeds 7.5% of adjusted gross income (AGI).

Line 27: If you have self-employment income (for income tax purposes) from the church or from other sources, you can open and contribute to a SEP (simplified employee pension) plan as late as the filing deadline including extensions—and still earn a 1996 write-off. Your SEP contributions top out at 15% of your gross self-employment earnings. Keogh contributions are also shown on this line.

- **Tax computation (lines 32 to 40). Line 34:** Claim the standard deduction only if the amount exceeds what you could write off in itemizing expenses on Schedule A. For 1996, the standard deduction is $6,700 joint, $5,900 head of household and $4,000 single (that's up from $6,550, $5,750, and $3,900 last year). The amounts are higher if you or your spouse is 65 or older or legally blind.

- **Other taxes (lines 47 to 54). Line 47:** If you are a qualified minister and have not opted out of social security, you are self-employed for social security tax purposes. Your social security is not withheld by your church but is calculated on Schedule SE if you had net earnings of $400 or more and paid with Form 1040. The tax is 15.3% of the first $62,700 of 1996 self-employment income and 2.95% of income above $62,700. If your total wages and self-employment earnings were less than $62,700, you can probably save time and headaches by filing the Short Schedule SE on the front of the SE form.

Line 51: You will owe the tax on qualified plans plus the 10% penalty on the amount you withdrew from your IRA or another retirement plan if you were under $59^{1}/_{2}$, unless you meet certain exceptions.

- **Payments (lines 55 to 61). Line 55:** Did you have a voluntary withholding arrangement whereby your employing church withheld federal income tax from your compensation? Then show the amount of federal income tax the church withheld along with other federal income tax withholding from other employment of you or your spouse here.

Line 56: Don't get confused: Even though you made your fourth-quarter 1996 estimated tax payment in 1997, it's counted on your 1996 return.

Line 57: Enter your earned income credit here or let the IRS calculate it for you. If you have a qualifying child, you must complete Schedule EIC.

If you made 403(b) tax sheltered annuity contributions, received a cash housing allowance in 1996, or were furnished housing by the church, enter the amount(s) received that were excluded from income and the value of the housing received and description as additional information on line 57.

- **Refund or amount you owe (lines 62 to 66). Line 65:** The IRS assumes you must pay the estimated tax penalty if you owe $500 or more beyond what you've paid through withholding or estimated tax and the amount due is more than 10% of your 1996 tax bill. You may qualify for one of several exceptions, however. Use Form 2210 to prove your case.

Schedule A (Itemized Deductions)

If you live in church-provided housing, you often cannot itemize. But run down Schedule A just to see whether you might have more write-offs than the standard deduction will permit.

● **Medical and dental expenses (lines 1 to 4).** In figuring whether these expenses exceed 7.5% of your AGI and can thus be deducted, don't overlook the cost of getting to and from the doctor or druggist. Write off 9 cents a mile, plus the cost of parking. If you didn't drive, deduct your bus, train, or taxi fares. The cost of trips to see out-of-town specialists and as much as $50 a day for the cost of lodging when you're out of town to get medical care count toward the 7.5%.

● **Taxes you paid (lines 5 to 9).** Even though your real estate taxes are a housing expense excludable under the housing allowance, you are still entitled to deduct them on line 6 as an itemized deduction—one of the few "double deductions" allowed in the tax law.

● **Interest you paid (lines 10 to 14). Line 10:** If you bought a house during 1996, review your escrow or settlement papers for any mortgage interest you paid that was not shown on your lender's year-end statement. If you paid interest on a second mortgage or line of credit secured by your home, include the interest expense here.

As with real estate taxes, it is possible to deduct mortgage interest as an itemized deduction even if the interest is included in housing expenses subject to a housing allowance. Interest paid on a secured mortgage is deductible on Schedule A regardless of how the proceeds of the loan are used. However, the only mortgage interest properly includable as housing expense under a housing allowance is when the loan proceeds were used to provide housing. For example, interest on a second mortgage used to finance your child's college education is deductible on Schedule A but does not qualify as a housing expense for housing allowance purposes.

Don't overlook points you paid to get the mortgage. All of the points are generally deductible as interest here. Points paid for a refinancing must be amortized over the life of the loan. But you can deduct on your 1996 return the portion of all points paid that correspond with the percentage of your refinancing used for home improvements.

● **Gifts to charity (lines 15 to 18). Line 15:** For gifts you made in 1996, you must have written acknowledgments from the charity of any single gifts of $250 or more.

Line 16. Deduct your charitable mileage for any volunteer work at the rate of 12 cents a mile.

● **Job expenses and other miscellaneous deductions (lines 20 to 27).** Don't assume you can't surmount the 2% AGI floor on these miscellaneous deductions. A wealth of employee business, investment, and tax-related expenses—from job-hunting costs to tax preparation fees—are deductible here. And if you bought business equipment required by your church and you were not reimbursed, you can write off its entire cost in 1996, as much as $17,500.

The 1040 Challenge

Completing Form 1040 can be very challenging and take hours to complete. Although it may not seem entirely logical, the 1040 and its accompanying schedules will lead you through the process of figuring your income and deductions and computing your tax.

Exemptions reduce your income by letting you subtract a fixed amount of money for yourself, your spouse, and each of your dependents.

Total Income includes:
Compensation from the church paid to you as an employee-minister for income tax purposes shown on Form W-2. Net earnings from Schedule C (C-EZ) for income from speaking engagements, marriages, and funerals (Schedule C will include all ministerial income and expenses if you are reporting as self-employed for income tax purposes).

Adjustments

Adjusted Gross Income (AGI)

The 1040 Challenge

Form 1040 (1996) Page **2**

Tax Computation

32 Amount from line 31 (adjusted gross income) **32**

33a Check if: ☐ **You** were 65 or older, ☐ Blind; ☐ **Spouse** was 65 or older, ☐ Blind.
Add the number of boxes checked above and enter the total here . . . . ▶ **33a**

b If you are married filing separately and your spouse itemizes deductions or you are a dual-status alien, see instructions and check here . . . . . . ▶ **33b** ☐

34 Enter the **larger** of your: { **Itemized deductions** from Schedule A, line 28, **OR** **Standard deduction** shown below for your filing status. **But** see the instructions if you checked any box on line 33a or b **or** someone can claim you as a dependent.
• Single—$4,000 • Married filing jointly or Qualifying widow(er)—$6,700
• Head of household—$5,900 • Married filing separately—$3,350 } **34** — Minus — **Itemized or Standard Deductions**

35 Subtract line 34 from line 32 . . . . **35**

If you want the IRS to figure your tax, see the line 37 instructions.

36 If line 32 is $88,475 or less, multiply $2,550 by the total number of exemptions claimed on line 6d. If line 32 is over $88,475, see the worksheet in the inst. for the amount to enter . **36** — Minus — **Exemptions**

37 **Taxable income.** Subtract line 36 from line 35. If line 36 is more than line 35, enter -0- . **37** — **Taxable Income**

38 **Tax.** See instructions. Check if total includes any tax from a ☐ Form(s) 8814 b ☐ Form 4970 c ☐ Form 4972 . . . . ▶ **38** — Equals — **Gross Income Tax**

Credits

39 Credit for child and dependent care expenses. Attach Form 2441 **39**
40 Credit for the elderly or the disabled. Attach Schedule R . . **40**
41 Foreign tax credit. Attach Form 1116 . . . . . . **41**
42 Other. Check if from a ☐ Form 3800 b ☐ Form 8396 c ☐ Form 8801 d ☐ Form (specify) **42**
43 Add lines 39 through 42 . . . . **43** — Minus — **Credits**
44 Subtract line 43 from line 38. If line 43 is more than line 38, enter -0- . . . . ▶ **44**

Other Taxes

45 Self-employment tax. Attach Schedule SE **45**
46 Alternative minimum tax. Attach Form 6251 . . . . **46**
47 Social security and Medicare tax on tip income not reported to employer. Attach Form 4137 . **47**
48 Tax on qualified retirement plans, including IRAs. If required, attach Form 5329 . . . . **48** — Plus — **Other Taxes** All ministers must show their social security tax due on line 47.
49 Advance earned income credit payments from Form W-2 . . . . . . **49**
50 Household employment taxes. Attach Schedule H **50**
51 Add lines 44 through 50. This is your **total tax** . . . . ▶ **51**

Proof as of July 1996 (subject to change)

Payments

52 Federal income tax withheld from Form(s) W-2 and 1099 . . **52**
53 1996 estimated tax payments and amount applied from 1995 return . **53**
54 **Earned income credit.** Attach Schedule EIC if you have a qualifying child. Nontaxable earned income: amount ▶ and type ▶ **54**
55 Amount paid with Form 4868 (extension request) **55**
56 Excess social security and RRTA tax withheld (see inst.) . . **56**
57 Other payments. Check if from a ☐ Form 2439 b ☐ Form 4136 **57**
58 Add lines 52 through 57. These are your **total payments** . . . . ▶ **58** — Minus — **Tax Already Paid**

Attach Forms W-2, W-2G, and 1099-R on the front.

Refund

59 If line 58 is more than line 51, subtract line 51 from line 58. This is the amount you **OVERPAID** **59**
60a Amount of line 59 you want **REFUNDED TO YOU** . . . . ▶ **60a** — Equals — **Refund or Tax Payment Due**
b Routing number c Type: ☐ Checking ☐ Savings
d Account number
61 Amount of line 59 you want **APPLIED TO YOUR 1997 ESTIMATED TAX** ▶ **61**

Send it right to your bank! See inst. and fill in 60b, c, and d.

Amount You Owe

62a If line 51 is more than line 58, subtract line 58 from line 51. This is the **AMOUNT YOU OWE.** For details on how to pay and use **Form 1040-V**, see instructions . . . . ▶ **62a**
b Are you paying the amount on line 62a **in full** with Form 1040-V? . . ▶ ☐ **Yes** ☐ **No**
63 Estimated tax penalty. Also include on line 62a **63**

Sign Here

Under penalties of perjury, I declare that I have examined this return and accompanying schedules and statements, and to the best of my knowledge and belief, they are true, correct, and complete. Declaration of preparer (other than taxpayer) is based on all information of which preparer has any knowledge.

Keep a copy of this return for your records.

Your signature	Date	Your occupation
Spouse's signature. If a joint return, BOTH must sign.	Date	Spouse's occupation

Paid Preparer's Use Only

Preparer's signature	Date	Check if self-employed ☐	Preparer's social security no.
Firm's name (or yours if self-employed) and address		EIN	
		ZIP code	

CHAPTER ONE

Taxes for Ministers

Ministers receive special tax treatment!

In This Chapter
- Ministers serving local churches
- Evangelists and missionaries
- Members of religious orders
- Ministers in denominational service, administrative, and teaching positions
- Individuals not qualifying for ministerial tax treatment
- Social security status of ministers
- Income tax status of ministers
- Forms and schedules for the minister
- Importance of the employee vs. self-employed decision
- Recommended filing status

Understanding how the various parts of the tax law fit together is your primary challenge. With the big picture in mind, you can plan your tax liability instead of just letting it happen.

The key to understanding the federal tax system that applies to ministers is to focus on tax rules that primarily benefit ministers (such as the housing allowance) and other provisions that are available to most taxpayers (like tax-free or tax-deferred fringe benefits).

There are several special tax provisions for ministers:

✓ Exclusion for income tax purposes of the housing allowance and the fair rental value of a church-owned parsonage provided rent-free to clergy.

✓ Exemption of clergy from self-employment social security tax under very limited circumstances.

✓ Treatment of clergy (who do not elect social security exemption) as self-employed for social security tax purposes for income from ministerial services.

- ✓ Exemption of clergy compensation from mandatory income tax withholding.

- ✓ Eligibility for a voluntary income tax withholding arrangement between the minister-employee and the church.

- ✓ Potential "double deduction" of mortgage interest and real estate taxes as itemized deductions and as housing expenses for housing allowance purposes for ministers living in minister-provided housing.

The six special tax provisions (see above) apply only to individuals who

- ✓ qualify as ministers of the gospel under federal tax rules and

- ✓ are performing services that qualify in the exercise of ministry under federal tax rules.

Ministers Serving Local Churches

You may believe you are a minister, your church may consider you a minister, your denomination may classify you as a minister, but what does the IRS consider you? For tax purposes, the opinion of the IRS is the one that counts. But even the IRS does not consistently apply the same rules in determining who is a minister in a local church setting.

Knowing whether you are a minister for tax purposes is very important. It determines how you prepare your tax return for income and social security tax purposes. A qualified minister is eligible for the housing allowance. This alone can exclude thousands of dollars from income taxation. Ministers pay self-employment social security tax (SECA) while nonministers pay FICA social security tax.

How can I tell whether the IRS will treat me as a minister?

If you are ordained, commissioned, or licensed and meet the following four tests, the IRS will generally consider you a minister. You

- ✓ administer the sacraments (such as performing marriage and funeral services, dedicating infants, baptizing, and serving communion),

- ✓ are considered to be a religious leader by your church,

- ✓ conduct religious worship, and

- ✓ have management responsibility in the "control, conduct, or maintenance" of your church.

If you meet some but not all of these four tests, the IRS may or may not consider you a minister. Under a 1989 tax court case, not all four factors had to be satisfied. However, more recent court cases and an IRS Private Letter Ruling have required that all four factors must be satisfied. Some youth pastors and ministers of music, education, or administration will not meet all four tests.

There is no requirement that you must be qualified to perform and actually perform every sacrament or rite of your religion. If you are qualified to perform certain sacraments and actually perform or could perform some of the sacraments on occasion, you will generally meet this test. A similar test applies to conducting religious worship and providing management services. If you currently conduct religious worship and provide management services, have done it in the past or could do it in the future, the test will generally be met.

Job titles have little significance for tax purposes. A licensed, commissioned, or ordained minister may have a job title that implies a ministry function. However, the actual responsibilities of the position will determine if the four-factor test is met. Ministers performing services of a routine nature, such as those performed by secretaries, clerks, and janitors, generally do not qualify as ministers for tax purposes.

Because of the inconsistency of these rulings, if you are a minister serving in a local church who does not clearly meet all four factors, you should discuss your situation with a qualified professional adviser before filing your income tax returns.

What about licensed or commissioned ministers?

Some religious groups license, commission, and ordain ministers. Other groups only ordain, or only license and ordain, ministers or provide some other combination of the three types of special recognition of ministers.

Will you be treated as a minister by the IRS if you are only licensed or commissioned? Yes, if you administer the sacraments, conduct worship services, and perform services in the "control, conduct, or maintenance of a church." If you do not perform, or are not qualified to perform, all three duties, your status depends on which court decision or ruling is followed by the IRS.

Example: Rev. Smith is an ordained minister who serves as a minister of counseling at his church. He does not preach or conduct worship services and never administers the sacraments. He has management responsibility for the operation of a counseling center in the local church. He occasionally makes hospital visits. While he qualifies under the "control, conduct, and maintenance of the church" test, he does not administer the sacraments or conduct worship services. With professional advice, he must decide whether he qualifies as a minister for tax purposes.

Evangelists and Missionaries

The qualifications for itinerant evangelists for the special ministerial tax provisions are generally the same as for ministers serving local churches.

Most evangelists are self-employed both for income tax and self-employment social security tax purposes. The only exception is the evangelist who has formed a corporation and is an employee of the corporation. In this instance, the evangelist is an employee for income tax purposes but remains self-employed for social security tax purposes.

Missionaries are also subject to the same rules to qualify for ministerial status for tax purposes. If a licensed, commissioned, or ordained missionary meets all four qualifying tests (see page 20), the special tax treatments for ministers will apply. Qualifying for benefits such as a housing allowance is often not so important for a minister-missionary because of the foreign earned income exclusion. However, the determination of ministerial tax status is vitally important to determine if the minister is subject to FICA or SECA for social security tax purposes. The foreign earned income exclusion affects income tax but not social security tax.

Members of Religious Orders

The IRS has developed stringent characteristics to determine whether an organization is a religious order. They are as follows:

✓ The organization is described in section 501(c)(3) of the Internal Revenue Code.

✓ The members of the organization, after successful completion of the organization's training program and probationary period, make a long-term commitment to the organization (normally more than two years).

✓ The organization is, directly or indirectly, under the control and supervision of a church or convention or association of churches or is significantly funded by such an entity.

✓ The members of the organization normally live together as part of a community and are held to a significantly stricter level of moral and spiritual discipline than that required of church lay members.

✓ The members of the organization work or serve full-time on behalf of the religious, educational, or charitable goals of the organization.

✓ The members of the organization participate regularly in activities such as public or private prayer, religious study, teaching, care of the aging, missionary work, or church reform or renewal.

There are two types of members of religious orders:

✓ Members who are ordained, licensed, or commissioned

• by a church that is separate from the religious order, or

- by the religious order, if authorized by its organizing documents.

✓ Non-ordained, non-licensed, or non-commissioned (lay) members.

Housing for members of religious orders generally falls into the following categories:

✓ Housing provided by the religious order on its premises and the member is required to live in the housing.

✓ Other housing.

- The member is allowed to live in religious-order-provided housing that is not located on the immediate premises of the religious order.

- The member is allowed to live in housing other than housing provided by the religious order (housing provided by the member).

Members of religious orders qualify for many of the special tax provisions afforded to qualified ministers. However, there are some key exceptions. The following chart summarizes the general application of these provisions:

Special Tax Provisions	Application to Religious Order Members
•Exclusion for income tax purposes of the housing allowance and the fair rental value of religious-order-owned housing provided rent-free to a member.	•If a member is required to live on the immediate premises of the order "for the convenience of the employer," the rental value of the housing is generally tax-free for income tax purposes. If a member does *not* live on the immediate premises of the order, the following guidelines generally apply: **Lay members.** The rental value of religious-order-provided housing or a housing allowance is generally subject to income tax. **Ordained, licensed, or commissioned members.** If the religious order is a church or an integral agency of a church or a church denomination, the rental value of religious-order-provided housing or a housing allowance is generally tax-free for income tax purposes.

Special Tax Provisions	Application to Religious Order Members
	If the religious order is not a church or a church denomination, the rental value of religious-order-provided housing or a housing allowance is generally tax-free for income tax purposes only if the work performed by the member includes sacerdotal functions.
●Exemption of members from self-employment social security tax in very limited circumstances.	●The same rules apply to members as to clergy.
●Treatment of members (who do not elect social security exemption) as self-employed for social security tax purposes for income from the religious order.	●The same rules apply to members as to clergy.
●Exemption of member compensation from mandatory income tax withholding.	●The same rules apply to members as to clergy.
●Eligibility for a voluntary income tax withholding arrangement between the member-employee and the religious order.	●The same rules apply to members as to clergy.

Ministers in Denominational Service, Administrative, and Teaching Positions

Ordained, commissioned, or licensed ministers *not* serving local churches may qualify as "ministers" for federal tax purposes in the following situations:

Denominational service

This category encompasses the administration of church denominations and their integral agencies, including teaching or administration in parochial schools, colleges, or universities that are under the authority of a church or denomination.

The IRS uses the following criteria to determine if an institution is an integral agency of a church:

- ✓ Did the church incorporate the institution?

- ✓ Does the corporate name of the institution suggest a church relationship?

- ✓ Does the church continuously control, manage, and maintain the institution?

- ✓ If dissolved, will the assets be turned over to the church?

- ✓ Are the trustees or directors of the institution approved by, or must they be approved by, the church and may they be removed by the church?

- ✓ Are annual reports of finances and general operations required to be made to the church?

- ✓ Does the church contribute to the support of the institution?

Assignment by a church

Services performed by a minister for a parachurch organization based upon a substantive assignment or designation by a church may provide the basis for ministerial tax treatment. The housing allowance should be designated by the employing organization, not the assigning church.

The following characteristics must be present for an effective assignment:

- ✓ There must be sufficient relationship between the minister and the assigning church to justify the assignment of the minister.

- ✓ There must be an adequate relationship between the assigning church and the parachurch organization to which the minister is assigned to justify the assignment.

To substantiate the relationship between the minister and the church, the church must answer the question of "why is there authority, power, or legitimacy in the church to assign this particular minister?" Such matters as being the ordaining church, providing ongoing supervision, denominational affiliation, contributing significant financial support, or being the long-term "home church" would all appear to support this relationship.

In addressing the second characteristic, the relationship between the church and the organization, the church must answer the question of "why should the church assign a minister to this particular ministry?" Essentially, the assignment of the minister must accomplish the church's ministry purposes.

In considering an assignment, it is important to distinguish between the *process* of assigning and the *documentation* of the assignment. The process of assigning expresses the church's theology, philosophy, and policy of operation: its way of doing ministry. The documentation of the assignment only provides evidence that the church is doing ministry through the particular individual assigned. The keys to a proper assignment are:

- ✓ A written policy describing the specific requirements for addressing the relationship of the church both to the minister being assigned and to the parachurch organization to which the minister is assigned. This would include the church's theological and policy goals for the assignment.

- ✓ A formal review to confirm that the minister and the proposed ministry with a parachurch organization qualify.

- ✓ A written assignment coupled with guidelines for supervision of and reporting by the minister and the parachurch agency.

- ✓ A periodic (at least annual) formal review of the minister's activities to confirm that the assignment continues to comply with the policy.

A sample assignment letter is included in the 1997 edition of the *Zondervan Church and Nonprofit Organization Tax & Financial Guide*.

Other service

If a church does not assign or designate your services, you will qualify for the special tax treatments of a minister only if your services substantially involve performing sacerdotal functions or conducting religious worship.

For example, if you are an ordained or licensed minister and are engaged full-time in conducting worship services or Bible studies, counseling, or performing baptisms, you may qualify for the housing allowance exclusion even though the services were not performed for a church, church-controlled organization, or other religious organization.

Individuals Not Qualifying for Ministerial Tax Treatment

You do not qualify as a "minister" for federal income tax purposes if you are

- ✓ a theological student who does not otherwise qualify as a minister,

- ✓ an unordained, uncommissioned, or unlicensed church official,

- ✓ an ordained, commissioned, or licensed minister working as an administrator or on the faculty of a nonchurch-related college,

- ✓ an ordained, commissioned, or licensed minister working as an executive of a nonreligious, nonchurch-related organization, and

✓ a civilian chaplain at a VA hospital (**NOTE:** The tax treatment of ministers who are chaplains in the armed forces is the same as for other members of the armed forces.)

Social Security Status of Ministers

Ministers engaged in the exercise of ministry are *always* treated as self-employed for social security purposes. This is true whether you are an employee of your church or self-employed for income tax purposes.

Ministers pay social security under the Self-Employment Contributions Act (SECA) instead of under the Federal Insurance Contributions Act (FICA). It is possible to become exempt from SECA if you meet strict exemption requirements (see pages 106-109). The request for exemption must be filed using Form 4361 within a specified time from the beginning of your ministry. The request for exemption must be approved by the IRS.

Your earnings that are *not* from the exercise of ministry are generally subject to social security tax under FICA or SECA as applied to all workers.

Income Tax Status of Ministers

Is a particular minister an employee or self-employed (independent contractor) for income tax purposes? The answer will vary by minister, but the decision has many ramifications for what and how a church and the minister reports to the IRS.

Employees report their compensation on Form 1040, line 7. Self-employed individuals report compensation on Schedule C or C-EZ. Employees receive Form W-2 each year, while Form 1099-MISC is used to report compensation received by a self-employed individual (if at least $600 of compensation is paid in a calendar year).

Employees deduct unreimbursed business expenses, and expenses reimbursed under a nonaccountable plan, on Form 2106 (2106-EZ) with the amount carried forward to Schedule A as an itemized deduction. The expense is subject to a 2% of adjusted gross income limitation, and only 50% of business meals and entertainment expenses may be included. Self-employed individuals deduct expenses on Schedule C or C-EZ whether or not they are eligible to itemize deductions. Expenses are not subject to the 2% of adjusted gross income limitation, but the 50% of business meals and entertainment limit still applies.

The IRS applies a common-law test to ministers (and nonministers) to determine whether they are employees or self-employed for income tax purposes. Ministers are generally considered employees for income tax purposes if they

✓ must follow the church's work instructions;

✓ receive on-the-job training;
✓ provide services that must be rendered personally;

- ✓ provide services that are integral to the church;
- ✓ hire, supervise, and pay assistants for the church;
- ✓ have an ongoing work relationship with the church;
- ✓ must follow set hours of work;
- ✓ work full-time for the church;
- ✓ work on the church's premises;
- ✓ must do their work in a church-determined sequence;
- ✓ receive business expense reimbursements;
- ✓ receive routing payments of regular amounts;
- ✓ need the church to furnish tools and materials;
- ✓ don't have a major investment in job facilities;
- ✓ cannot suffer a loss from their services;
- ✓ work for one church at a time;
- ✓ do not offer their services to the general public;
- ✓ can be fired by the church;
- ✓ may quit work at any time without penalty.

Some of the above factors are often given greater weight than others. Generally a minister is an employee if the church has the legal right to control both what and how work is done, even if the minister has considerable discretion and freedom of action. The threshold level of control necessary to find employee status is generally lower when applied to professional services than when applied to nonprofessional services.

Recent tax court cases have adopted the following seven-factor test to determine if you are an employee or self-employed for income tax purposes:

- ✓ How much control does the church exercise over your work?

  - Do you have the authority to establish your own church?

  - Are you required to give an account of your pastoral ministries to an annual convention or conference at a district, state, or regional level?

- Are you amenable to a local church board?

✓ Does the church or the minister invest in the facilities used in the work?

- Who provides the church facilities?

- Who provides an office, equipment, library, and so on?

✓ Does the minister have the opportunity for profit or loss?

- Is the minister paid a fixed salary?

✓ Does the church have the right to discharge the minister?

- Can the minister be removed if the church believes the minister is unacceptable?

✓ Is the work performed by the minister a part of the regular business of the church?

- Is the work of the minister an integral part of the work of the church?

✓ How permanent is the relationship between the church and the minister?

- Does the minister offer his or her services to the general public as would an independent contractor?

- Does the church provide retirement benefits (such as contributions to a pension plan) for the minister?

✓ What relationship does the church and the minister believe they have created?

- Does the church withhold federal income tax from the minister's salary and provide Form W-2?

- Does the church provide the minister with a home or a cash housing allowance to provide his or her own home?

Based on this seven-factor test, most ministers serving local congregations will be determined by the IRS to be employees for income tax purposes. It is also generally advantageous for ministers to file as employees for income tax purposes to qualify for certain tax-free fringe benefits and for a number of other reasons outlined in the next section of this chapter.

Forms and Schedules for the Minister

You may need to file a variety of other forms in addition to the 1040. Here are some of the forms ministers typically need to file.

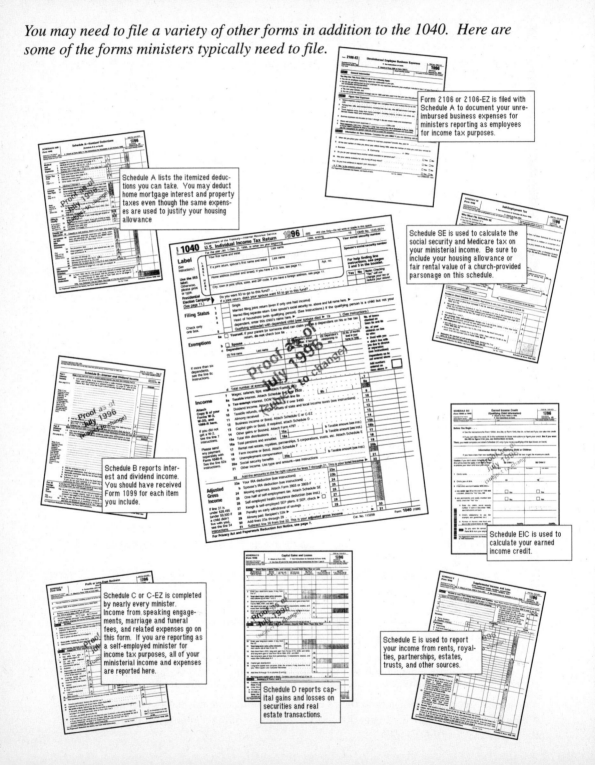

Form 2106 or 2106-EZ is filed with Schedule A to document your unreimbursed business expenses for ministers reporting as employees for income tax purposes.

Schedule A lists the itemized deductions you can take. You may deduct home mortgage interest and property taxes even though the same expenses are used to justify your housing allowance

Schedule SE is used to calculate the social security and Medicare tax on your ministerial income. Be sure to include your housing allowance or fair rental value of a church-provided parsonage on this schedule.

Schedule B reports interest and dividend income. You should have received Form 1099 for each item you include.

Schedule EIC is used to calculate your earned income credit.

Schedule C or C-EZ is completed by nearly every minister. Income from speaking engagements, marriage and funeral fees, and related expenses go on this form. If you are reporting as a self-employed minister for income tax purposes, all of your ministerial income and expenses are reported here.

Schedule D reports capital gains and losses on securities and real estate transactions.

Schedule E is used to report your income from rents, royalties, partnerships, estates, trusts, and other sources.

Importance of the Employee vs. Self-Employed Decision

Determining if you are an employee or self-employed for income tax purposes will resolve several other tax-related issues:

✓ Minister-employees must be given Form W-2 and report their compensation on page 1 of Form 1040. They are eligible to claim unreimbursed business expenses and expenses reimbursed under a nonaccountable plan on Schedule A (nonaccountable plan reimbursements must be included in compensation on Form W-2). If you itemize deductions, business and professional expenses are deductible only to the extent that such expenses exceed 2% of adjusted gross income (AGI). Deductible business meals and entertainment expenses are limited to 50%.

Self-employed ministers must be given Form 1099-MISC (if they receive at least $600 in compensation) and report compensation and business expenses on Schedule C or C-EZ. Business expenses are deductible regardless of itemized deductions and are not subject to the 2%-of-AGI floor. The 50% limitation on business meals and entertainment applies to expenses claimed on Schedule C or C-EZ.

✓ Health, accident, and long-term care insurance premiums paid directly by an employer or reimbursed by an employer, after the minister provides substantiation, are not reportable as income to the minister-employee but must be reported as taxable income to the self-employed minister.

Minister-employees report health, accident, and long-term care insurance premiums paid personally, and not reimbursed by the church, on Schedule A as a medical and dental expense, subject to a 7.5% limitation of adjusted gross income.

A deduction is available on page 1 of Form 1040 for 30% of the health, accident, and long-term care insurance premiums paid by the self-employed minister. The remaining 70% may be claimed on Schedule A as a medical and dental expense, subject to the 7.5% limitation.

✓ Group-term life insurance, provided by an employer, of $50,000 or less is tax-free to employees but represents taxable income for the self-employed.

✓ Contributions to Keogh plans are available only to the self-employed. IRAs may be used by both employees and the self-employed.

✓ A voluntary arrangement to withhold income tax may be used by a minister-employee but may not be used by the self-employed.

✓ Adjusted gross income ordinarily will be higher if a minister reports as an employee and claims unreimbursed business expenses on Schedule A as miscellaneous deductions. Self-employed ministers deduct business expenses in computing adjusted gross income.

Adjusted gross income is an amount that is important for many reasons. For example, the percentage limitations applicable to charitable contributions, medical expenses, and miscellaneous deductions relate to adjusted gross income.

✓ The accountable expense reimbursement rules apply only to employer/employee relationships (see page 85). However, it is often wise to apply the same guidelines for payments to ministers considered self-employed for income tax purposes.

✓ A minister will have a lower audit risk if filing as an employee versus filing as self-employed for income tax purposes.

Recommended Filing Status

Most local church ministers qualify as employees for income tax purposes. It is generally wise for ministers to file as employees for income tax purposes unless you can clearly demonstrate that you qualify for self-employed status.

Since some ministers believe that they are self-employed for income tax purposes, this book has examples for both the employee and self-employed approaches.

Churches must provide a W-2 to ministers it considers to be employees and provide a Form 1099-MISC to ministers it considers to be self-employed for income tax purposes. Yet the minister may take an exception to the reporting of the church. For example, if the church gives the minister Form 1099-MISC or provides no Form 1099-MISC or W-2, the minister may report as an employee on line 7, page 1, Form 1040 and attach a statement to explain that the church did not provide a W-2.

Even though the minister might take an exception to the reporting of the church, the church has a responsibility under the law to determine the proper filing method and proceed accordingly.

Action Steps

■ Determine if the special tax provisions for ministers are applicable to you.

■ Determine whether the church considers you an employee or self-employed for income tax purposes. The IRS considers almost all ministers to be employees.

■ If you qualify as a minister, pay your social security tax (SECA) based on the annual completion of Schedule SE. The church should *never* withhold FICA tax from your pay.

■ If you are a qualified minister, request that an appropriate amount be designated as a parsonage or housing allowance whether you provide your own housing or live in church-provided housing.

CHAPTER TWO
Compensation and Financial Planning
Use fringes that really benefit!

In This Chapter
- How much should a minister be paid?
- Can pay be too high?
- Plan your compensation
- Avoid recharacterization of income
- Use fringe benefits wisely
- Use accountable expense reimbursements
- Use key money management concepts

The structure of a minister's compensation may be more important than the amount. Maximizing the housing allowance and other tax-free benefits will save many dollars.

When it comes to compensation, the clergy are like no other category of taxpayers. For example:

✓ While treated as self-employed for social security purposes, most pastors (but not all) file as employees for income tax purposes.

✓ Ministers have a category of income (potentially excludable from income tax) that few others enjoy: the housing allowance.

✓ Although a housing allowance excludes some pay from income tax, it does not provide any exclusion from self-employment social security tax (SECA).

✓ Ministers, unlike other employees, are not required to have income taxes deducted from their paychecks (and should never have social security taxes deducted); they file quarterly estimated taxes unless a *voluntary* withholding arrangement is used.

With the special treatment of minister's compensation often comes confusion and improper tax reporting. Some of the most prevalent myths are shown below.

Ministerial Compensation Myths

Myth #1 All fringe benefits are tax-free. Fact: All fringe benefits are taxable unless specifically exempted from tax.

Myth #2 Fringe benefits are treated the same whether a minister files as an employee or self-employed for income tax purposes. Fact: In several instances, ministers filing as employees for income tax purposes receive favorable treatment compared with self-employed ministers.

Myth #3 The designated housing allowance may be automatically excluded from income whether or not the funds are totally expended for housing purposes. Fact: The exclusion cannot exceed the amount spent for housing. The fair rental value of the housing is typically the most limiting factor.

Myth #4 Expense allowances do not represent taxable income. Fact: Unless allowances are treated under the accountable expense plan rules, they must be added to gross compensation.

Myth #5 Supplying only a list of business expenses to the church provides adequate substantiation of expenses. Fact: Substantiation of expenses is complete only when the minister provides adequate supporting documentation.

Myth #6 The "highly-compensated" employee rules (see page 47) never apply to ministers. Fact: Ministers will often be classified as "highly-compensated" and ineligible for many tax-free fringe benefits.

Myth #7 A church does not have to offer the same fringe benefits to all employees. Fact: Certain fringe benefits that would normally be tax-free become taxable if the church discriminates against certain employees.

How Much Should a Minister Be Paid?

Ministerial compensation is a two-edged sword: A minister should be paid what he is worth, but the minister should be worth what he is paid.

Compensation paid to the minister should be fair and a reasonable indication of the congregation's evaluation of the minister's worth. Above all, compensation should reflect the congregation's assessment of how well the minister handles a multitude of problems and effectively serves a diverse congregation. Pay should relate to the responsibilities, the size of the congregation, the economic level of the locale, and the experience of the pastor.

Consideration also should be given to the ability of the church to pay a pastor's compensation. Churches run the gamut, from very small to very large. It may be impossible for some very small churches to pay an adequate compensation package. But some congregations may be hiding behind their relatively small size to avoid paying better salaries.

In reporting to the congregation, many churches include the pastor's expense reimbursements and fringe benefits with gross pay and report the total on one line of the church financial report labeled "pastor's salary." This is very unfair to the pastor and inaccurate. Professional expense allowances and reimbursements and fringe benefits should be stated on a nonsalary line and not be shown as ministerial compensation. The cash housing allowance and the fair rental value of a parsonage are properly included in the salary category.

If a church does not increase the pastor's pay each year, it has reduced the pay. Inflation is in single digits, but it is still there, even at about three or four percent. It does cost more each year to live. And just as laypersons expect their employer to provide them with a cost-of-living pay increase each year, a pastor should expect the same.

Can Pay Be Too High?

Few ministers receive unreasonably high compensation for their work. But excessive compensation can result in private benefit and may jeopardize the tax-exempt status of the church.

There is very little specific guidance for what constitutes unreasonable compensation. The facts of each situation determine reasonableness.

Reasonable compensation is based on what would ordinarily be paid for like services by a similar organization under similar circumstances. It includes all forms of compensation.

Total compensation may be much higher than taxable income. The IRS includes the housing allowance *and* tax-free fringe benefits to determine total compensation.

Plan Your Compensation

Who reviews the package?

The participation of an individual or a small group for compensation discussions with the pastor is crucial. The entire congregation may ultimately approve the annual budget that includes pastoral pay, benefits, and reimbursements. But the pay package needs to be carefully developed before it reaches the congregational approval stage. Even the entire church board is too large a forum for the initial compensation discussions.

MINISTER'S COMPENSATION WORKSHEET

	This Year	Next Year

SALARY:
- A. Cash salary, less designated housing/furnishings allowance $_____ $_____
- B. If parsonage owned by church, fair rental value including utilities and any housing/furnishings allowance _____ _____
- C. If parsonage not owned by church, cash housing allowance provided (plus utilities, maintenance, or any other housing expenses paid directly by church) _____ _____
- D. Tax-deferred payments (TSA, 401(k), IRA) _____ _____
- E. Cash bonus _____ _____
- F. Other _____ _____
- **Total Salary** $_____ $_____

FRINGE BENEFITS:
- A. Denominational pension fund $_____ $_____
- B. Social security reimbursement _____ _____
- C. Medical expense reimbursement _____ _____
- D. Insurance premiums paid by church
  1. Health _____ _____
  2. Disability _____ _____
  3. Long-term care _____ _____
  4. Group-term life _____ _____
  5. Dental/vision _____ _____
  6. Professional liability _____ _____
  7. Malpractice _____ _____
- E. Other _____ _____
- **Total Fringe Benefits** $_____ $_____

PROFESSIONAL EXPENSE REIMBURSEMENTS:
(limited to ordinary, necessary, and actual expenses)
- A. Auto/travel $_____ $_____
- B. Books/subscriptions/tapes _____ _____
- C. Continuing education _____ _____
- D. Conventions/conferences _____ _____
- E. Professional dues _____ _____
- F. Church-related entertainment _____ _____
- G. Child care _____ _____
- H. Other _____ _____
- **Total Professional Expense Reimbursements** $_____ $_____

NOTE: Tax-deferred payments are shown under the salary category on this form. This presentation seems to be appropriate because it is often an option of the minister to receive the funds as salary or have them paid into a deferred plan.

When to review the package

An annual review of a pastor's pay is vital. The pastor should know exactly what to expect from the congregation during the coming year. It is inexcusable to wait until the new church year begins or later to decide the new pay plan for the pastor.

Late in 1997 is the time for the committee responsible for recommending compensation matters to get busy to put a plan together for the new church year that might begin in early to mid-1998. A representative or a small committee from the church board should meet with the pastor, talk about pay expectations, review past pay patterns, discuss the tax consequences of compensation components, then make recommendations to the appropriate body. The discussions should focus on the reimbursement of professional expenses, fringe benefits, housing, and salary, in that order. This will insure covering all the items in a pay plan in an orderly, systematic way.

The church board should act on the recommendations by March for a fiscal year beginning in mid-1998. Then the compensation package may be included in the congregational budget for the next year. The detail elements of the pay plan, while fully disclosed to the church board, are often summarized for presentation to the congregation.

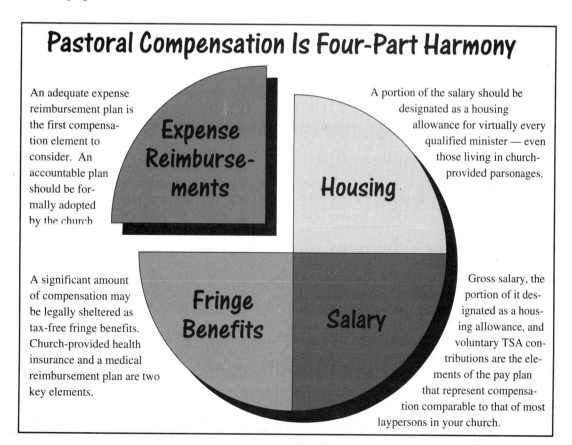

Pastoral Compensation Is Four-Part Harmony

Expense Reimbursements — An adequate expense reimbursement plan is the first compensation element to consider. An accountable plan should be formally adopted by the church.

Housing — A portion of the salary should be designated as a housing allowance for virtually every qualified minister — even those living in church-provided parsonages.

Fringe Benefits — A significant amount of compensation may be legally sheltered as tax-free fringe benefits. Church-provided health insurance and a medical reimbursement plan are two key elements.

Salary — Gross salary, the portion of it designated as a housing allowance, and voluntary TSA contributions are the elements of the pay plan that represent compensation comparable to that of most laypersons in your church.

Elements of the package to review

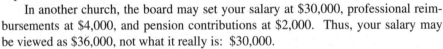

In some congregations, the board may say, "We can pay you $40,000. How do you want the money divided among salary, housing allowance, fringe benefits, and expense reimbursements?"

In another church, the board may set your salary at $30,000, professional reimbursements at $4,000, and pension contributions at $2,000. Thus, your salary may be viewed as $36,000, not what it really is: $30,000.

Some congregations may choose to boost your salary 4% this year, leaving other elements of the pay package as they are. This practice presumes that your base salary for the previous year was adequate. This may or may not have been true.

An accountable expense reimbursement plan should be provided to every minister. An ideal policy provides for the full reimbursement for all professional expenses. Alternately, the plan should provide for reimbursements up to a specified annual limit. It is generally counter-productive to set expense plan limits by segments of expense like automobile, meals and entertainment, dues, and so on. If an expense limit is set, use one limit for all business and professional expenses. (See chapter 5.)

After the reimbursement policy and the fringe benefit items are decided, housing and salary should be reviewed. Housing and salary are the true "compensation" items of the pay plan. Reimbursements are not a part of salary. Reimbursements are simply a form of church operating expenses. Fringe benefits are not salary even if they are taxable. They are simply benefits.

Just as laypersons do not include the payments made by their employers to pension or health plans as part of their salary, a congregation should not add those costs as part of the pastor's salary. True, they are a real cost for having a pastor, but they are benefits, not salary. *Housing, salary, church-funded IRA payments, and voluntary TSA or 401(k) contributions are generally the only elements that represent compensation comparable to most laypersons in your church.*

Avoid Recharacterization of Income

Some churches fund expense reimbursements through a salary reduction arrangement falsely believing this creates a tax benefit for the minister. Under this method, the church determines the combined cash salary and the reimbursable-expense dollar limit. Then substantiated expenses are subtracted from compensation.

Example: The church and minister agree that the combined cash salary and reimbursable-expense limit is $30,000. The church places no limit on the amount of expenses that may be reimbursed. The minister substantiates $8,000 of church-related business expenses. The church reduces the $30,000 combined total by the $8,000 of expenses and provides the minister with a Form W-2 or 1099-MISC reflecting $22,000 of compensation. This is improper reporting of the minister's compensation. Since specific salary and expense plan amounts were not separately stated by the church when the compensation plan was drawn, Form W-2

COMPENSATION AND FINANCIAL PLANNING

or 1099-MISC must show compensation of $30,000. The minister may deduct the $8,000 of expenses on Form 2106/Schedule A or Schedule C (C-EZ), subject to limitations.

Reimbursements through salary reduction are not an effective method to reduce gross compensation. The only valid approaches for funding expense reimbursements are as follows:

✓ The church may reimburse substantiated business expenses *without limitation* under the "accountable plan" rules discussed in chapter 5.

Example: The church agrees to provide the minister-employee with a salary of $30,000 per year plus an unlimited reimbursement of business expenses. Following the "accountable reimbursement rules," the minister substantiates expenses of $8,473 during the year. The church gives the minister a Form W-2 reflecting compensation of $30,000. The expenses of $8,473 are not reported by the church or the minister to the IRS.

✓ The church may reimburse substantiated business expenses up to certain limits under the "accountable plan" rules discussed in chapter 5.

Example: The church agrees to provide the minister-employee with a salary of $30,000 per year and reimburse business expenses up to $8,500 per year. Following the "accountable reimbursement rules," the minister substantiates $8,500 of expenses during the year. Additionally, the minister incurs $385 of business expenses beyond the $8,500 plan limit. The $385 of expenses are not reimbursed. The church gives the minister a Form W-2 showing compensation of $30,000. The $8,500 of reimbursed expenses are not reported by the church or the minister to the IRS. The $385 of unreimbursed business expenses may be claimed by the minister on Form 2106 (2106-EZ) and carried forward to Schedule A, miscellaneous deductions.

As a part of a church plan to reimburse a minister for business expenses, the church also may establish guidelines about the rate for auto mileage or apply per diem rates instead of paying actual expenses for meals and lodging (see chapter 5).

Use Fringe Benefits Wisely

There are several key fringe benefits that many churches consider for ministers:

✓ **Tax-deferred accounts**. Contribute as much as you can (see chapter 3 for limitations) to tax-deferred accounts such as tax-sheltered annuities (TSAs) or 401(k) plans. Also, encourage your church to pay in the maximum to a denominational pension plan if one is available to you.

Contributions to TSAs, 401(k)s, and denominational pension plans are generally not taxable income currently. Tax is deferred until distributions are later received, usually at retirement.

Pension plans, TSAs, and 401(k)s sponsored by a denomination also have another tremendous advantage over other independently purchased retirement products. The IRS still permits pension boards to designate retirement benefits paid through a pension, TSA, or 401(k) plan they sponsor as a housing allowance. This allows a minister to exclude actual housing expenses from income tax (and generally from social security tax)—even when retired!

✓ **Health insurance**. With the spiraling cost of health insurance premiums, the provision of health coverage at the congregation's expense is a must. Some churches also pay for dental and eye insurance.

If the church pays the premiums in addition to salary, the benefit is tax-free to the minister. It is preferable for the church to pay the premiums directly to the insurance carrier. However, a reimbursement to the minister for health insurance premiums is tax-free if based on substantiation.

✓ **Long-term care insurance.** Effective for 1997, long-term care coverage provided by the church for a minister is tax-free to the minister. Churches should consider adding long-term care to their fringe benefit package.

✓ **Social security reimbursement**. All ministers pay self-employment social security tax of 15.3% on the first $62,700 of income in 1996. The Medicaid tax of 2.9% is due for all income above this limit. The only exception is for the few ministers who qualify, file, and are approved for social security exemption.

Churches often provide a reimbursement or allowance to assist the pastor in paying a portion or all of the social security tax. These payments must be made directly to the minister, not the IRS. The payments are taxable for income and social security tax purposes.

✓ **Other benefits**. There are many other fringe benefits that may be provided to a minister. Chapter 3 includes an extensive list of these possibilities.

Use Accountable Expense Reimbursements

With the IRS taking the position that most ministers are employees for income tax purposes, an adequate accountable reimbursement plan is vital.

All ministers incur travel expenses while conducting the ministry of the local church. Ministers also incur other business expenses such as entertainment, professional books and magazines, membership dues, and supplies. Some churches reimburse their ministers in full for these expenses. Other churches reimburse the minister for these expenses up to certain limits.

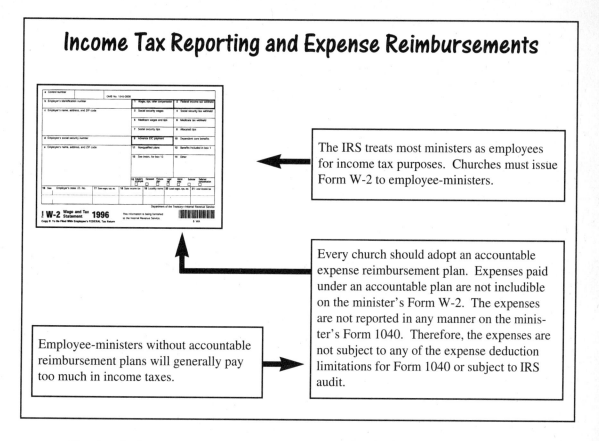

The church should establish a fair and equitable reimbursement plan, comparable to most business situations. The reimbursement plan should meet the rules for accountable plans explained in chapter 5. Full reimbursement of reasonable professional expenses should be the goal. If the church does not reimburse you for 100% of professional expenses, the unreimbursed expenses probably will not be fully deductible for tax purposes and perhaps not deductible at all.

Besides the adoption of an accountable reimbursement plan by the church, you must keep proper records and provide substantiation to the church for the expenditure of funds. The failure to account adequately for the expenses may be very expensive to you in terms of income taxes.

Use Key Money Management Concepts

A minister must seek to live within his or her means. This takes practice and discipline. The apostle cautioned, "I have learned to be content whatever the circumstances" (Philippians 4:11). For some ministers, driving a luxury car is living within their means. Many others will be more "content" driving a mid-range or compact. Each has a responsibility to be a wise manager of God's resources and live moderately.

The key to worry-free money management is learning good spending habits. Money can be used to honor God in every part of your life. Learn to control your spending. Paying high interest rates on past spending is not God's plan. Depending on Him to pay for what you consumed yesterday is wrong. Depending on Him for income to pay for today's needs and future needs is the sign of a good steward.

Slow and steady ways to build your cash

Saving is setting aside a portion of your earnings on a regular basis. It involves spending less in the short-term and investing for long-term benefits. Those benefits may include a vacation, automobile, or a down payment on that "dream home."

Procrastination is pure poison for ministers. If you begin now and put away $250 a month in an account earning 3% after taxes, you will have $16,402 in just five years. Wait until this time next year to begin saving that amount, and you will accumulate only $12,733 by the same date.

The key to keeping more of what you earn is *self-discipline*—not self-denial. First, get a clear picture of your cash-spending and your cash-earning potential. Then use discipline:

✓ Take all credit cards—except one or two for emergencies and out-of-town travel—out of your wallet. Don't let credit cards become a way to finance your daily living.

✓ Don't carry your checkbook around. Write yourself one allowance check every week. Cash the check—and don't spend more than that for routine expenses during the week. Become your own banker, and learn how to say no.

✓ Make a list of your outstanding credit-card debts. Pay them off one at a time. Celebrate when you finish paying off the outstanding debt by cutting your card in half.

✓ Track where your money goes. You start out with $40 in your wallet, but a few things here and a few things there and the next thing you know, it is all gone. Sound familiar?

✓ Get yourself a spiral notebook. Then write down every penny you spend for two months. Then review your expenses and label them "O" for optional and "E" for essential. The challenge is to eliminate the optional expenses that give you the least value for your money.

✓ Reduce auto expenses. Buy a used car, or a new car you can maintain for 10 years. Getting rid of your car after a couple of years is simply throwing away money.

✓ Save money on auto and homeowners insurance. Increase your deductibles (providing you could afford to pay the deductible amount if you had to) and lower your total insurance premiums.

Use debt cautiously

Heavy indebtedness is caused by presuming on your future ability to pay an obligation. You may be falling into the debt trap by buying a home or driving an automobile that you cannot afford.

The amount of debt a minister can adequately handle varies from one minister to another. Because of limited finances, some may not be able to positively handle ANY debt.

Credit-card debt should be avoided because of the high interest rates. Credit-card interest rates are almost always higher than what you can reasonably expect to earn after paying taxes on a very good investment.

Overextended credit-card balances are often one of the greatest heartaches for the minister's family. Using credit cards and paying the balance in full is different from avoiding credit-card debt. Using them for convenience and recordkeeping may even be a good money-management practice for you.

Take a long-term view

Take a long-term view toward your money management. It is the steady, consistent approach that pays huge dividends. If you only have a short-term view of your investments, you will likely jump out of your mutual fund every time the Dow-Jones drops 100 points.

One of the primary advantages of taking the long-term view is harnessing the power of time. As several small streams make a mighty river, your modest but steady saving and investing over a longer period allows your money to grow and "compound."

Taking the long-term view will protect you from putting your money into some get-rich-quick scheme. You may be tempted by a friend telling you about a new investment where you can receive 100% return on your money in a year, for example. "Not many people know about the opportunity yet, and you can get in on the ground floor!" But with the long-term view, you are more likely to keep your focus on your goals. It's a proven principle: If the investment is too good to be true, it probably *is* just that.

Saving, investing, and spending wisely doesn't guarantee carefree living in later years. However, failure to save will reduce your options (whether or not you will need to work). Increased physical limitations may prevent you from working, even though you may need the income.

God's providing and our planning go hand in hand. "The man who plants and the man who waters have one purpose, and each will be rewarded according to his own labor. For we are God's fellow workers" (1 Corinthians 3:8, 9).

Publishers note: For a clear guide on gaining control of your finances, see *The Christian's Guide to Worry-Free Money Management* by Daniel D. Busby, Kent E. Barber, and Robert L. Temple at your favorite Christian bookstore.

Action Steps

- Encourage your church board to perform an annual review of the entire pay package.

- Segregate salary, fringe benefits, and reimbursements when the pay package is designed.

- Do not use a salary reduction arrangement to fund expense reimbursements.

- Encourage church leaders to adopt an accountable expense reimbursement plan.

- Have an adequate cash housing allowance designated, even if you live in church-provided housing.

- File as an employee for income tax purposes in virtually every instance.

- Shift as much taxable income as possible into tax-free or tax-deferred fringe benefits.

- Keep detailed records of auto miles and business expenses.

- If you are not saving money on a regular basis, get started now.

- Avoid credit-card debt.

- Harness the power of time in your investing.

CHAPTER THREE
The Pay Package
More than meets the eye!

In This Chapter
- Should you delay paying tax on a portion of your salary?
- How much income can you defer?
- Can churches discriminate when providing fringe benefits?
- Tax treatment of compensation, fringe benefits, and reimbursements
- Table of compensation, fringe benefits, and reimbursements

Ask most ministers how much they get paid and they will tell you the amount of their salary and housing allowance. Usually there is more to it than that. Not only is your salary subject to tax, but so are many fringe benefits that you may receive.

What are fringe benefits? A fringe benefit is any cash, property, or service that an employee receives from an employer in addition to the regular salary or wage. The term "fringe benefits" is really a misnomer because employees have come to depend on them as a part of the total compensation package. Most fringe benefits are taxable as wages to employees unless specifically exempted by the Internal Revenue Code.

Many fringe benefits can be provided by a church to a minister without any dollar limitation (health insurance is an example), while other fringe benefits are subject to annual limits (dependent care is an example). (See the discussion later in this chapter to determine annual limits by fringe benefit type.)

Should You Delay Paying Tax on a Portion of Your Salary?

Following conventional advice, a minister should defer as much income as possible. Deferring income postpones reckoning with taxes until a future year.

You should come out ahead if you invest 100% of your money, pay no current taxes on earnings and then pay taxes on both the principal and earnings a number of years later. Your option is to pay the taxes on all your income, including earnings, as you go.

But the principle of deferring income and taxes relies on one key assumption: the playing field remains level over the time period the income is deferred. If tax rates stay the same or go down, deferring income is generally wise. However, if tax rates go up, you could actually lose money by using this technique. Any significant change in the favorable tax rules available to ministers today, such as the housing allowance, would also impact the benefit of deferring income.

Many ministers have an extra potential benefit from deferring income over non-ministers. If a minister has funds placed in a denominationally-sponsored pension, tax-sheltered annuity, or 401(k) plan, the benefits received at retirement are eligible for exclusion under the housing allowance rules.

How Much Income Can You Defer?

The basic annual limit for elective deferrals is $9,500. If you have completed at least fifteen years of service with a church, the $9,500 limit is increased each tax year up to a limit of $12,500.

The annual limit for non-elective deferrals is 20% of compensation after deducting the housing allowance but before making deferred payments. This limit relates to payments to denominational pension programs and all other deferrals. Most ministers can defer a minimum of $3,000 regardless of their level of compensation.

Can Churches Discriminate When Providing Fringe Benefits?

To qualify for exclusion from income, many fringe benefits must be nondiscriminatory. In other words, the benefits must be offered to all employees or all employees in certain classes. A fringe benefit subject to the nondiscrimination rules that is offered by a church only to the senior pastor, when other individuals are employed by the church, would be clearly discriminatory. This is particularly true for some benefits for certain key employees.

Failure to comply with the nondiscrimination rules does not disqualify a fringe benefit plan entirely. Only the highly compensated or key employees lose the tax-free benefit. Other employees will still receive the benefit tax-free.

The nondiscrimination rules apply to several types of fringe benefit plans, such as

- qualified tuition and fee discounts,
- eating facilities on or near the employer's premises,

- ✓ educational assistance benefits,
- ✓ dependent care plans,
- ✓ group-term life benefits,
- ✓ self-insured medical plans, and
- ✓ cafeteria plans (including medical reimbursement plans).

A "highly compensated employee" for 1996 is

- ✓ paid more than $100,000,
- ✓ paid more than $66,000 and in the top 20% of paid employees for the year,
- ✓ an officer and paid more than $59,400, or
- ✓ the highest-paid officer if there is no one paid over $59,400.

Tax Treatment of Compensation, Fringe Benefits, and Reimbursements

- ✓ **Awards**. Ministers rarely receive awards based on performance. But such awards are generally taxable income unless the value is insignificant. If an award is made to the minister in goods or services, such as a vacation trip, the fair market value of the goods or services is includable in income.

- ✓ **Bonuses**. A bonus received by a minister is taxable income.

- ✓ **Books**. A church may reimburse a minister for ministry-related books as a tax-free benefit.

- ✓ **Business and professional expense payments without adequate accounting**. Many churches pay periodic allowances to the minister for car expenses, library, entertainment, and so on. Other churches reimburse the minister for professional expenses with no requirement to account adequately for the expenses. (These are both nonaccountable plans.)

    Allowances or reimbursements under a nonaccountable plan must be included in the taxable income of the minister. For an employee, the expenses related to a nonaccountable reimbursement plan are deductible only if the minister itemizes expenses on Schedule A. Even then, the business expenses, combined with other miscellaneous deductions, must exceed 2% of adjusted gross income. If self-employed, the expenses are deductible on Schedule C (C-EZ).

✓ **Business and professional expenses reimbursed with adequate accounting.** If the church reimburses the minister under an *accountable* plan for employment-related professional or business expenses (auto, other travel, subscriptions, entertainment, and so on), the reimbursement is not taxable compensation and is not reported to the IRS by the church or the minister. Per diem allowances up to IRS-approved limits also qualify as excludable reimbursements.

✓ **Child care.** (See dependent care.)

✓ **Clothing.** Ordinary clothing (not vestments) worn in the exercise of your duties for the church are personal expenses and not deductible as business expenses or reimbursable by the church under an accountable plan.

If you wear clothing for your ministry that is not adaptable to general use, it is deductible or reimbursable as a business expense.

✓ **Computers.** The value of the business use of a church-provided computer for home use may be excludable from your gross income as a "working condition" fringe benefit. In order for the exclusion to apply, your business use of the computer must

- relate to the work of the church,

- entitle you to a business deduction if you purchased the computer personally, and

- be more than 50% of your total use.

You must include the value of the benefit of a computer in income if

- your use is nonbusiness,

- your use does not qualify as a working condition fringe benefit (see the three requirements shown above), or

- you do not keep records to substantiate business use.

✓ **Continuing education.** (See educational reimbursement plans.)

✓ **Conventions.** Expenses incurred for you to attend a ministry-related convention or seminar are generally deductible. (See chapter 5 for rules for the expenses of your spouse and children.)

If the convention is held outside the North America area, expenses are deductible only if the attendance is ministry-related and it is as reasonable for the convention to be held outside the North America area as within it.

When a minister travels away from home to attend a convention and

THE PAY PACKAGE

combines personal activities with ministry activities, the deduction for convention expenses may be subject to certain limitations.

When a minister attends a convention on a cruise ship, expenses incurred in connection with the convention are deductible only if the convention is ministry-related, the cruise ship is registered in the United States, and the ship does not stop at a port outside the United States or one of its possessions. Additionally, there is a $2,000 limit on expenses that may be deducted for a convention of this type.

✓ **Deferred compensation.** A church may maintain a retirement or other deferred compensation plan for employees that is not qualified (under the Internal Revenue Code) and is not a tax-sheltered annuity or a "rabbi trust." If the plan is unfunded (the church makes a promise, not represented by a note, to pay at some time in the future), contributions to the plan are generally not taxable currently.

Funds placed in an investment account (other than in a tax-sheltered annuity or "rabbi trust") under the church's control to provide retirement funds for the minister have no tax consequence to the minister until the funds are paid or available to the minister.

Nonqualified deferred compensation plans established after July 1, 1986 generally limit deferrals of compensation to amounts deferred before they are earned and deferral of the lesser of $7,500 or one-third of the employee's includible compensation (reduced by amounts deferred under a 403(b), 401(k), or SEP-IRA plan).

If the church funds the plan (such as purchasing an annuity contract), the contributions are generally taxable currently.

✓ **Dependent care.** If the church provides you with child care (for dependents under age 13) or disabled dependent care services to allow you to work, you can exclude the amount of this benefit from income within certain limits. The amount excludable is limited to the smaller of

- your earned income,

- your spouse's earned income, or

- $5,000 ($2,500 if married filing separately).

The dependent care assistance must be provided under a separate written plan of your employer that does not favor highly compensated employees and that meets other qualifications.

Dependent care assistance payments are excluded from income if the payments cover expenses that would be deductible if the expenses were not reimbursed. If the minister is married, both spouses must be employed. There are special rules if one spouse is a student or incapable of self-care.

For a sample dependent care assistance plan, see the 1997 edition of the *Zondervan Church and Nonprofit Organization Tax & Financial Guide.*

✓ **Disability insurance.** If the church pays the disability insurance premiums (and the minister is the beneficiary) as a part of your compensation package, the premiums are excluded from your income. Any disability policy proceeds must be included in your gross income.

Conversely, if you pay the disability insurance premiums or have the church withhold the premiums from your salary, any disability benefits paid under the policy are not taxable to you.

Most claims for social security disability benefits are denied. This is all the more reason to secure disability insurance coverage.

✓ **Disability pay.** (See Sick or disability pay.)

✓ **Discretionary fund.** Churches often establish a fund to be disbursed upon the discretion of the pastor. If the funds are used for church business or the needs of individuals associated with the church in a benevolent manner, and a proper accounting is made, there is no tax impact on the minister. If there is no accounting to the church, and if it is permissible to distribute some of the funds to the minister, money placed in the fund becomes additional taxable income to the minister in the year the money is transferred by the church to the discretionary fund.

✓ **Dues and memberships.** Membership fees paid to ministry-related professional organizations generally qualify as business expense if there is a clear relationship to the ministry of the church or the minister.

Club dues are reimbursable tax-free to the extent that the use of the club is for bona fide business purposes and the dues are reimbursed under an accountable business expense reimbursement plan. This rule applies to all types of clubs, including athletic and country clubs, and hotel and airline clubs.

Dues for downtown luncheon clubs, such as Kiwanis, Lions, Rotary, and so on, generally do not result in income to an employee. Dues for country clubs generally will result in income to the employee, particularly when there is substantial use of the club by the employee's family and personal guests.

If the church pays the health, fitness, or athletic facility dues for a minister, the amounts paid are includable in the minister's income.

✓ **Educational assistance programs.** An educational assistance program is a separate written plan of a church to provide educational assistance to employees. A program may include job-related courses or courses that are part of a degree program. Graduate-level courses begun after June 30, 1996 will be excluded for purposes of this benefit. The program must be nondiscriminatory.

No benefits may be provided to the employee's spouse or dependents. The church should exclude from income the first $5,250 of any qualified educational assistance paid for you during the year. This provision expired on December 31, 1994 but the benefit has been extended to 1995, 1996, and 1997.

THE PAY PACKAGE

✓ **Educational reimbursement plans.** If your church requires the educational courses or they are job-related, and your church either pays the expenses directly to the educational organization or reimburses you for the expenses after you make a full accounting, you may not have to include in income the amount paid by your church.

While there are no specific dollar limits on educational expenses paid under a nonqualified reimbursement plan, the general ordinary and necessary business expense rules do apply. These types of payments may be discriminatory.

Though the education may lead to a degree, expenses may qualify as excludable if the education

- is required by your church or the law to keep your salary, status, or job (and serves a business purpose of your church), or

- maintains or improves skills required in your present work.

Even if you meet the above qualification, education expenses do not qualify if the education

- is needed to meet the minimum educational requirements of your present work, or

- is part of a program of study that can qualify you for a new trade or business, even if you have no plans to enter that trade or business.

It may be possible for you to deduct as itemized deductions unreimbursed educational expenses or those reimbursed under a nonaccountable plan.

✓ **Equity allowance.** If the church owns the parsonage, only the church is building up equity. If the church provides a cash allowance for the minister to purchase a home, the minister may establish some equity.

An equity allowance is an amount paid to the minister living in a church-owned parsonage. This allowance may partially or fully offset the equity that the minister would have accumulated in a personally owned home.

An equity allowance that you are paid is fully taxable and not excludable as a housing allowance. However, the church could make the equity payments into a tax-sheltered annuity (TSA) or 401(k) plan. This would be consistent with the desire of a congregation to provide funds for housing at retirement. Under current law, the funds received at retirement from church-sponsored TSA or 401(k) plans may be eligible for tax-free treatment as a housing allowance.

✓ **Entertainment expenses.** A minister may deduct ministry-related entertainment expenses. Entertainment expenses must be directly related to or associated with the work of the church. Entertainment expenses are not deductible if they are lavish or extravagant.

Business meal and entertainment expenses are limited to 50% of such expenses unless reimbursed by the church based on substantiation. If the church reimburses the expenses, a 100% reimbursement may be made.

✓ **Flexible spending arrangements**. "Cafeteria" or flexible spending plans are separately written plans that allow employee participants to choose between two or more qualified fringe benefits.

The only taxable benefit that a cafeteria or flexible spending plan can offer is cash. A qualified (nontaxable) benefit to the participant includes any benefit that is not currently taxable upon receipt. Examples of these benefits are group-term life insurance up to $50,000, coverage under an accident or health plan, and coverage under a dependent care assistance program.

A cafeteria or flexible spending plan cannot discriminate in favor of highly compensated participants for contributions, benefits, or eligibility to participate in the plan. Churches with fewer than 25 employees generally do not find these plans feasible.

✓ **Forgiveness of debt**. (See Loan-grants.)

✓ **401(k) plans.** A church may offer a 401(k) plan to its employees starting in 1997 (see pages 7-8). Under a 401(k) plan, an employee can elect to have the church make tax-deferred contributions to the plan or make a taxable cash distribution directly to the employee.

✓ **Frequent flyer awards**. Free travel awards used personally that are received as frequent flyer miles on business travel paid by the church are taxable when the awards are used. The IRS is not aggressively monitoring the reporting of the value of these awards, but IRS examiners can raise the issue during an audit and assess tax for the value of awards.

✓ **Gifts/personal**. Money that a minister receives directly from an individual is usually considered a personal gift and may be excluded from income if the payments are intended for the personal benefit of the minister and not in consideration of any services rendered. If the gift is a check, it should be made payable directly to the minister to qualify for tax exclusion for the minister. A personal gift of this nature will not qualify as a charitable contribution by the donor.

Checks made out to the church for the benefit of the minister will typically represent taxable income to the minister at the point the minister receives the funds.

✓ **Gifts/special occasion**. Christmas, anniversary, birthday, retirement, and similar gifts paid by a church to its minister are typically taxable compensation. This is true if the gift came from the general fund of the church or from an offering in which tax-deductible contributions were made to the church for the benefit of the minister.

To qualify as a nontaxable gift, the transfer must meet the requisites of a gift. A gift is based on detached and disinterested generosity, out of affection, respect, admiration, charity, or like impulses. The transferor's intention is the most critical factor. Also, it must be made without consideration of services rendered.

The church may announce an all-cash offering with a clear understanding that all proceeds will be paid directly and personally to the minister and that amounts given will not be receipted as charitable contributions. If the amounts given are not entered on the church books as contributions, they may qualify as tax-free gifts to the minister.

If the church gives you a turkey, ham, or other item of nominal value at Christmas or other holidays, the value of the gift is not income. But if the church gives you cash or an item that you can easily exchange for cash, such as a gift certificate, the gift is extra compensation regardless of the amount involved.

✓ **Health insurance**. If the church pays the medical insurance premiums directly to the insurance carrier or reimburses the minister-employee for the premiums based on substantiation, the premiums are tax-free to the minister. However, if similar payments are made for a self-employed minister, the payments represent additional taxable income.

If a church makes a lump-sum payment to a minister-employee to provide health insurance coverage and the minister does not substantiate the expense, the payment is taxable income.

Church medical plans funded solely through insurance contracts are not subject to the nondiscrimination rules. Premium payments by an employer may be excluded from the gross income of employees if the plan only covers one or more of the church's employees. Benefits received under the plan are also tax-free.

Churches are *exempt* from the requirements imposed on other employers to refrain from discriminating in favor of more highly paid individuals for health insurance programs handled through an insurance carrier.

✓ **Home office.** If their home is the principal place of business, certain taxpayers can deduct a portion of their home expenses such as depreciation, utilities, repairs, and so on. However, the home office rules generally have no benefit for ministers as it relates to housing expenses.

A home provided by a minister does not generate any home-office deductions if the church designates a housing allowance and all housing expenses are excluded. With the exclusion of the housing allowance from salary, the housing expenses—including the housing element of home-office expenses—have already been treated as tax-free.

The status of a home office as a regular or principal place of business may have a direct bearing on the status of commuting versus business transportation expenses. (See page 94 for further discussion of this issue.)

✓ **Housing allowance**. A properly designated housing allowance may be excluded from income subject to certain limitations. The fair rental value of a parsonage provided to a minister is not taxable for income tax purposes but is includable for social security tax purposes.

Any housing allowance paid to a minister that is more than the excludable amount is taxable compensation. The excess must be determined by the minister and reported on Form 1040, page 1. The church does not have a reporting requirement to the minister or the IRS regarding any portion of the designated housing allowance that exceeds the amount actually excluded.

✓ **Individual Retirement Accounts.** Amounts contributed by a church for a minister-employee's Individual Retirement Account (IRA) are includable in the employee's compensation on the Form W-2 and are subject to self-employment tax. Minister-employees may generally deduct church contributions to an IRA up to the lesser of $2,000 or 100% of compensation. Other limits often apply if the minister or spouse is an active participant in a retirement plan. Participation in a denominational pension plan generally does not disqualify a minister from making tax-deductible IRA contributions.

✓ **Keogh plans**. If a minister has self-employment income for income tax purposes, a Keogh (also known as H.R. 10) plan may be used.

Amounts contributed to a Keogh plan are not taxed until distribution if the contribution limits are observed. If you withdraw money from your Keogh plan before you reach the age of 59½, you will be subject to a 10% early withdrawal penalty.

✓ **Life insurance**. The rules covering life insurance fall into two categories:

- **Whole life or universal life**. If the church pays the premium on a whole life or universal life insurance policy on the life of the minister and the minister names personal beneficiaries, all the premiums paid are taxable income to the minister.

- **Group-term life**. If the group life coverage provided under a nondiscriminatory plan does not exceed $50,000 for the minister, the life insurance premiums are generally tax-free to the employee-minister. For an employee, group-term life insurance coverage of more than $50,000 provided to the minister by the church is taxable under somewhat favorable IRS tables. If self-employed, all group-term life premiums are taxable income. Group-term life insurance is term life insurance protection that

    ■ provides a general death benefit that can be excluded from income,

THE PAY PACKAGE

- covers a group of employees (a "group" may consist of only one employee),

- is provided under a policy carried by the employer, and

- provides an amount of insurance for each employee based on a formula that prevents individual selection.

If you pay any part of the cost of the insurance, your entire payment reduces, dollar for dollar, the amount the church would otherwise include in income.

If your group-term life insurance policy includes permanent benefits such as a paid-up or cash surrender value, you must include in income the cost of the permanent benefits, reduced by the amount you pay for them.

If you are a retired minister, you also should include in income any payments for group-term life insurance coverage over $50,000 made by a former employing church, unless you otherwise qualify to exclude the payments.

✓ **Loan-grants**. Churches may provide a loan-grant to a minister relating to moving expenses, the purchase of a car, or the purchase of other property. In these instances, compensation is reported on Form W-2 or 1099-MISC for the minister based on the amount of the loan forgiven in a calendar year. The rules on compensation-related loans (see below) apply to loan-grants over $10,000.

✓ **Loans**. If the church provides a below-market compensation-related loan to a minister-employee or to a self-employed minister, additional compensation for the foregone interest must be included on the minister's Form W-2 or 1099-MISC. The minister must also attach a statement to the return showing the amount of imputed interest and the name, address, and employer identification number of the lender.

If the loan proceeds were used for housing and you itemize your deductions, you may be able to deduct the imputed interest as mortgage interest. The interest is also eligible for inclusion in housing expenses for housing allowance purposes.

A "compensation-related" loan is any direct or indirect loan of over $10,000 made below market interest rates that relates to the performance of services between a church and a minister.

For term loans, the additional compensation is considered as received on the date the loan was made. For demand loans, the foregone interest is added to compensation each year, quarter by quarter, that the loan is outstanding.

Loans to ministers may be prohibited by state law. Check with legal counsel before making such a loan. Even if a loan is legal under state law, the IRS could consider it to be private inurement, thereby jeopardizing the church's tax-exempt status.

✓ **Long-term care insurance.** Long-term care or nursing home insurance premiums paid or reimbursed by the church represent additional taxable income to the minister for 1996 and prior years. However, these payments are tax-free in 1997 and later years. If the premiums are paid by the minister in 1997 and not reimbursed by the church, they are deductible as medical expenses subject to annual limits based on your age.

✓ **Love offerings.** (See Gifts/special occasion.)

✓ **Meals.** If meals provided to you by the church are a means of giving you more pay and there is no other business reason for providing them, their value is extra income to you.

If the meals are furnished by the church for the church's convenience (e.g., such as having a minister on call), a minister does not include their value in income if the benefits are nondiscriminatory. However, the benefits are taxable for social security purposes.

✓ **Medical insurance.** (See Health insurance.)

✓ **Medical expense reimbursement plan.** A properly designed, *written* employee medical expense reimbursement plan (MERP) under which the church pays the medical expenses of the minister, spouse, and dependents may be nontaxable to the minister-employee. See the 1997 Edition of the *Zondervan Church and Nonprofit Organization Tax & Financial Guide* for a sample plan and other requirements for a MERP.

MERPs may be funded by church-provided funds or by a reduction of the minister's salary. If funded by salary reduction, excess funds in the MERP cannot be paid to the minister without causing all the benefits under the plan to be treated as taxable compensation. Excess money in a church-funded MERP can be carried over to a future year without any tax implications to the minister. Typical expenses covered by such a plan are deductibles and co-insurance and non-covered amounts paid by the individual.

MERPs may not discriminate in favor of highly compensated employees, with regard to either benefits or eligibility. For example, a plan that covers the church pastor but not the full-time secretary would be discriminatory.

MERPs are only available to minister-employees (and other nonminister employees).

✓ **Memberships.** (See Dues and memberships.)

✓ **Minimal fringe benefits.** If the fringe benefits are so small (*de minimis*) in value that it would be unreasonable or impractical to account for them, the minister does not have to include their value in income. If the value of the benefit is not small, you must include its entire value in your income.

De minimis fringe benefits include traditional holiday gifts with a low

THE PAY PACKAGE

fair market value, occasional typing of personal letters by the church secretary, or occasional personal use of the church copy machine.

Example: You use the church copy machine for personal items. The machine is used at least 85% of the time for business purposes since the church restricts personal use of the copy machine. Though you use the machine for personal purposes more than other employees, your use is small and not taxable.

✓ **Moving expenses** (paid by the church). Moving expenses paid directly or reimbursed by the church are excludable from gross income (reported on Form W-2, only in Box 13, using Code P to identify them as nontaxable reimbursements) for minister-employees. Amounts are excludable only to the extent that they would be deductible as moving expenses, i.e., only the cost of moving household goods and travel, other than meals, from the old residence to the new residence.

If self-employed, you must include in gross income (and the church must report on your Form 1099-MISC) all reimbursements of, or payments for, moving expenses. Include the moving expense payments on line 1 of Schedule C (C-EZ). To claim a deduction for moving expenses, complete Form 3903 (3903-F for foreign moves) and enter your deduction on line 24, page 1, of Form 1040.

Moving expenses do not qualify as business expenses. Therefore, moving expenses are not deductible in computing self-employment tax on Schedule SE for ministers considered to be self-employed for income tax purposes. For ministers filing as employees for income tax purposes, there is no requirement to add moving expense reimbursements, excluded on Form W-2, to Schedule SE income.

Example 1: You report as an employee for income tax purposes. Your church paid a moving company $2,200 in 1996 for your move. The church also reimbursed you $350 for miscellaneous moving expenses. The church should report $2,550 on Form W-2, only in Box 13, using Code P.

Example 2: You report as self-employed for income tax purposes. Your church reimburses you $3,000 for your 1996 move. The church must include $3,000 in your Form 1099-MISC and provide you with Form 4782. You must include the $3,000 income on Schedule C or C-EZ (subject to social security) and deduct the moving expenses on line 24, page 1, of Form 1040.

✓ **Nursing home insurance.** (See Long-term care insurance.)

✓ **Office in the home.** (See Home office.)

57

✓ **Parking**. You do not have to include in income the value of free parking facilities provided to you on or near the church premises if it is $165 or less for 1996. This also applies for reimbursements from the church for renting a parking space on or near the church premises. A church can also sell transit passes or tokens to ministers at discounts of up to $65 per month tax-free or just give cash up to $65 for passes and tokens tax-free.

✓ **Pension plans**. Contributions to certain pension and retirement plans are excludable or deductible by a minister for income tax purposes. In these instances, there is generally no tax consequence until the funds are distributed to the minister.

- **Denominational plans**. When the church makes contributions to a denominational pension plan for you, the contributions are not included in your taxable income. Upon retirement, the benefits represent taxable income unless excluded as a parsonage allowance.

- **Nonqualified deferred compensation plans.** (See Deferred compensation.)

- **Pension payroll deductions.** You cannot generally exclude from income amounts that you pay directly or pay into a pension plan through payroll deductions. The amounts provided by salary reductions to 403(b) tax-sheltered annuities or 401(k) plans are excluded from income for income tax purposes.

- **Other.** (See Individual Retirement Accounts, Keogh plans, Simplified Employee Pension plans, and Tax-sheltered annuities.)

✓ **Pre-employment expense reimbursements**. Prospective ministers are sometimes reimbursed for expenses related to seeking a position with a particular church. Expenses related to interviews (meals, lodging, and travel) are not includable in the prospective employee's gross income whether or not the minister is subsequently employed.

✓ **Property transfers/restricted**. To reward good work, a church may transfer property to a minister subject to certain restrictions. The ultimate transfer of the property will occur only if the restrictions are met at a later date.

Property that is subject to substantial risk of forfeiture and is nontransferable is substantially not vested. No tax liability will occur until title to the property is vested with the minister. This simply represents a deferral of the tax consequences.

When restricted property becomes substantially vested, the minister must include in income an amount equal to the excess of the fair market value of the property at the time it becomes substantially vested, over the amount the minister pays for the property.

For tax planning purposes, the "vesting" of a restricted property transfer

THE PAY PACKAGE

to a minister should be staggered over several years. The reporting of a sizeable restricted gift in one year may have significant tax consequences.

Example: A church transfers a house to a minister subject to the completion of twenty years of pastoral service to the church. The minister does not report any taxable income from the gift until the calendar year that includes the twentieth anniversary of the agreement.

✓ **Property transfers/unrestricted.** If a church transfers property (for example, a car, equipment, or other property) to a minister at no charge, this constitutes taxable income to the minister. The amount of income is generally the fair market value of the property transferred as of the date of the transfer.

If you buy property from the church at a price below its fair market value, you must include in compensation the difference between the property's fair market value and the amount you paid for it and liabilities that you assumed.

✓ **Rabbi trust.** Deferred compensation plans that use a trust are commonly referred to as "rabbi trusts." The IRS has issued a model form for these trusts. If the model trust is used, contributions to the trust will generally not be taxed currently.

✓ **Recreational expenses.** A minister may incur expenses that are primarily recreational, e.g., softball or basketball league fees, greens fees, and so on. Even if there is an element of ministry purpose, the deduction or reimbursement of such fees as business expenses is generally not justified.

✓ **Retirement gifts.** Gifts made to a minister at retirement are usually taxable compensation. This is particularly true for minister-employees. Retirement gifts made by an individual directly to a minister may be tax-free to the minister, but they will not qualify as charitable contributions by the donor.

✓ **Salary.** The cash salary (less the properly designated and excludable housing allowance amount) is taxable income.

✓ **Savings Incentive Match Plans for Employees (SIMPLE Plans).** Starting in 1997, churches with 100 or fewer employees who received at least $5,000 in compensation from the church in a preceding year may adopt a SIMPLE plan, if they do not currently maintain another qualified plan. The plan allows employees to make elective contributions of up to $6,000 per year and requires churches to make matching contributions. Assets in the account are not taxed until they are distributed to an employee. SIMPLE plans are not subject to the nondiscrimination rules.

✓ **Scholarship fund.** The church may provide a scholarship fund for the benefit of the minister's children when they attend college or a pre-college private school. When the church makes the payment to the college, the funds are taxable income to the minister. If the church withholds money from your pay and forwards the funds to a college for the education of your child, the amount withheld does not reduce your taxable compensation. See the 1997 edition of the *Zondervan Church and Nonprofit Organization Tax & Financial Guide* for more information on scholarship funds established by churches.

✓ **Seminars**. (See Conventions.)

✓ **Severance pay**. A lump-sum payment for cancellation of your employment contract is income in the tax year you receive it and must be reported with your other compensation.

✓ **Sick or disability pay**. Amounts you receive from your church while you are sick or disabled are part of your compensation (sick or disability pay is distinguished from payments for injury provided under Workers' Compensation insurance, which are normally not taxable). You must also include in income any payments made by an insurance company if the church paid the premiums.

If you paid the premiums on an accident or health insurance policy or if the premiums paid by your church were treated as part of your taxable compensation, the benefits you receive under the policy are not taxable.

✓ **Simplified Employee Pension Plans (SEPs)**. Through an SEP, the church may contribute amounts to your IRA if you are an employee or self-employed for income tax purposes. But there are many nondiscriminatory limitations on SEP contributions that most churches will find insurmountable. The maximum annual contribution is effectively 13.04%.

✓ **Social security tax reimbursement**. Churches commonly reimburse ministers for a portion or all of their self-employment social security (SECA) tax liability. Any social security reimbursement must be reported as taxable income.

Because of the deductibility of the self-employment tax in both the income tax and self-employment tax computations, a full reimbursement is effectively less than the gross 15.3% rate:

Your Marginal Tax Rate	Effective SECA Rate
0%	14.13%
15	13.07
28	12.15
31	11.94

It is usually best to reimburse the minister for self-employment tax on a monthly or quarterly basis. An annual reimbursement may leave room for misunderstanding between the church and the minister. This is especially true if the minister moves to another church before the reimbursement is made.

For missionaries who are not eligible for the income tax deduction of one-half of the self-employment tax due to the foreign earned income exclusion,

THE PAY PACKAGE

the full reimbursement rate is effectively 14.13%.

✓ **Subscriptions**. A church may reimburse a minister for ministry-related magazine subscriptions as a tax-free benefit. Unreimbursed subscriptions may be deducted on Schedule A or C.

✓ **Tax-sheltered annuities (TSAs)**. Minister-employees may have a Section 403(b) salary reduction arrangement based on a written plan. Churches and elementary or secondary schools, controlled, operated, or principally supported by a church or convention or association of churches, are not subject to the stringent nondiscrimination rules. For a sample TSA plan, see the 1997 Edition of the *Zondervan Church and Nonprofit Organization Tax & Financial Guide*.

Both nonelective and elective employer contributions for a minister to a TSA are excludable for income and social security tax (SECA) purposes. The housing allowance amount must be excluded from gross pay before multiplying 20% times compensation to determine the maximum TSA annual contribution. See page 46 for other TSA limitations.

Withdrawals from a denominationally-sponsored TSA plan qualify for designation as a housing allowance and are generally not subject to social security (SECA) tax.

A minister can roll funds tax-free from one TSA to another TSA. However, funds cannot be rolled from a qualified pension plan to a TSA.

✓ **Telephone/cellular**. If a cellular telephone is provided by the church, the same rules apply as in the case of computers provided by the church. (See Computers.)

✓ **Travel expenses**. Travel expenses of a minister are deductible as business expenses if they are ordinary and necessary and incurred while traveling away from the minister's tax home for business-related reasons. Expenses that are for personal or vacation purposes, or that are lavish or extravagant, may not be deducted.

Travel expenses incurred outside the United States may be subject to a special business vs. personal travel expense allocation of the transportation costs to and from the business destination. This allocation can apply even when foreign travel expenses are incurred primarily for business purposes. Expenses incurred for travel as a form of education, such as a tour of the Holy Land, are not deductible (see pages 88-89).

Under proposed IRS regulations, if a minister incurs travel expenses for a spouse or child, the minister may deduct or receive a tax-free reimbursement for the spouse's children's expenses if

- the travel of the spouse or child is for a bona fide business purpose; and

- the employee-minister substantiates the time, place, amount, and business purpose of the travel under an accountable business expense reimbursement plan.

✓ **Tuition and fee discounts**. If you are an employee of a church-operated elementary, secondary, or undergraduate institution, certain tuition and fee discounts provided to a minister, spouse, or dependent children may be tax-free. The discounts must be nondiscriminatory and relate to an educational program.

If you are employed by the church and not by the church-operated private school, tuition and fee discounts that you receive may be taxable income. You may wish to obtain professional counsel on this matter.

✓ **Vacation pay**. Payments made by the church to you for vacations are taxable income.

✓ **Vehicles/personal use of church-owned vehicle.** The personal use of a church-provided vehicle is considered a taxable fringe benefit. The fair market value of the personal use must be included in the minister's gross income unless the minister fully reimburses the value to the church.

Example: Your church provides a vehicle for your use for a full year. The vehicle cost was $16,000 and the annual lease value for the year is $4,600. You drive 6,000 miles during the year for the church and 2,000 miles for personal use. The value of the working condition fringe is 6,000 (business miles) divided by 8,000 (total miles) times $4,600 (total value) equals $3,450. The $3,450 value of the working condition fringe is excluded from income. The remaining $1,150 value is for the personal use of the vehicle and must be included in your income. You must also add 5.5 cents per mile unless you paid for the fuel when the vehicle was used for personal purposes.

Many churches use the annual lease value rule to set a value on the use of a church-provided vehicle. (There are also several other valuation rules that are available). If the church provides the fuel, 5.5 cents per mile must be added to the annual lease value. See IRS Publication 535 for more information.

✓ **Vehicle use/nonpersonal**. The total value of the use of a qualified nonpersonal-use vehicle is excluded from income as a working condition fringe. The term "qualified nonpersonal-use vehicle" means any vehicle that is not likely to be used more than a small amount for personal purposes because of its nature or design.

Example: A church provides you with a vehicle to use for church business. You do not qualify for a home office and leave the car parked at the church when it is not being driven for business purposes. There is a written agreement with the church that prohibits your personal use of the vehicle. Only in an emergency is the car driven for personal benefit. This vehicle should qualify under the nonpersonal-use provision, and

THE PAY PACKAGE

the entire value of the vehicle would be excluded from your income.

✓ **Wage continuation**. Generally, payments to an employee from a wage continuation plan are treated as compensation for income tax purposes. For the treatment of special types of wage continuation plans, see the explanations under Disability insurance and Workers' Compensation.

✓ **Withholding**. Amounts withheld from your pay or put into your bank account under a voluntary withholding agreement for income tax or savings bonds are compensation as though paid directly to you. They must be included on your Form W-2 or 1099-MISC in the year they were withheld. The same generally is true of amounts withheld for taxable fringe benefits.

If the church uses your wages to pay your debts, or if your wages are garnisheed, the full amount is compensation to you.

✓ **Workers' Compensation**. A minister who receives Workers' Compensation benefits due to his job-related injuries or sickness may generally exclude the benefits from gross income. In addition, the minister is not taxed on the value of the insurance premium paid by the church.

Employee-ministers should be covered under Workers' Compensation laws in many states. It is often important to cover ministers under Workers' Compensation insurance even if it is not a state requirement. For work-related injuries of minister-employees, many health benefit plans will not pay medical expenses unless the minister is covered by Workers' Compensation insurance. For more information, see the 1997 edition of the *Church and Nonprofit Organization Tax & Financial Guide*.

Action Steps

■ Understand the different treatment of certain fringe benefits depending on whether you are an employee or self-employed for income tax purposes.

■ Determine which fringe benefits are taxable vs. tax-free. Focus on the tax-free benefits.

■ Be aware of the nondiscrimination rules for certain fringe benefits. Many fringe benefits for ministers are taxable under these rules.

■ Structure your pay package to include as many tax-free fringe benefits as possible while minimizing your taxable salary.

Compensation, Fringe Benefit, and Reimbursement Reporting for Income Tax Purposes

Compensation, fringe benefits, or reimbursement	Employee-Minister	Self-Employed Minister
Bonus or gift from church	Taxable income/Form W-2	Taxable income/Form 1099-MISC
Business and professional expenses reimbursed with adequate accounting	Tax-free	Tax-free. Accountable expense plan rules are not applicable
Business and professional expense payments without adequate accounting	Deduction on Schedule A, Miscellaneous Deductions. Subject to 2% of AGI and 50% meals and entertainment limits	Deduction on Schedule C (C-EZ), Part II. 50% meal and entertainment limit applies
Club dues paid by the church	Taxable income/Form W-2 (exception for dues for civic and public service groups)	Taxable income/Form 1099-MISC (exception for dues for civic and public service groups)
Compensation reported to minister by church	Form W-2	Form 1099-MISC
Dependent care assistance payments	Tax-free	Tax-free
Earned income tax credit (EITC)	May be eligible for EITC	May be eligible for EITC
Educational assistance programs	May be eligible to exclude up to $5,250 of qualified assistance	Ineligible for this benefit
401(k) plan	Eligible for 401(k)	Eligible for 401(k)
Gifts/personal (not handled through church)	Tax-free	Tax-free
Housing allowance	Tax-free. Subject to limitations	Tax-free. Subject to limitations
IRA payments by church	Taxable income/Form W-2	Taxable income/Form 1099-MISC

Compensation, Fringe Benefit, and Reimbursement Reporting for Income Tax Purposes

Compensation, fringe benefits, or reimbursement	Employee-Minister	Self-Employed Minister
Insurance, disability, paid by church, minister is beneficiary	Premiums are tax-free. Proceeds are taxable	Taxable income/Form 1099-MISC
Insurance, disability, paid by minister, minister is beneficiary	Proceeds are tax-free	Proceeds are tax-free
Insurance, group-term life, paid by church	First $50,000 of coverage is tax-free	Taxable income/Form 1099-MISC
Insurance, health	Tax-free if directly paid by church or reimbursed to minister upon substantiation. If paid by minister and not reimbursed by church, deduct on Schedule A.	Taxable income if paid by church. 30% deducted on Form 1040, page 1/remaining 70% claimed on Schedule A
Insurance, life, whole or universal, church is beneficiary	Tax-free	Tax-free
Insurance, life, whole or universal, minister designates beneficiary	Taxable income/Form W-2	Taxable income/Form 1099-MISC
Insurance, long-term care	Tax-free if directly paid by church or reimbursed to minister on substantiation. If paid by minister and not reimbursed by church, deduct on Schedule A subject to limitations.	Taxable income if paid by church. Deduct on Schedule A, subject to limitations.
Loans, certain low-interest or interest-free to minister over $10,000	Imputed interest is taxable income/Form W-2	Imputed interest is taxable income/Form 1099-MISC
Medical expense reimbursement plan	Tax-free	Taxable income/Form 1099-MISC
Moving expenses paid by the church	Reported on Form W-2, only in Box 13, using Code P. Not added back to income on Schedule SE for social security purposes	Included on Form 1099-MISC. Offset as an adjustment to income on page 1, Form 1040. Not deductible for social security purposes on Schedule SE

Compensation, Fringe Benefit, and Reimbursement Reporting for Income Tax Purposes

Compensation, fringe benefits, or reimbursement	Employee-Minister	Self-Employed Minister
Pension payments to a denominational plan for the minister by the church	Tax-deferred. No reporting required until the funds are withdrawn or pension benefits are paid	Tax-deferred. No reporting required until the funds are withdrawn or pension benefits are paid
Per diem payments for meals, lodging, and incidental expenses	May be used for travel away from home under an accountable reimbursement plan	Ineligible to use the per diem rates for lodging
Professional income (weddings, funerals)	Taxable income/Schedule C(C-EZ)	Taxable income/Schedule C(C-EZ)
Property transferred to minister at no cost or less than fair market value	Taxable income/Form W-2	Taxable income/Form 1099-MISC
Retirement or farewell gift to minister from church	Taxable income/Form W-2	Taxable income/Form 1099-MISC
Salary from church	Report salary on page 1, Form 1040	Report compensation on Schedule C or C-EZ
Social Security reimbursed by church to minister	Taxable income/Form W-2	Taxable income/Form 1099-MISC
TSA, Sec. 403(b) tax-sheltered annuity	Eligible for TSA	Eligible for TSA
Travel paid for minister's wife by the church	May be tax-free if there is a business purpose	Taxable income/Form 1099-MISC
Tuition and fee discounts	May be tax-free in certain situations	Ineligible for this benefit
Value of home provided to minister	Tax-free	Tax-free
Vehicles/personal use of church-owned auto	Taxable income/Form W-2	Taxable income/Form 1099-MISC
Voluntary withholding	Eligible for voluntary withholding agreement	Ineligible for voluntary withholding agreement

CHAPTER FOUR
Home Sweet Home

The housing allowance is easily the best of all tax benefits for clergy!

In This Chapter
- Types of housing arrangements
- Structuring the housing allowance
- Reporting the housing allowance to the minister
- Accounting for the housing allowance
- Other housing allowance issues
- Housing allowance worksheets

Ministers are eligible to receive lodging from the church free of income tax liability. Maximizing housing benefits requires careful planning. Used properly, the housing allowance can truly be the minister's best tax friend.

Every minister should have a portion of salary designated as a housing allowance. For ministers living in church-owned housing, a housing allowance covering expenses such as furnishings, personal property insurance on contents, utilities, and so on could save several hundred dollars of income taxes annually. A properly designated housing allowance may be worth thousands of dollars in income tax savings for ministers living in their own homes or rented quarters. For a minister without a housing allowance, every dollar of compensation is taxable for federal income tax purposes.

The housing allowance provides an opportunity to exclude dollars from gross income. The excluded amount should be subtracted from compensation before the church completes the data on Form W-2 or 1099-MISC. The excluded portion of the housing allowance is not entered on Form 1040 or related schedules (except Schedule SE) since it is not a deduction for income tax purposes nor is it an adjustment to income at the bottom of Form 1040, page 1.

If you receive a cash housing allowance, the exclusion is commonly referred to as a *housing* allowance. If you live free of charge in a church-owned home, the exclusion is often called a *parsonage* allowance. In either instance, the exclusion

Church-Provided Housing

The fair rental value of the parsonage plus utilities (if paid by church) is
- Excludable for federal income tax purposes
- Includable for social security (SECA) purposes

A parsonage allowance may be provided a minister living in church-provided housing. It is a designation of the cash salary. The parsonage allowance may cover certain housing expenses paid by the minister (see the worksheet on page 80).

Minister-Provided Housing

The excludable portion of a housing allowance is not taxable for federal income tax purposes. The entire housing allowance is taxable for social security tax (SECA) purposes. See the worksheets on pages 81-82 for excludable expenses.

The excludable housing allowance is the lowest of these factors:
- Reasonable compensation
- Fair rental value of the home furnished plus utilities
- Amount used from current ministerial income to provide the home
- Amount properly designated by the church

If a designated housing allowance exceeds these four factors, the excess is reportable as additional income for income tax purposes.

relates to income tax, not self-employment tax.

Ministers are eligible to exclude the fair rental value of church-provided housing, for income tax purposes, without any official action by the church. However, a cash housing allowance related to church-provided or minister-provided housing is only excludable under the following rules:

✓ The allowance must be officially designated by the church. The designation should be stated in writing, preferably by board resolution, in an employment contract, or, at a minimum, in the church budget and payroll records. If the only reference to the housing allowance is in the church budget, the budget should be formally approved by the official board of the church. See the 1997 edition of the *Zondervan Church and Nonprofit Organization Tax & Financial Guide* for examples of housing allowance resolutions.

Tax law does not specifically say an oral designation of the housing allowance is unacceptable. In certain instances, the IRS accepted an oral housing designation. Still, the use of a written designation is preferable and highly recommended. The lack of a written designation significantly weakens the defense for the housing exclusion upon audit.

✓ The housing allowance must be designated prospectively by the church. Cash housing allowance payments made prior to a designation of the housing allowance are fully taxable for income tax purposes. Carefully word the resolution so that it will remain in effect until a subsequent resolution is adopted.

✓ Only actual expenses can be excluded from income. The expenses must be paid from ministerial income earned in the current year. The most limiting factor for minister-provided housing is generally the fair rental value of the home furnished plus utilities (see page 70). For church-provided housing, the limiting factor is often the fair rental value of minister-provided furnishings (see page 70).

Types of Housing Arrangements

Minister living in a parsonage owned by or rented by a church

If you live in a church-owned parsonage or housing rented by the church, do not report the fair rental value of the housing for income tax purposes. The fair rental value is subject only to self-employment tax.

You may request a housing allowance to cover expenses incurred in maintaining the church-owned or church-rented housing. The cash housing allowance excludable, for income tax purposes, is the *lowest* of (1) the fair rental value of minister-provided furnishings (see pages 78-79), or (2) actual housing expenses paid from current ministerial income, or (3) the amount properly designated.

Examples of allowable expenses are utilities, repairs, furnishings, and appliances. If the actual expenses exceed the housing allowance declared by the church, or the fair rental value of minister-provided furnishings, the excess amount cannot be excluded from income.

The expenses shown on the worksheet on page 80 qualify as part of the housing allowance for a minister living in housing owned or rented by the church. The expenses may be excluded from income.

It is appropriate for the minister's out-of-pocket expenses relating to repairs and utilities, for example, for a church-owned parsonage to be reimbursed by the church if a full accounting is made. Such reimbursements do not relate to a housing allowance. If such expenses are not reimbursed, they could be excludable from income under a housing allowance.

If the church owns the parsonage, the church may wish to provide an equity allowance to help compensate the minister for equity not accumulated through home ownership. An equity allowance is taxable both for income and social security tax purposes *unless* directed to a 403(b) tax-sheltered annuity, 401(k) plan, or certain other retirement programs.

Minister owning or renting own home

If you own or rent your own home, you may exclude, for income tax purposes, a cash housing allowance that is the *lowest* of (1) reasonable compensation, (2) the fair rental value of the home furnished plus utilities, (3) the amount used to provide a home from current ministerial income, or (4) the amount properly designated. If you live in rented housing, there is no need to apply the fair rental value test.

The expenses shown on the worksheet on page 81 qualify as part of the housing allowance for a minister owning or buying his home. Page 82 shows a similar worksheet for a minister renting his own home.

Many ministers make the mistake of automatically excluding from income (for income tax purposes) the total designated housing allowance, even though the fair rental value of the home furnished plus utilities or actual housing expenses are less than the designation. This practice may cause a significant underpayment of income taxes.

The housing expenses related to a minister-owned house should not be reimbursed by the church. These expenses may be covered by the minister under a cash housing allowance paid by the church.

Example: A minister lives in a personally owned home. The church prospectively designated $18,000 of the salary as housing allowance. The minister spends $17,000 for housing-related items. The fair rental value of the home furnished plus utilities is $17,500.

Since the amount spent is lower than the designated housing allowance or the fair rental value, the excludable housing is $17,000. Therefore, $1,000 ($18,000 less $17,000) must be added by the minister to taxable income on Form 1040, page 1, line 21. Unless the minister has opted out of social security, the entire $18,000 is reportable for social security purposes on Schedule SE.

Structuring the Housing Allowance

Before paying compensation

The church should take the following steps to designate a housing allowance *before* paying compensation:

- ✓ Verify the qualified status of the minister. Does the minister meet the tests found on pages 20 and 21?

- ✓ Verify the qualified nature of the minister's services. These services are explained on page 21.

- ✓ Determine the extent to which payment of housing expenses will be the responsibility of the minister. For example, will the utilities for a church-owned parsonage be paid by the church or the minister?

- ✓ Request that the minister estimate the housing-related expenses expected in the coming year.

- ✓ Adopt a written designation based on the minister's estimate. This designation may be included in minutes or resolutions of the board, an employment contract, annual budget, or another appropriate document if official action on the document is recorded.

- ✓ Decide whether and how a cash housing allowance will be paid to the minister, e.g., weekly, monthly, and so on.

During the calendar year

The following actions should be taken during the year (after designating the housing allowance):

- ✓ The minister should keep records of allowable housing expenses.

- ✓ The minister should make payments to the IRS to cover the self-employment tax (SECA) on the entire housing allowance (and other income subject to SECA) plus federal income tax on any anticipated unexpended portion of the allowance and other taxable income, or he should make arrangements for voluntary income tax withholding by the employer.

- ✓ The minister should identify any significant change in housing expenses and estimate the amount by which the total actual expenses may exceed the amount designated as the housing allowance.

✓ When housing expenses are running higher than anticipated or are expected to do so, the minister should ask the church to *prospectively* increase the housing allowance designation. A *retroactive* housing allowance increase is ineffective.

✓ The church should *prospectively* amend the minister's housing allowance as appropriate to reflect the anticipated change in financial circumstances.

After each calendar year

The following steps should be taken after the close of each calendar year with respect to the housing allowance:

✓ The church should report the minister's compensation to federal, state, and local governments according to applicable laws.

✓ The church should provide the minister with copies of Form W-2 or 1099-MISC, depending if the church determines the minister to be an employee or self-employed for income tax purposes. An approved housing allowance paid to the minister should be excluded from the compensation amount. The Form W-2 or 1099-MISC should not include any reference to the excluded housing allowance.

✓ The church should provide the minister with a separate statement showing the amount of any housing allowance *paid* to or for the minister.

✓ The minister who provides his own housing should compare the amount designated for housing, the housing expenses substantiated, and the fair rental value of the house furnished plus utilities. The *lowest* of these amounts is excluded for income tax purposes.

Ministers living in church-provided housing must compare the amount designated, actual housing expenses, and the fair rental value of minister-provided furnishings and exclude the lowest of the three amounts.

Designation limits

The IRS does not place a limit on how much of a minister's compensation may be *designated* as a housing allowance by the employing church. In a few extreme instances, as much as 100% of the compensation may be designated. But practical and reasonable limits usually apply.

A housing allowance must not represent "unreasonable compensation" to the minister. Unfortunately, neither the IRS nor the courts have provided a clear definition of unreasonable compensation. The IRS takes the total compensation package into account, including the housing allowance and taxable and nontaxable fringe benefits. This amount is often compared with the church's annual budget and may be compared with other similar-sized churches.

For a minister-owned home, the lower of actual expenses or the fair rental value of the home furnished plus utilities will usually be the limiting factor. For a minister renting a home, the actual expenses will typically be the limit.

As a practical matter, it is typically unwise for the employing church to exclude 100% of compensation unless the minister is employed part-time or receiving a very low salary. A 100% exclusion may result in very unusual reporting to the IRS that may draw questions and an audit. Officers of financial organizations often give extra scrutiny to loan or home mortgage applications of ministers where Form W-2 income is unusually low.

> **Example 1:** A minister receives a salary of $10,000 per year and provides his home. Actual housing costs are $12,000 and the fair rental value is $11,000. If the church sets the housing allowance at 100% of compensation, or $10,000, the minister may exclude $10,000 for federal income tax purposes. If the church had set the housing allowance at 50% of compensation, or $5,000, he could exclude only $5,000. A housing allowance equal to 100% of the minister's compensation is appropriate in this example.

> **Example 2:** An employee-minister has a voluntary withholding arrangement with the church, and the church sets the housing allowance at 100% of compensation. Form W-2 would show no salary (ignoring other compensation factors) but would reflect federal income tax and possibly state income tax withheld. While Form W-2 would be correctly stated, its appearance would be most unusual.

It is best to overdesignate your parsonage allowance by a reasonable amount to allow for unexpected expenses and increases in utility costs unless you provide your own housing and you are limited by the fair rental value of the home furnished plus utilities. If actual expenses are less than the designation, the excess should be shown as income on line 21 of Form 1040 for employees or line 6 of Schedule C or line 1 of Schedule C-EZ if self-employed for income tax purposes.

Amending the housing designation

If a minister's actual housing expenses are or will be higher than initially estimated and designated, the church may *prospectively* amend the designation during the year.

> **Example:** The church sets the housing allowance at $1,000 per month on January 1, but housing expenses are averaging $1,200 per month. On July 1, the church board approves an increase in the housing allowance to $1,600 per month. Therefore, the housing allowance for the year totalled $15,600 ($6,000 for the first six months and $9,600 for the other six months). Actual housing costs were $14,400 ($1,200 for each month). The fair rental value of the house was $15,000. The minister

could exclude $13,200 for federal income tax purposes ($6,000 for the first six months because of the designation limit and $7,200 for the last six months as limited by the actual housing costs).

Multiple ministers of one church receiving housing allowances

There is no limit on how many ministers may be given housing allowances by one church. If there are multiple pastors on a church staff, the church may designate a housing allowance for each of them. When housing allowances are provided for more than one minister, the allowance should vary according to the estimated housing expenses of the respective ministers. A lump-sum housing allowance covering multiple ministers of one church, without any designation of the amount relating to specific individuals, is not an appropriate designation.

Housing allowance as a percentage of salary

Some churches set the housing allowance by applying a percentage to the total cash salary. Housing allowance percentages are often in a range of 40% to 60% of the total cash salary. Setting the housing designation based on an estimate of housing expenses for each minister is highly preferred to the percentage method. By using the percentage approach, the church may unintentionally permit an excessive housing exclusion from income or preclude a legitimate exclusion.

Housing allowance adopted by denomination

If the local congregation employs and pays you, a resolution by a national or area office of your denomination does not constitute a housing allowance designation for you. The local congregation must officially designate a part of your salary as a housing allowance.

But a resolution of your denomination can designate your housing allowance if you are employed *and* paid by a national or area office or if you are a retired minister receiving retirement funds from a denominational retirement plan.

Reporting the Housing Allowance to the Minister

A church should report the designated housing allowance to a minister by providing a statement separate from Form W-2 or 1099-MISC. This may be in a memo or letter. The statement should not be attached to your income tax returns.

The inclusion of the housing allowance (description or amount) on Form W-2 or 1099-MISC and on the face of Form 1040 or Schedule C (or C-EZ) often is confusing to the IRS. If the housing allowance is questioned, you should ultimately have the housing allowance exclusion upheld. But the omission of the housing allowance from Form W-2 or 1099-MISC may save or shorten an IRS audit.

Your church may erroneously include the housing allowance on your Form W-2, box 5, or 1099-MISC, box 7. If this happens, the church should prepare a corrected form. If a corrected form is not prepared, you should deduct your actual housing expenses, subject to the housing allowance limitations, on line 21 of Form 1040, line 6 of Schedule C, or line 2 of Schedule C-EZ.

Although not required by law, the minister may account to the church for the actual housing expenses and the fair rental value (for nonchurch-owned housing). The church then prepares Form W-2 or 1099-MISC with the adjusted housing allowance excluded. Under this approach, the excluded housing is always equal to or less than the housing designation.

Accounting for the Housing Allowance

Determining fair rental value

The determination of the fair rental value for church-provided housing is totally the responsibility of the minister. The church is not responsible to set the value. The fair rental value should be based on comparable rental values of other similar, furnished residences in the immediate neighborhood or community.

Housing allowance in excess of actual expenses or fair rental value

Some ministers erroneously believe that they may exclude every dollar of the housing *designation* adopted by the church without limitation. The housing designation is merely the starting point. If actual expenses or the fair rental value is lower, the lowest amount is eligible for exclusion from income.

> **Example:** A minister living in a home owned personally receives cash compensation from the church of $25,000. The church prospectively designates $20,000 as a housing allowance. Actual housing expenses for the year are $14,000. The fair rental value of the home plus utilities is $15,000. The amount excludable from income is limited to the actual housing expenses of $14,000.

Actual expenses in excess of fair rental value

Actual housing expenses that exceed the fair rental value limitation are not deductible. There are no provisions to carry over "unused" housing expenses to the next year. When housing expenses are projected to exceed the fair rental value, spreading some housing costs over two or more years may save some deductions. This approach reduces your taxable income by maximizing your exclusion.

> **Example:** A minister living in a home owned personally receives cash compensation from the church of $30,000. The church formally designates $20,000 of the $30,000 as a housing allowance. Actual housing expenses were $25,000. The expenses were unusually high because of a down payment on a house. The fair rental value of the home plus utilities was $18,000. The amount excludable from income is the fair rental value plus utilities, or $18,000. There is no carryover of the $7,000 of actual expenses in excess of the fair rental value to the next tax year.

The fair rental value test is applied by the IRS but it has not been tested in court. Consult a tax professional before choosing to ignore this test.

Determining actual expenses

Actual amounts expended for housing and furnishings is limited to amounts expended in the current calendar year. Amounts expended in a prior year cannot be carried forward to a following year through depreciation or by carrying forward actual expenses that exceeded the fair rental value or amounts designated in a prior year.

Second mortgages and home equity loans

If all home mortgages are paid off, a minister has lower housing expense to exclude under a housing allowance than if there is a mortgage. Also, there is no double deduction of the mortgage interest as an itemized deduction and as housing expense for purposes of the housing allowance exclusion if there are no mortgages.

Some ministers have an equity loan or second mortgage that generates principal and interest payments. The loan or mortgage payments are excludable as housing expenses *only* if the loan proceeds are used for housing expenses. The exclusion is not available if the loan proceeds are used for personal expenses such as the purchase of an auto or for a child's college education.

> **Example:** A minister paid off the home mortgage in 1995. In 1996, he obtained a loan of $20,000 secured by the residence. The money was used in 1996 as follows: $10,000 for a new car and $10,000 to add a deck and screened-in porch. The mortgage payments relating to funds used to purchase the new car are not excludable as housing expenses. Since the other $10,000 was used for housing, the mortgage payments relating to this portion of the loan qualify as housing expenses.

Other Housing Allowance Issues

Payment of the housing allowance to the minister

It is immaterial whether the payment of a properly designated cash housing allowance is a separate payment or is part of a payment that also includes other compensation. A cash housing allowance usually is included with the minister's salary check.

Cost of the housing allowance to the church

Some churches mistakenly believe that providing a housing allowance to their minister will increase the church budget. This is not true. If a portion of the minister's compensation is designated as a housing allowance, it costs the church nothing.

> **Example:** A church is paying a minister $30,000 per year but does not presently designate a housing allowance. The minister provides the home. The minister requests that the church designate a housing allowance of $10,000 per year. The church adopts a resolution reflecting compensation of $30,000 per year, of which $10,000 is a designated housing allowance. Before the designation, Form W-2 or 1099-MISC for the minister would have shown compensation of $30,000. After the designation, Form W-2 or 1099-MISC would reflect compensation of $20,000. The cash spent by the church is the same before and after the designation.

Double deduction of interest and taxes

Ministers who own their homes and itemize their deductions are eligible to deduct mortgage interest and property taxes on Schedule A even though these items are excluded from taxable income as part of the housing allowance. This is often referred to as a "double deduction."

Housing allowances for retired ministers

Pension payments, retirement allowances, or disability payments paid to a retired minister from an established plan are generally taxable as pension income. But a denomination can designate a housing allowance for retired ministers to compensate them for past services to the local churches of the denomination or to the denomination. The housing allowance designated relates only to payments from the denominationally-sponsored retirement program.

Withdrawals from a denominationally-sponsored tax-sheltered annuity (TSA) or 401(k) plan qualify for designation as a housing allowance. Withdrawals from a TSA or 401(k) plan that is not sponsored by a local church are not eligible for designation as a housing allowance. Benefits from a TIAA-CREF plan for a minister formerly employed by a church-related college *do not* qualify for the housing allowance.

Also, retired ministers may exclude the rental value of a home furnished by a church or a rental allowance paid by a church as compensation for past services.

If the denomination body reports the gross amount of pension or TSA payments on Form 1099-R and designates the housing allowance, the recipient may offset the housing expenses and insert the net amount on page 1, Form 1040. A supplementary schedule such as the following example should be attached to the tax return:

Pensions and annuity income (Form 1040, line 16a)	$10,000
Less housing exclusion	8,000
Form 1040, line 16b	$2,000

NOTE: The amount excluded is limited to the lowest of (1) the fair rental value of the home furnished plus utilities, (2) the amount used to provide a home, or (3) the properly designated housing allowance.

A surviving spouse of a retired minister *cannot* exclude a housing allowance from income. If a minister's surviving spouse receives a rental allowance, it is includable in gross income.

Housing allowances for evangelists

Traveling evangelists may exclude a portion of the amounts they receive from various churches as nontaxable housing allowances to the extent that each church designates all or a portion of the minister's honorarium as a housing allowance in advance of payment to the minister. Honoraria payments of $600 or more to the evangelist (besides the properly designated housing allowance) require the church to issue Form 1099-MISC.

> **Example:** William Dalton, an ordained evangelist, preaches at Westside Church for ten days. Westside Church paid Mr. Dalton $1,500 consisting of $300 travel expenses (documentation provided to the church), a properly designated housing allowance of $500, and a $700 honorarium. Since the honorarium exceeded $600, the church issued Mr. Dalton a Form 1099-MISC for $700.

Some itinerant evangelists form nonprofit corporations for their ministries. The evangelist's nonprofit corporation may designate a housing allowance for him. This eliminates the need for each church to provide the housing designation. If an evangelist purchases a house and rents it out while traveling, only the housing expenses relating to the time at home are excludable.

Furnishings as a housing expense

The actual cost of furnishings purchased for church-provided or minister-provided housing may be excluded for income tax purposes in the current year under a properly designated housing allowance. Examples of furnishings that may qualify for the exclusion are rugs, wall hangings, appliances, and furniture.

The fair rental value of furnishings purchased in a prior or current year cannot be counted as actual housing expenses for the current year. The fair rental value of minister-provided furnishings is only a factor in determining the limits of the overall housing exclusion.

> **Example:** The minister excludes, under a properly designated housing allowance, the current expenses of providing the home but also excludes the fair rental value of minister-owned furnishings (some of the furnishings were purchased in the current year and some in prior years). This is incorrect and would not be allowed by the IRS. Only the amounts paid for furnishings in the current tax year are excludable under a housing allowance.

Action Steps

- The church should adopt a written housing designation based on the minister's estimate of housing expenses.

- The minister should request a housing designation even if living in church-provided housing.

- The church should never approve a retroactive adjustment in the housing designation.

- The minister should keep a record of actual allowable housing expenses.

- If the home is owned by the minister, include in income any housing allowance paid that is more than the *lowest* of (1) the fair rental value of the home, furnished plus utilities, (2) the amount used to provide the home from current ministerial income, (3) the amount properly designated by the church, or (4) reasonable compensation.

- If the house is rented by the minister, include in income any housing allowance paid that is more than the *lowest* of (1) the amount used to provide the home from current ministerial income, (2) the amount properly designated by the church, or (3) reasonable compensation.

- If the minister lives in church-provided housing, include in income any housing allowance paid that is more than the *lowest* of (1) the fair rental value of furnishings owned by the minister, (2) the amount used to provide the home from current ministerial income, (3) the amount properly designated by the church, or (4) reasonable compensation.

- Include the entire housing designation in the computation of your social security tax on Schedule SE (unless you have opted out of social security).

Housing Allowance Worksheet
Minister Living in a Parsonage
Owned by or Rented by the Church

Minister's Name: _____

For the period _____, 199__ to _____, 199__

Date designation approved _____, 199__

Allowable Housing Expenses *(expenses paid by minister from current income)*

	Estimated Expenses	Actual
Utilities *(gas, electricity, water)* and trash collection	$_____	$_____
Local telephone expense *(base charge)*	_____	_____
Decoration and redecoration	_____	_____
Structural maintenance and repair	_____	_____
Landscaping, gardening, and pest control	_____	_____
Furnishings *(purchase, repair, replacement)*	_____	_____
Personal property insurance on minister-owned contents	_____	_____
Personal property taxes on contents	_____	_____
Umbrella liability insurance	_____	_____
Subtotal	_____	
10% allowance for unexpected expenses	_____	
TOTAL	$_____	$_____ (A)

Fair rental value of furnishings owned by the minister $_____ (B)
Properly designated housing allowance $_____ (C)

Note: The amount excludable from income for federal income tax purposes is the *lowest* of A, B, or C.

Housing Allowance Worksheet
Minister Living in Home
Minister Owns or Is Buying

Minister's Name: _____

For the period _____, 199__ to _____, 199__

Date designation approved _____, 199__

Allowable Housing Expenses *(expenses paid by minister from current income)*

	Estimated Expenses	Actual
Down payment on purchase of housing	$ _____	$ _____
Housing loan principal and interest payments	_____	_____
Real estate commission, escrow fees	_____	_____
Real property taxes	_____	_____
Personal property taxes on contents	_____	_____
Homeowner's insurance	_____	_____
Personal property insurance on contents	_____	_____
Umbrella liability insurance	_____	_____
Structural maintenance and repair	_____	_____
Landscaping, gardening, and pest control	_____	_____
Furnishings *(purchase, repair, replacement)*	_____	_____
Decoration and redecoration	_____	_____
Utilities *(gas, electricity, water)* and trash collection	_____	_____
Local telephone expense *(base charge)*	_____	_____
Homeowner's association dues/condominium fees	_____	_____

Subtotal _____

10% allowance for unexpected expenses _____

TOTAL $ _____ $ _____ (A)

Fair rental value of home furnished
plus utilities $ _____ (B)

Properly designated housing allowance $ _____ (C)

Note: The amount excludable from income for federal income tax purposes is the *lowest* of A, B, or C.

Housing Allowance Worksheet
Minister Living in Home
Minister Is Renting

Minister's Name: _____

For the period _____, 199__ to _____, 199__

Date designation approved _____, 199__

Allowable Housing Expenses *(expenses paid by minister from current income)*

	Estimated Expenses	Actual
Housing rental payments	$ _____	$ _____
Personal property insurance on minister-owned contents	_____	_____
Personal property taxes on contents	_____	_____
Umbrella liability	_____	_____
Structural maintenance and repair	_____	_____
Landscaping, gardening, and pest control	_____	_____
Furnishings *(purchase, repair, replacement)*	_____	_____
Decoration and redecoration	_____	_____
Utilities *(gas, electricity, water)* and trash collection	_____	_____
Local telephone expense *(base charge)*	_____	_____
Mobile home space rental	_____	_____
Subtotal	_____	
10% allowance for unexpected expenses	_____	
TOTAL	$ _____	$ _____ (A)
Properly designated housing allowance.		$ _____ (B)

Note: The amount excludable from income for federal income tax purposes is the *lower* of A or B.

CHAPTER FIVE
Business Expenses
How to avoid the unreimbursed business expense trap

In This Chapter
- Accountable and nonaccountable expense reimbursement plans
- Documenting and reporting business expenses
- Travel and transportation expenses
- Auto expense deductions
- Other business and professional expenses
- Allocation of business expenses

Most ministers spend thousands of dollars each year on church-related business expenses. Auto expenses are a major cost. You only have two choices: try to deduct the expenses for tax purposes or have them reimbursed by the church. Reimbursed business expenses will almost always save you money.

Business and professional expenses fall into three basic categories: expenses reimbursed under an accountable plan, expenses reimbursed under a nonaccountable plan, and unreimbursed expenses. The last two categories are treated the same for tax purposes.

The reimbursement of an expense never changes the character of the item from personal to business. If personal expenses are reimbursed, it creates taxable income to the minister.

Accountable and Nonaccountable Expense Reimbursement Plans

An accountable plan is a reimbursement or expense allowance arrangement, established by your church, that requires (1) a business purpose for the expenses, (2) substantiation of expenses to the church, and (3) the return of any excess reimbursements.

The substantiation of expenses and return of excess reimbursements must be handled within a reasonable time. The following methods meet the "reasonable time" definition:

✓ The fixed date method applies if

- an advance is made within 30 days of when an expense is paid or incurred;

- an expense is substantiated to the church within 60 days after the expense is paid or incurred; and

- an excess amount is returned to the church within 120 days after the expense is paid or incurred.

✓ The periodic statement method applies if

- the church provides employees with a periodic statement that sets forth the amount paid under the arrangement that is more than substantiated expenses;

- the statements are provided at least quarterly; and

- the church requests that the employee provide substantiation for any additional expenses that have not yet been substantiated and/or return any amounts remaining unsubstantiated within 120 days of the statement.

If you substantiate your business expenses and any unused payments are returned, expense reimbursements have no impact on your taxes. The expenses reimbursed are not included on Form W-2 or 1099-MISC or deducted on your tax return.

Example 1: Your church adopts an accountable reimbursement plan using the "fixed date method." The church authorizes salary of $26,000 plus business expenses up to $10,000.

During the year, you substantiate expenses under the accountable guidelines of $9,000. The church provides you with a Form W-2 or 1099-MISC reflecting compensation of $26,000. The substantiated expenses of $9,000 are not reported to the IRS by the church or on your tax return.

The church retains the $1,000 difference between the amount budgeted by the church and the amount reimbursed to the minister. (See page 86 for an example where the church pays the balance in the expense budget to the minister.)

Example 2: Your church authorizes a salary of $23,000 plus an auto allowance of $5,000 and $3,000 for other business expenses. The church does not require or receive any substantiation for the auto or other business expenses. This is a nonaccountable reimbursement plan.

The church should provide you with a Form W-2 or 1099-MISC reflecting compensation of $31,000. The auto and other business expenses you incur will need to be claimed on Form 2106 (2106-EZ) and Schedule A as miscellaneous deductions if you are reporting as an employee for income tax purposes. The expenses may be claimed on Schedule C (C-EZ) if you are reporting as self-employed for income tax purposes.

The IRS disallows deductions for unreimbursed business expenses to the extent they are allocable to a tax-exempt housing allowance (see allocation of business expenses on pages 99-100). This is another reason that every minister should comply with the accountable expense reimbursement rules. The goal should be to eliminate all unreimbursed business expenses.

Although not required, ministers filing as self-employed for income tax purposes will also find it advantageous to comply with the guidelines. A minister who has not complied with these rules and is reclassified by the IRS from self-employed to an employee, for income tax purposes, could face a significant tax bill.

Nonaccountable expense reimbursement plans

If your business expenses are not reimbursed, if you do not substantiate your expenses to the church, or if the amount of the reimbursement exceeds your actual expenses and the excess is not returned to the church within a reasonable period, your tax life becomes more complicated.

Nonaccountable reimbursements and excess reimbursements over IRS mileage or per diem limits must be included in your gross income and reported as wages on Form W-2 or Form 1099-MISC for self-employed ministers.

Unreimbursed expenses or expenses reimbursed under a nonaccountable plan can be deducted only as itemized miscellaneous deductions and only to the extent that they, with your other miscellaneous deductions, exceed 2% of your adjusted gross income. Unreimbursed expenses are not deductible if you are an employee for income tax purposes and do not itemize. If you are filing as self-employed for income tax purposes, unreimbursed expenses or those reimbursed under a nonaccountable plan are deductible on Schedule C (C-EZ).

Excess reimbursement retained as a "bonus"

If your church allows you to keep excess reimbursements by calling them a "bonus," a plan becomes nonaccountable. This is also referred to as a "recharacterization of income." All payments under a nonaccountable plan are reportable as compensation on Form W-2 or 1099-MISC.

Example: Your church sets your salary at $25,000 and agrees to reimburse your business expenses under an accountable plan for up to $10,000. If your reimbursed expenses are less than $10,000, the church will give you a bonus for the difference between $10,000 and reimbursed expenses. Because of the "bonus" arrangement, all reimbursements made under the plan become nonaccountable. The entire $35,000 must be reported by the church as compensation on Form W-2 or 1099-MISC.

Expense allowances

If your church pays you an allowance for entertainment, dues and subscriptions, or other business expenses, you must keep records of all expenses in order to claim the expenses on Form 2106 (2106-EZ) or Schedule C (C-EZ). An allowance not based upon actual expenses does not meet the adequate accounting requirements for an accountable plan and must be included in your income.

Documenting and Reporting Business Expenses

Documenting business expenses

For expenses to be allowed as deductions, you must show that you spent the money and that you spent it for a legitimate business reason. To prove that you spent the money, you generally need to provide documentary evidence that can be confirmed by a third party. Canceled checks or credit card slips are excellent evidence. To the IRS, third-party verification is important; if business expenses are paid in cash, be sure to get a receipt.

Documenting a business expense can be time-consuming. The IRS is satisfied if you note the five W's on the back of your credit card slip or other receipt:

- ✓ Why (business purpose)
- ✓ Who (names of persons present)
- ✓ What (description, including itemized accounting of cost)
- ✓ When (date)
- ✓ Where (location)

The only exception to the documentation rules is if your individual outlays for business expenses, other than for lodging, come to less than $75. The IRS does not require receipts for such expenses, although the five W's are still required. You *always* need a receipt for lodging expenses regardless of the amount.

Use of a church credit card constitutes reimbursement of expenses. However, the use of a credit card does not automatically provide substantiation without additional documentation, e.g., business purposes and business relationship.

While you are traveling out of town as an employee, your church may use a per diem for reimbursements instead of actual costs of meals (see pages 89-90 for current rates). The per diem is not subject to the 50% limitation on meal and entertainment expenses.

Forms on which expenses are reportable

Only the portion of business and professional expenses directly attributable to your Schedule C (C-EZ) income (self-employment activities) should be deducted on Schedule C (C-EZ). The portion of these expenses related to activities as an employee of the church should be deducted on Form 2106 (2106-EZ). If you receive reimbursement for any business or professional expenses and adequately account to the church under an accountable plan, you should not report the expenses on Form 2106 (2106-EZ) or Schedule C (C-EZ).

Travel and Transportation Expenses

The terms "transportation" and "travel" are often used interchangeably, but each has a distinct meaning for tax purposes. Travel is the broader category, including not only transportation expenses, but the cost of meals, lodging, and incidental expenses as well. To deduct travel expenses—including expenses you incur for meals, phone calls, cab fares, and so forth on the road—the business purpose must take you away from home overnight or require a rest stop. If you do not spend the night, you can deduct only your transportation costs.

Travel expenses

Many different expenses can add up on a business trip: air and taxi fares, costs of lodging, baggage charges, rental cars, tips, laundry and cleaning, and telephone expenses. You can deduct 100% of these expenses plus 50% of the meal and entertainment expenses you incurred while you were away, provided you meet certain guidelines:

✓ The trip must have a business purpose.

✓ The expenses cannot be "lavish and extravagant."

✓ You must be away from home long enough to require sleep or rest.

Deriving some personal pleasure from a trip doesn't disqualify it from being deductible. The IRS does, however, apply some important twists to the tax treatment of foreign travel expenses.

If you are traveling within the United States, you can deduct all transportation costs, plus the costs of business-related meals (subject to the 50% limit) and lodging, if business was the primary reason for the trip. If you need to stay over Saturday night to get a lower airfare, the hotel and meal expenses for Saturday will generally be deductible. If the trip is primarily personal, none of your transportation costs can be deducted, but you can deduct other business-related travel expenses.

Travel expenses must be divided between your self-employment activities reported on Schedule C (C-EZ) and activities as an employee reported on Form 2106 (2106-EZ). Any travel expense that is also a meal or entertainment expense is subject to the 50% limitation for business meals and entertainment.

If you are reimbursed for travel expenses and adequately account to the church, you should not report your travel expenses on Form 2106 (2106-EZ) or Schedule C (C-EZ). Further, you are not subject to the 50% limitation for business meals and entertainment.

International travel

Costs are deductible if you took the trip for business reasons. If your trip is seven days or less, you can deduct your entire airfare even if you spend most of your time on personal activities. If you spend extra days for personal reasons, your hotel, car-rental, and meal costs are not deductible for those days. If your trip is more than seven days and you spend more than 25% of your time on personal activities, you must allocate your expenses between business and personal time.

Trips to the Holy Land

Ministers often travel to the Holy Land to more closely identify with the area where Christ taught, preached, and ministered. In spite of all the obvious ministerial advantages of visiting the Holy Land, the applicability of tax deductions or tax-free reimbursements for such trips is not as clear.

Generally, no deduction is allowed for travel as a form of education. This rule applies when a travel deduction would otherwise be allowable only on the ground that the travel itself served educational purposes. However, it does not apply when a deduction is claimed with respect to travel that is a necessary factor to engaging in an activity that gives rise to a business deduction relating to education.

A number of factors must be considered before the tax status of a Holy Land trip may be determined. To qualify as a deductible ministry-related expense or as a tax-free reimbursement by your church, the trip has to meet the general educational expense rules outlined on page 96. Holy Land trips are subject to the international travel rules as described above.

If you can answer "Yes" to the following questions, your expenses are more likely to qualify for reimbursement or as a deduction:

BUSINESS EXPENSES

- ✓ Did the employing church require (or strongly suggest) that you make the trip to the Holy Land?

- ✓ Is this your first trip to the Holy Land (versus a pattern of making the pilgrimage every few years)?

- ✓ Will you be receiving college credit for the trip from a recognized educational institution? Is there a course syllabus?

- ✓ Did you go on the trip with a group organized for the purpose of study in the Holy Land and led by a Bible scholar?

- ✓ Did you take notes and pictures of places visited (versus pictures of sites with family members in most of the pictures)?

A tax deduction or reimbursement by a church for a minister's trip to the Holy Land should be made only after careful consideration of the facts and circumstances and the applicable tax rules.

Travel expenses of your spouse or children

If your spouse or children accompany you on your business trip, their expenses are reimbursable tax-free or deductible if

- ✓ the travel of the spouse or dependent is for a bona fide business purpose; and

- ✓ the employee substantiates the time, place, amount, and business purpose of the travel under an accountable business expense reimbursement plan.

Furlough travel

A missionary on furlough may qualify for travel status. The purpose of the travel must be primarily business, such as deputation reporting to constituents, or education, and the missionary's primary residence must remain in another country. Incidental costs for personal travel such as vacation, nonbusiness spousal costs, and travel costs of children are not deductible. If these expenses are paid by a church or missions organization, they should be included in compensation on Form W-2 or 1099-MISC.

Per diem allowance

The federal per diem rate is the sum of the federal lodging rate and meals and incidental expenses rate. It is $152 for 1996 for the 61 high-cost areas and $95 per day for all other areas. The federal meals and incidental expense rate is $36 for the high-cost areas and $28 for any other locality. The federal lodging rate is $116 for the high-cost areas and $67 for other localities. The high-cost areas are identified in IRS Publication 463.

Per diem allowances apply to employer reimbursements. These rates may not be used to claim deductions for unreimbursed expenses.

Auto Expense Deductions

Few ministers put only business miles on cars. When the odometer reading includes commuting from home to church or trips to the grocery store and the playground, an allocation must be made between your personal and business mileage. It is possible to use a car 100% of the time for business purposes, but it is highly unusual. It is apt to draw IRS scrutiny and perhaps an audit.

Mileage and actual expense methods

In determining your deduction for the business use of a personal car, you can use one of two methods to figure your deduction: the standard mileage rate or the actual expense method. Generally, you can choose the method that gives you the greater deduction, but there are two exceptions. You must use the actual-expense method if you have a leased car or if you used the actual-cost method in the first year your car was placed in service.

Standard mileage rate method

If you are paid a fixed mileage allowance of 31 cents per mile (1996 maximum IRS rate) or less and you provide the time, place, and business purpose of your driving, you have made an adequate accounting of your automobile expenses.

The standard mileage rate may generate a lower deduction than using actual expenses in some instances. But the simplicity of the standard mileage method is a very compelling feature.

If the church does not reimburse you for auto expenses or reimburses you under a nonaccountable plan, you may deduct business miles on Form 2106 (2106-EZ). The total from Form 2106 (2106-EZ) is carried to Schedule A, Miscellaneous Deductions. If you are self-employed for income tax purposes, report these expenses on Schedule C (C-EZ).

The standard mileage rate, which includes depreciation and maintenance costs, is based on the government's estimate of the average cost of operating an automobile. Depending upon the age and cost of the car, the mileage rate may be more or less than your actual auto expense. If you use the mileage rate, you also may deduct parking fees and tolls and the business portion of personal property tax (and the business portion of interest if filing as self-employed for income tax purposes).

Using the standard mileage rate reduces the tax basis of your car. You must reduce the basis by 11 cents a mile. This comprises the depreciation portion of the standard mileage allowance.

All auto-related taxes must be claimed on Schedule A for employees. For self-employed persons, the business portion of auto-related interest and taxes should be claimed on Schedule C (C-EZ) and the personal portion of taxes on Schedule A.

✓ **Conditions on Use of Mileage Rate.** You may not use the mileage rate if

- you lease your car,

- you have claimed depreciation under MACRS, ACRS, or another accelerated method,

- you have claimed additional first-year depreciation, or

- you have claimed first-year expenses under Section 179

✓ **Use of Mileage Rate in First Year.** If you choose the standard mileage rate for the first year the car is in service, you may use the standard mileage rate or actual expense method in later years.

By choosing to use the mileage rate in the first year your car is in service, you may not use the MACRS method of depreciation for the car in a later year. Also, you may not claim a deduction under Section 179. If you switch to the actual expenses method in a later year before your automobile is fully depreciated, you must use the straight-line method of depreciation.

If you do not choose the standard mileage rate in the first year, you may not use it for that car in any year.

Actual expense method

If you have kept accurate records, determining your deduction for most expenses should be straightforward. Generally, the amount of depreciation you may claim and the method you use to calculate it depends on when you purchased your auto and began to use it for ministerial purposes.

Under the actual expense method, you can use either accelerated or straight-line depreciation. As the names imply, the accelerated method front-loads the depreciation, giving you larger deductions sooner. The straight-line method gives you the same depreciation deduction every year.

With either method, you calculate your depreciation deduction just as you would for any other asset used for business purposes. Your "depreciable basis" is the purchase price of the car multiplied by the percentage you use it for business purposes.

Allowable expenses under the actual expense method include

gas and oil	interest on auto loan
repairs	lease payments

tires
batteries
insurance
license plates

automobile club membership
car washes and waxes
supplies, such as antifreeze
parking fees and tolls

Depreciating your car

Depreciation is an allowance for wear and tear on your car. To compensate for this loss of value, the tax law allows you to recover the cost of your car over a period of five years.

Your depreciation is computed using the 200% declining balance method. You take only half a year's depreciation in the first year, no matter when actual use began, and half a year when the car is sold or traded in. This is the half-year convention. This rule spreads the depreciation deduction over 6 years.

The following percentages represent the allowed depreciation by year:

1st year	20.00%
2nd year	32.00%
3rd year	19.20%
4th year	11.52%
5th year	11.52%
6th year	5.76%
	100.00%

The so-called "luxury auto limit" places a ceiling on the annual depreciation deduction you can claim for a passenger automobile based on the date you place the automobile in service. For 1996, a "luxury" auto is one that costs over $15,500. The depreciation deduction cannot exceed the dollar limits indicated based on the year a car is placed in service:

Placed in service	1994	1995	1996
Year one	$2,960	$3,060	$3,060
Year two	4,700	4,900	4,900
Year three	2,850	2,950	2,950
Each subsequent year	1,675	1,775	1,775

The luxury car limitations do not permanently deprive you from recovering the cost of your car. They merely postpone a portion of depreciation deductions to later years by placing a cap on the amount of depreciation that may be claimed in any year. The part of an otherwise allowable deduction may be taken after the normal recovery period.

If your car is used for both business and personal driving, depreciation is computed only on the business portion of the car's basis. Because depreciation is computed on the business portion of your car, your basis can change each year if your percentage of business use varies.

BUSINESS EXPENSES

Example: You purchased a new car on May 15, 1996, for $15,900. During 1996, you drove the car a total of 10,000 miles. Ministerial miles were 6,000. Your depreciation deduction is $1,836. If the car had cost over $15,900, the depreciation would still have been $1,836 because of the luxury car limit.

✓ Percentage of business use
    Business miles   6,000
    Total miles   10,000 = 60%

✓ Business portion of basis
    Purchase price $15,900
    Times business percentage   60%
                                 $ 9,540

✓ Depreciation deduction
    Business portion of basis $ 9,540
    MACRS percentage/1st year   20%
                                 $ 1,908

✓ Maximum allowable depreciation
       $3,060 x 60% business   = $ 1,836

Leasing your car

You may not depreciate property you do not own. So you never depreciate a leased car. You deduct your lease payments instead. The tax law is designed to bring lease payments in line with the "luxury auto" limits placed on depreciation deductions for purchased cars. This applies to autos that cost more than $15,500 and are first leased in 1996. So, leasing a "luxury" car does not give you a tax-break over buying one.

Driving a church-owned vehicle

If you drive a church-owned car, the church must report the value of your personal use of the car as income on your W-2 form or 1099-MISC. If you reimburse the church for a portion of the personal use value, the reimbursement is offset against the auto value to determine your additional compensation.

Commuting

Personal mileage is never deductible. Commuting expenses are nondeductible personal expenses.

Unless your home-office qualifies under all four requirements of a home-office (see page 97), travel from home to church (a *regular* work location) and return for church services and other work at the church is commuting and not deductible. But the cost of traveling between your home and a *temporary* work location may be deductible regardless if your home qualifies as an office. Once you arrive at the first work location, temporary or regular, you may deduct trips between work locations.

A regular place of business is any location at which you work or perform services on a regular basis. A temporary place of business is any location at which you perform services on an irregular or short-term (i.e., generally a matter of days or weeks) basis.

If you make calls in a certain nursing home nearly every day, it would qualify as a regular work location. However, if you only visit the nursing home a few days each month, it would generally qualify as a temporary work location.

You are considered as performing services at a particular location on a regular basis whether you perform services at that location every week or on a set schedule. Thus, daily transportation expenses you incur in going between a church-sponsored school and your office at the church or between your home and a temporary work location such as a hospital to call on a church member are deductible business expenses.

> **Example 1:** A minister, not qualifying for an office at home, drives from his home to the church. This trip is commuting and treated as personal mileage.
>
> The minister leaves the church and drives to a hospital to call on a member. From the hospital, he drives to the home of a prospect to make a call. These trips qualify for business mileage regardless if the hospital qualifies as a regular or a temporary work location.
>
> From the prospect's house, the minister drives to his home. This trip is also deductible since the minister is driving from a temporary work location.
>
> **Example 2:** A minister, not qualifying for an office at home, drives from his home to a hospital to call on a member. The hospital is a temporary work location. This trip is deductible.
>
> The minister then drives to a member's office to make a call and then returns to the minister's office at the church. The trips to this point are deductible as business expenses because they are all trips between work locations. The minister then drives to his home. This trip is commuting and is not deductible because the minister is driving from a regular work location to a nonwork location.

Documentation of auto expenses

To support your automobile expense deduction or reimbursement, automobile expenses must be substantiated by adequate records. A weekly or monthly mileage log that identifies dates, destinations, business purposes, and odometer readings in order to allocate total mileage between business and personal use is a basic necessity if you use the mileage method. If you use the actual expense method, a mileage log and supporting documentation on expenses is required.

Reporting auto expenses

If you are reimbursed for automobile expenses under an accountable expense plan, you should not report your travel expenses on Form 2106 (2106-EZ) or Schedule C (C-EZ). This type of reimbursement eliminates the need for income or social security tax reporting by the church or the minister. If you *do not* have an accountable expense reimbursement plan, automobile expenses are reported on Form 2106 (2106-EZ) for minister-employees and Schedule C (C-EZ) for ministers reporting as self-employed for income tax purposes.

Other Business and Professional Expenses

There are many other allowable miscellaneous business and professional expenses that may be deductible if unreimbursed or submitted to the church for reimbursement under a nonaccountable plan.

✓ **Business gifts**. You can deduct up to $25 per donee for business gifts to any number of individuals every year. Incidental costs, such as for engraving, gift wrapping, insurance, and mailing do not need to be included in determining whether the $25 limit has been exceeded.

The gifts must be related to your ministry. Gifts to church staff or board members would generally be deductible. Wedding and graduation gifts are generally personal instead of business.

✓ **Charitable contributions as business expenses**. Denominations or local churches often impose some type of tithing (10% of gross income) requirement on ministers. In some instances, the requirement is rigidly enforced based on periodic reviews. Ministers are dismissed for noncompliance. At other times, a more cursory review (such as the completion of an annual report form) is made to enforce the policy. Tithing records are not checked and ministers are rarely if ever dismissed for noncompliance.

Tithes and other offerings are generally deductible by ministers as charitable contributions. If there is a contractual requirement for the minister to tithe to the church, it may be appropriate to withhold tithes from compensation payments since the minister is not legally entitled to keep required contribution amounts. If so, the Form W-2 or 1099-MISC reporting should reflect compensation net of the tithe deductions.

If tithes are paid by the minister to the church instead of withheld from compensation and the requirement to tithe meets certain stringent guidelines, it may be possible to deduct the tithe as a business expense (on Schedule A and Form 2106 [2106-EZ]). The reimbursement of a tithe under an accountable plan has not been directly addressed by the IRS or any court.

Qualifying the tithe as a business expense may have two advantages over a charitable deduction. Some ministers are unable to itemize their deductions, and charitable deductions offer no tax advantage. Also, business expenses are deductible for self-employment (SECA) social security purposes while charitable contributions do not offer this benefit.

Whether tithes qualify for a payroll deduction or as business expenses will vary based on the facts and circumstances of each case. For most ministers, deducting the tithe as business expense represents a very aggressive tax position. Since comparable tax treatments are not available for members of the church (not employed by the church), the concept often raises questions with lay leadership and it should be approached with extreme caution.

✓ **Clothing.** The cost of your clothing is deductible if the church requires the clothes and they are not suitable as normal wearing apparel. A regular suit worn into the pulpit on Sunday is not deductible, but vestments are deductible.

✓ **Education.** The cost of educational expenses incurred may be deductible if they are

- to meet the requirements of your church to keep your present position, or

- to maintain or improve skills in your present employment.

But no deduction is allowed, even though these requirements are met, if the education

- is required for you to meet the minimum educational requirements of your occupation, or

- is part of a program of study that will qualify you for a new occupation.

Deductible educational expenses include the cost of tuition, books, supplies, laboratory fees, correspondence courses, and travel and transportation expenses.

Expenses under a written "qualified educational assistance program" are discussed on pages 50-51.

✓ **Entertainment.** You may deduct meal and entertainment expenses if they are ordinary and necessary and are either directly related to or associated with your ministerial responsibilities.

Does deductible entertainment expense include your personal meal? Personal expenses are not deductible since you would be eating anyway.

Granted, you might not be spending $10 for your lunch, but you would be eating. Only the amount over what you normally spend for breakfast, lunch, or dinner is deductible. But the IRS has decided not to enforce this part of the tax law. Unless a taxpayer is deducting outrageous amounts of personal expenses, 50% of the cost of the meals while entertaining will be allowed.

Certain entertainment expenses incurred in your home may be deductible if you can show a ministry relationship. Since it is difficult to precisely document the cost of meals served in the home, a reasonable cost per meal is generally allowable (for you and your guests). Keep a log including date(s), names of guests, ministry purpose, and estimated cost.

✓ **Home-office**. Rarely is it advantageous or even appropriate for a minister to claim office-in-the-home deductions (Form 8829). A home-office provided by a minister does not generate any deductible expenses if all the housing expenses are already treated as tax-free via a housing allowance. If no housing allowance is provided or the housing allowance provided is inadequate, the home-office must meet the following criteria to substantiate a deduction:

- Be exclusively used in the minister's business.

- Be used on a regular basis in the minister's business.

- Be used for the convenience of the church.

- Be the minister's principal place of business.

Even if there is no home-office expense deduction available to a minister, qualifying the home-office under the four criteria will permit a minister to treat otherwise personal commuting mileage as business mileage (see page 94).

✓ **Interest expense**. The business portion of interest expense on an auto loan is deductible on Schedule C (C-EZ) for ministers who use this form to report their primary ministerial income and expense. For a minister-employee, all auto-related interest expense is personal interest, which is not deductible.

✓ **Moving expenses**. Moving expenses reimbursed by a church to a minister-employee are excludable from gross income.

For minister-employees, when moving expense reimbursements have been excluded from income, there is no requirement to add these amounts to determine a minister's net earnings from self-employment, and therefore they are not subject to self-employment tax.

For ministers filing as self-employed for income tax purposes, the reimbursement or payment of moving expenses is includable in income on Form 1099-MISC. However, the expenses are deductible (reimbursed or unreimbursed) on page 1, Form 1040, line 24 (based on completing Form 3903 or

3903-F). The expenses are not deductible in calculating self-employment income and are therefore subject to social security tax.

Moving expense reimbursements or payments are excludable only to the extent that they would qualify for a moving expense deduction if they had been paid by the minister and not reimbursed. The definition of deductible moving expenses is very restrictive. For example, meals while traveling and living in temporary quarters near the new workplace are not deductible. If a minister is reimbursed for nondeductible moving expenses, the amounts paid are additional taxable compensation (whether the minister files as an employee or self-employed for income tax purposes).

✓ **Personal computers and cellular telephones**. Personal computers and cellular telephones you own and use more than 50% for ministry may be depreciated as five-year recovery property or deducted under Section 179 up to the annual limit of $17,500 ($18,000 for 1997) on a joint return.

As a minister-employee, your use of the computer or cellular telephone must be

- for the "convenience of the church," and

- required as a "condition of employment."

If a computer is provided by the church in the church office but you prefer to work at home on your personal computer, it is not being used for the church's convenience.

If you meet the "convenience of employer" and "condition of employment" tests but do not use your computer or cellular telephone more than 50% of the time for your work, you must depreciate these items using the straight-line method. If you qualify under the office-in-the-home rules, the 50% test does not apply to you.

Records of the business use of your computer or cellular telephone should be maintained to substantiate your deductions.

✓ **Section 179 deductions**. In the year of purchase, you may choose to deduct up to $17,500 ($18,000 for 1997) on a joint return of the cost of tangible personal property used for business. Section 179 generally has limited use for automobiles because of the $3,060 (1996 rate) luxury auto limit on annual auto depreciation. While Section 179 may be used by ministers to deduct expenses, the deduction is not includable under an accountable expense reimbursement plan.

✓ **Subscriptions and books**. Subscriptions to ministry-related periodicals are deductible. If the information in a periodical relates to your ministerial preparation, news magazines may even qualify for a deduction.

Books related to your ministry with a useful life of one year or less may be deducted. The cost of books (such as commentaries) with a useful life of more than one year may be depreciated over the useful life. There is an option to deduct the books in the year of purchase under Section 179.

BUSINESS EXPENSES

✓ **Telephone expenses**. You may not deduct, as a business expense, any of the basic local service charge (including taxes) for the first telephone line into your home. Long-distance calls, a second line, special equipment, and services such as call-waiting used for business are deductible. If you are out of town on a business trip, the IRS will not challenge a reasonable number of telephone calls home.

Although your basic local telephone service is not deductible for tax purposes, it is includable as housing expense for housing allowance purposes.

Allocation of Business Expenses

The IRS is becoming aggressive in preventing ministers from deducting unreimbursed business expenses to the extent that they are "allocable" to a tax-exempt housing allowance. Recent tax court cases clearly document their position. IRS Publication 517 (Social Security and Other Information for Members of the Clergy and Religious Workers) explains this topic in detail and includes the concept in a completed tax return example. The draft of the new Tax Guide for Churches and Other Religious Organizations and the MSSP Audit Guide for Ministers' Returns, both issued by the IRS, clearly apply the expense allocation concept.

Under these guidelines, if you receive a rental or parsonage allowance that is tax-free, you must allocate the expenses of operating your ministry. You cannot deduct expenses that are allocable to your tax-free rental or parsonage allowance. This rule does not apply to your deductions for home mortgage interest or real estate taxes.

If you receive a tax-free rental or parsonage allowance and have ministerial expenses, attach a statement to your tax return. The statement must contain all the following information:

✓ A list of each item of taxable ministerial income by source (such as wages, salary, honoraria from weddings, baptisms, etc.) plus the amount.

✓ A list of each item of tax-free ministerial income by source (parsonage allowance) plus the amount.

✓ A list of each item of otherwise deductible ministerial expense plus the amount.

✓ How you figured the nondeductible part of your otherwise allowable deductions.

✓ A statement that the other deductions on your tax return are not allocable to your tax-free income.

This limitation requires the following calculation:

1. Amount of tax-exempt income (the fair rental value of a church-provided parsonage and the housing allowance excluded from gross income; this may be less than the church designated housing allowance) $_____

2. Total income from ministry:

   Salary (including the fair rental
   value of a church-provided parsonage
   and the housing allowance excluded
   from gross income) $_____
   Fees   _____
   Allowances (nonaccountable plan)   _____

                                              $_____

3. Divide line 1 amount by line 2 amount = nontaxable income %   _____%

4. Total business and professional expenses less 50% of meals and entertainment expenses (for which the minister was not required to "account" to the church) $_____

5. Multiply line 4 total by line 3 percentage (these are nondeductible expenses allowable to tax-exempt income). $_____

6. Subtract line 5 amount from line 4 amount (these are deductible expenses for federal income tax purposes on Form 2106 [2106-EZ] or Schedule C [C-EZ]). $_____

Action Steps

- Request your church to adopt an accountable expense reimbursement plan.

- Fully document all business expenses. Keep a log of auto miles driven for business purposes.

- Supply full substantiation for business expenses when submitting data to the church under an accountable reimbursement plan. The mere reporting of your expenses to the church does not constitute substantiation.

- If you are claiming unreimbursed business expenses, review the discussion in IRS Publication 517 on allocating expenses to tax-free income.

CHAPTER SIX

Social Security Tax

Ministers pay social security tax as self-employed persons.

In This Chapter
- Computing the self-employment tax
- Both spouses are ministers
- Self-employment tax deductions
- Use of voluntary withholding agreement to pay social security taxes
- Opting out of social security
- Working after you retire
- Canada Pension Plan

Calculating the portion of your income that is subject to social security is a complex process. For example, the housing allowance is taxable for social security purposes although potentially tax-exempt for income tax purposes. The IRS forms provide little help for ministers with this calculation.

Social security taxes are collected under two systems. Under the Federal Insurance Contributions Act (FICA), the employer pays one-half of the tax and the employee pays the other one-half. Under the Self-Employment Contributions Act (SECA), the self-employed person pays all the tax (self-employment tax). IRS Publication 517 provides information on social security taxes.

Compensation received by a minister for services performed in the exercise of ministry is self-employment income and always subject to self-employment tax (SECA). Ministerial income is exempt from SECA only if you have opted out of social security. Federal Insurance Contributions Act (FICA) social security tax should *never* be withheld from the compensation of a qualified minister.

Example: A church hires and pays you to perform ministerial services for it, subject to its control. Under the common law rules (pages 26–27), you are an employee of the church while performing those services. The church reports your wages on Form W-2 for income tax purposes, but no

SOCIAL SECURITY SYSTEM

FICA (Federal Insurance Contributions Act)	SECA (Self-Employment Contributions Act)
Non-minister employees of a church are all subject to FICA.	All qualified ministers are subject to SECA (unless they have opted out of social security).
Employee pays 7.65% Employer pays <u>7.65%</u> 15.30%	Self-employed individuals pay the full 15.3%.
The 15.3% is paid on a wage base of up to $62,700 for 1996 ($65,100 for 1997).	The 15.3% is paid on a wage base of up to $62,700 for 1996 ($65,100 for 1997).
Both the employer and employee pay a 1.45% tax rate on all wages.	The individual pays a 2.9% tax rate on all wages.

social security taxes are withheld. You are self-employed for social security purposes. You must pay self-employment tax (SECA) on those wages yourself unless you request and receive an exemption from self-employment tax. On Form W-2, box 12 for social security wages is left blank.

Many churches reimburse ministers for a portion or all of their SECA liability. SECA reimbursements represent additional taxable compensation in the year paid to the minister for both income and social security tax purposes.

Because of the SECA deductions (see page 105), a full SECA reimbursement is effectively less than the gross 15.3% rate.

Computing the Self-Employment Tax

When computing the self-employment tax, your net earnings from self-employment include the gross income earned from performing qualified services minus the deductions related to that income.

The following tax rates apply to net earnings from self-employment of $400 or more each year:

SOCIAL SECURITY TAX

	Tax Rate		Earnings Base	
Year	OASDI	Medicare	OASDI	Medicare
1994	12.4%	2.9%	60,600	no limit
1995	12.4%	2.9%	61,200	no limit
1996	12.4%	2.9%	62,700	no limit
1997 est.	12.4%	2.9%	65,100	no limit
1998 est.	12.4%	2.9%	67,800	no limit

OASDI = Old-age, survivors, and disability insurance, or social security.

Use the worksheet on page 104 to calculate net earnings from self-employment. Net earnings are transferred to Form SE, page 1, line 2, to calculate the SECA.

Example: You have the following ministerial income and expenses: church salary $30,000 (of which the housing allowance is $12,000); net Schedule C (C-EZ) income related to special speaking engagements, weddings, funerals, etc., $1,350; Schedule A employee business expenses (after offsetting 50% of nondeductible meal and entertainment) $1,800.

Your self-employment income is
Salary from church	$18,000
Church-designated housing allowance	12,000
Schedule C (C-EZ) net earnings	1,350
Schedule A employee business expenses	(1,800)
Total	$29,550

Only business expenses are deductible in determining income subject to SECA. The minister may deduct unreimbursed business expenses for the SECA computation even if deductions are not itemized on Schedule A.

Moving expenses do not qualify as business expenses. Therefore, moving expenses are not deductible in computing self-employment tax. However, for minister employees, reimbursed moving expenses are excludable from Form W-2. Therefore, the reimbursements are not included for income or social security tax purposes.

Both Spouses Are Ministers

If a husband and wife who are both duly ordained, commissioned, or licensed ministers have an agreement with a church that each will perform specific services for which they will receive pay, jointly or separately, they must divide the compensation according to the agreement. Such a division of income would have no impact on their income tax if they filed a joint return. But each of them could obtain social security coverage by dividing the compensation and subjecting the compensation to social security tax.

If the agreement for services is with one spouse only and the other spouse

Self-Employment Social Security Tax Worksheet

Inclusions:

Salary paid by church as reflected on Form W-2 $ _____

Net profit or loss as reflected on Schedule C or C-EZ
(includes speaking honoraria, offerings you receive
for marriages, baptisms, funerals, and other fees)   _____

Housing allowance excluded from salary on Form W-2 or from
income on Schedule C (C-EZ)   _____

Fair rental value of parsonage provided (including paid utilities)   _____

Nonaccountable business expense reimbursements
(if not included on Form W-2, Schedule C, or C-EZ)   _____

Reimbursement of self-employment taxes (if not
included on Form W-2, Schedule C, or C-EZ)   _____

Value of meals provided to you, your spouse, and your dependents
whether or not provided for your employer's convenience (these
amounts may have been excluded from gross income)   _____

Total inclusions   _____

Deductions:

Unreimbursed ministerial business and professional expenses
(included on Form W-2) or reimbursed expenses paid under
a nonaccountable plan (included on Form W-2)
     A.   Deductible on Schedule A before the 2% of AGI limitation
            whether or not you itemized[1] or   _____
     B.   Not deductible on Form 2106/2106 EZ or
            Schedule C/C-EZ because expenses were
            allocated to taxable/nontaxable income.   _____

Total deductions   _____

Net earnings from self-employment (to Schedule SE) $ _____

[1] The 50% unreimbursed meal and entertainment expense limitation applies to amounts subject to social security tax. In other words, if some of your meal and entertainment expenses were subjected to the 50% limit, the remainder cannot be deducted here.

Note 1:   Your net earnings from self-employment are not affected by the foreign earned income exclusion or the foreign housing exclusion or deduction if you are a U.S. citizen or resident alien who is serving abroad and living in a foreign country.

Note 2:   Amounts received as pension payments or annuity payments related to a church-sponsored tax-sheltered annuity by a retired minister are generally considered to be excluded from the social security calculation.

receives no pay for any specific duties, amounts paid for services are included only in the income of the spouse having the agreement.

If you have already filed a return and incorrectly divided, or failed to divide, the income for self-employment tax purposes, you may file an amended return showing the entire amount as self-employment income of that spouse.

If one spouse is ordained, commissioned, or licensed and the other is not, the "qualified" minister under the tax law generally receives 100% of the compensation from the church, and the spouse is considered a volunteer. This is true even though they may have been hired as a team and each spouse provides significant services to the church.

However, it may be legitimate to split the compensation from the church based on the duties of each spouse. Pay should *never* be split merely for the purpose of allowing a spouse to qualify for social security or to avoid exceeding the social security earnings limit for one spouse.

A minister's spouse who is not duly ordained, commissioned, or licensed as a minister of a church but who receives pay for performing services for the organization should not include the earnings with the minister's self-employment income. The nonminister spouse is an employee of the church for federal income tax and social security (FICA) tax purposes unless self-employment status for income tax purposes is appropriate.

Self-Employment Tax Deductions

You can take an income tax deduction equal to one-half of your self-employment tax liability. The deduction is claimed against gross income on line 25 of Form 1040, page 1.

You also may deduct about one-half of your self-employment tax liability in calculating your self-employment tax. This deduction is made on Schedule SE, line 4 by multiplying self-employment income by .9235.

The purpose of these deductions is to equalize the social security (and income) taxes paid by (and for) employees and self-employed persons with equivalent income.

Use of Voluntary Withholding Agreement to Pay Social Security Taxes

Under a voluntary withholding agreement, a minister-employee may ask the church to withhold a sufficient amount to cover federal income taxes plus enough for the self-employment taxes (SECA). The church must report all amounts withheld under such an arrangement as federal income taxes. The other option for the payment of income and social security taxes is to use the Form 1040-ES in paying quarterly estimated taxes.

A self-employed minister for income tax purposes is not eligible for the voluntary withholding agreement. The church could withhold from the minister's pay amounts for income and social security taxes and periodically pay these amounts to the minister. In turn, the minister would submit the funds to the IRS as estimated tax payments using Form 1040-ES.

Opting Out of Social Security

All ministers are automatically covered by social security (SECA) for services in the exercise of ministry unless an exemption has been received based on the filing with and approval by the IRS of Form 4361. You must certify that you oppose, either conscientiously or because of religious principles, the acceptance of any public insurance (with respect to services performed as a minister), including social security coverage. Either opposition must be based on religious belief. This includes an opposition to insurance that helps pay for or provide services for medical care (such as Medicare) and social security benefits.

To claim the exemption from self-employment tax, you must

✓ file Form 4361,

✓ be conscientiously opposed to public insurance because of your individual religious considerations (not because of your general conscience), or because of the principles of your religious denomination,

✓ file for *other than* economic reasons,

✓ inform the ordaining, commissioning, or licensing body of your church or order that you are opposed to public insurance if you are a minister,

✓ establish that the religious organization that ordained, commissioned, or licensed you or your religious order is a tax-exempt religious organization,

✓ establish that the organization is a church or a convention or association of churches, and

✓ sign and return the statement the IRS mails to you to verify that you are requesting an exemption based on the grounds listed on the statement.

Deadline for filing for an exemption

The application for exemption from self-employment tax must be filed by the date your tax return is due, including extensions, for the second year in which you had net ministerial income of $400 or more. These do not have to be consecutive tax years.

Example 1: A minister ordained in 1995 has net earnings of $400 in 1995

SOCIAL SECURITY TAX

Form 4361
(Rev. February 1994)
Department of the Treasury
Internal Revenue Service

Application for Exemption From Self-Employment Tax for Use by Ministers, Members of Religious Orders and Christian Science Practitioners

OMB No. 1545-0168
Expires 2-28-97

File Original and Two Copies

File original and two copies and attach supporting documents. This exemption is granted only if the IRS returns a copy to you marked "approved."

Please type or print

1 Name of taxpayer applying for exemption (as shown on Form 1040)
Harold T. Baldwin

Social security number
603 42 8941

Number and street (including apt. no.)
P. O. Box 123

Telephone number (optional)
( )

City or town, state, and ZIP code
Milton, PA 17847

2 Check ONE box: ☐ Christian Science practitioner ☒ Ordained minister, priest, rabbi
☐ Member of religious order not under a vow of poverty ☐ Commissioned or licensed minister (see line 6)

3 Date ordained, licensed, etc. (Attach supporting document. See instructions.)
7/ 1/ 97

4 Legal name of ordaining, licensing, or commissioning body or religious order
Christian General Conference

Number, street, and room or suite no.
P. O. Box 5002

Employer identification number
48-9017682

City or town, state, and ZIP code
Nashville, AR 71852

5 Enter the first 2 years, after the date shown on line 3, that you had net self-employment earnings of $400 or more, any of which came from services as a minister, priest, rabbi, etc.; member of a religious order; or Christian Science practitioner ▶ 19 96 19

6 If you apply for the exemption as a licensed or commissioned minister, and your denomination also ordains ministers, please indicate how your ecclesiastical powers differ from those of an ordained minister of your denomination. Attach a copy of your denomination's bylaws relating to the powers of ordained, commissioned, or licensed ministers.

7 I certify that I am conscientiously opposed to, or because of my religious principles I am opposed to, the acceptance (for services I perform as a minister, member of a religious order not under a vow of poverty, or a Christian Science practitioner) of any public insurance that makes payments in the event of death, disability, old age, or retirement; or that makes payments toward the cost of, or provides services for, medical care. (Public insurance includes insurance systems established by the Social Security Act.)

I certify that as a duly ordained, commissioned, or licensed minister of a church or a member of a religious order not under a vow of poverty, I have informed the ordaining, commissioning, or licensing body of my church or order that I am conscientiously opposed to, or because of religious principles, I am opposed to the acceptance (for services I perform as a minister or as a member of a religious order) of any public insurance that makes payments in the event of death, disability, old age, or retirement; or that makes payments toward the cost of, or provides services for, medical care, including the benefits of any insurance system established by the Social Security Act.

I certify that I did not file an effective waiver certificate (Form 2031) electing social security coverage on earnings as a minister, member of a religious order not under a vow of poverty, or a Christian Science practitioner.

I request to be exempted from paying self-employment tax on my earnings from services as a minister, member of a religious order not under a vow of poverty, or a Christian Science practitioner, under section 1402(e) of the Internal Revenue Code. I understand that the exemption, if granted, will apply only to these earnings. Under penalties of perjury, I declare that I have examined this application and to the best of my knowledge and belief, it is true and correct.

Signature ▶ *Harold T. Baldwin* Date ▶ 9/30/97

Caution: Form 4361 is **not** proof of the right to an exemption from Federal income tax withholding or social security tax, the right to a parsonage allowance exclusion (section 107 of the Internal Revenue Code), assignment by your religious superiors to a particular job, or the exemption or church status of the ordaining, licensing, commissioning body, or religious order.

For Internal Revenue Service Use

☐ Approved for exemption from self-employment tax on ministerial earnings
☐ Disapproved for exemption from self-employment tax on ministerial earnings

By ....
  (Director's signature) (Date)

Paperwork Reduction Act Notice.—We ask for the information on this form to carry out the Internal Revenue laws of the United States. You are required to give us the information. We need it to ensure that you are complying with these laws and to allow us to figure and collect the right amount of tax.

The time needed to complete and file this form will vary depending on individual circumstances. The estimated average time is:

Recordkeeping, 7 min.; **Learning about the law or the form,** 19 min.; **Preparing the form,** 16 min.; **Copying, assembling, and sending the form to the IRS,** 17 min.

If you have comments concerning the accuracy of these time estimates or suggestions for making this form more simple, we would be happy to hear from you. You can write to both the **Internal Revenue Service,** Attention: Reports Clearance Officer, PC:FP, Washington, DC 20224; and the **Office of Management and Budget,** Paperwork Reduction Project (1545-0168), Washington, DC 20503. **DO NOT** send this form to either of these offices. Instead, see **Where To File** on page 2.

General Instructions

Section references are to the Internal Revenue Code.

Purpose of Form.—File Form 4361 to apply for an exemption from self-employment tax if you are:

● An ordained, commissioned, or licensed minister of a church;

● A member of a religious order who has not taken a vow of poverty;

● A Christian Science practitioner; or

● A commissioned or licensed minister of a church or church denomination that ordains ministers, if you have authority to perform substantially all religious duties of your church or denomination.

This application must be based on your religious or conscientious opposition to the acceptance (for services performed as a minister, member of a religious order not under a vow of poverty, or Christian Science practitioner) of any public insurance that makes payments for death, disability, old age, or retirement; or that makes payments for the cost of, or provides services for, medical care, including any insurance benefits established by the Social Security Act.

If you are a duly ordained, commissioned, or licensed minister of a church or a member of a religious order not under a vow of poverty, prior to filing this form you must inform the ordaining, commissioning, or

(continued on page 2)

Cat. No. 41586H Form **4361** (Rev. 2-94)

Caution: Very few ministers qualify to file Form 4361. The filing must be based on the minister's conscience or religious principles, not because of a preference to invest retirement funds elsewhere.

and $500 in 1996. An application for exemption must be filed by April 15, 1997. If the minister does not receive the approved exemption by April 15, 1996, the self-employment tax for 1995 is due by that date.

Example 2: A minister has $300 in net clergy earnings in 1995 but earned $400 in both 1994 and 1996. An application for exemption must be filed by April 15, 1997. If the minister does not receive the approved exemption by April 16, 1995, the self-employment tax for 1994 is due by that date.

Example 3: A minister, ordained in 1994, earned $700 net for that year. In 1995, ministerial compensation was $1,000 and related expenses were over $1,000. Therefore, the 1995 net earnings were zero. Also in 1995, $7,000 in net self-employment earnings was received from nonministerial sources. In 1996, net self-employment earnings were $1,500 and $12,000 from nonministerial sources.

Because the minister had ministerial net earnings in 1994 and 1996 that were more than $400 each year, the application for exemption must be filed by April 15, 1997.

A minister must include with Form 4361 a statement that he has informed the ordaining body of his church of his opposition to the coverage.

If the request for exemption is approved, it is irrevocable, but it does not apply to nonministerial wages or to any other self-employment income.

Nullifying the exemption

If a minister has applied for exemption from self-employment tax and the IRS has approved the application, there is no stated procedure to nullify the exemption. If a minister filed the application for exemption in error, presumably he could appeal to the IRS to have the exemption nullified.

An appeal to nullify an exemption should be thoughtfully made. In initially applying for the exemption, the minister signs the form under penalties of perjury. Because of the three year statute of limitations, the IRS could assess three back years of social security tax against a minister who nullifies the exemption.

If you decide to opt back into social security, you might consider paying the social security tax for the next two years. Then, with the return for the third year, write the IRS and request that the exemption be nullified. This procedure could avoid the assessment of any back taxes.

Second ordination

A second ordination with a second church generally does not provide a second opportunity for a minister to opt out by filing Form 4361.

SOCIAL SECURITY TAX

Securing another copy of approved Form 4361

If a minister has lost the approved copy of the Form 4361, Application for Exemption from Self-Employment Tax, he may write the Internal Revenue Service Center where the form was filed and request a copy.

A copy of the Form 4361 also may be requested from the Social Security Administration, Office of Central Records Operations, Metro West Building, 300 North Green Street, Baltimore, MD 21201. In either case, include your name and social security number and the approximate date the form was filed.

Basis of filing for exemption

Neither economics nor any other nonreligious reason is a valid basis for the exemption. Many ministers are improperly counseled to opt out of social security because it may not be a "good investment." Your view of the soundness of the social security program has *absolutely no relationship* to the application for exemption.

Your first consideration in this issue is your ability to sign Form 4361 with a clear conscience. Key words in qualifying for exemption from social security coverage on ministerial earnings are "religious principles" and "conscientiously opposed to the *acceptance* of any public insurance." Religious principles cannot consist of simply the conviction that perhaps social security will not be there when you retire or that a better retirement can be purchased through an annuity or other retirement program. The belief must be an integral part of your religious system of beliefs, your theology.

Further, this religious principle must be one that would prevent you from ever asking for the benefits from such a plan based on your church salary. No basis exists for an objection related to paying the taxes or to the level of the taxes to be paid.

If you opt out and do not have sufficient credits from prior employment or from future nonministerial employment, neither you nor your dependents will be covered under social security benefits, survivors' benefits, or Medicare. If you opt out of social security, you should make alternate plans to provide for catastrophic illness, disability, or death as well as for retirement.

This is not a decision to be taken lightly. First, you must act on religious convictions. Second, the decision may be irreversible. Third, you must be prepared financially with alternatives to the benefits of social security coverage.

Although a minister may opt out of social security with respect to ministerial income, the minister may still receive social security benefits related to nonministerial wages or other self-employment income.

Working After You Retire

If you continue to work after you retire, your social security benefits are reduced if you earn over certain levels if you are between ages 62 and 69. When you reach age 70, your social security benefits are not reduced regardless of your earnings. The 1996 penalty levels are as follows:

Age	Social Security Benefits Will Be Reduced If Your Earnings Are Over
62-64	$8,280
65-69	11,520

If you are receiving social security benefits in the age 62 to 69 range and you are receiving a cash housing allowance or living in a parsonage, the Social Security Administration will generally include the housing allowance or value of the housing provided in your earnings to determine if your benefits will be reduced.

Canada Pension Plan

Under an agreement between the U.S. and Canada, a minister is subject to the laws of the country in which the services are performed for the purposes of U.S. social security and Canada Pension Plan, respectively. In other words, a Canadian citizen who moves to the U.S. to pastor a church generally must pay U.S. social security (SECA) tax.

There is one exception to the general rule: If the minister is required by a Canadian employer to transfer to a related organization in the U.S. on a temporary basis for a period not exceeding 60 months, with the intention of returning to the employment with the Canadian employer at the end of the temporary assignment. In this case, the Canadian employer must complete Form CPT 56. Revenue Canada has issued Information Circular No. 84-6 explaining these provisions. Copies may be obtained by writing Revenue Canada, Customs, Excise and Taxation, Ottawa, Ontario, K1A 0L8.

Action Steps

■ If you qualify for special tax treatment as a minister, be sure the church is not withholding or paying FICA tax for you.

■ Take advantage of all your allowable exclusions and deductions in computing income subject to SECA.

■ You may cover your SECA liability through a voluntary withholding arrangement by having the church withhold additional federal income tax.

■ Take your self-employment tax deduction on line 25 of Form 1040, page 1.

■ Do not opt out of social security because you don't think it is a good investment or you just prefer to handle the money yourself.

CHAPTER SEVEN
Paying Your Taxes
How to pay your taxes on time and avoid penalties

In This Chapter
- Tax withholding
- Estimated tax
- Excess social security withheld (FICA)
- Earned income tax credit
- Extension of time to file
- Extension of time to pay
- Filing an amended tax return

A minister has three choices in paying federal income taxes and social security taxes: tax withholding, quarterly estimated tax payments, or a combination of the two methods. IRS Publication 505 provides additional information on tax withholding and estimated taxes.

Tax Withholding

Federal income tax withheld from earnings as an employee should be reported to you on the appropriate form (W-2, W-2G, or 1099). The total amount withheld from all sources should be entered on line 55, Form 1040. Be sure to check the box to the left of the amount column on line 55 if you had any withholding from 1099 income.

Churches are *not required* to withhold income taxes from wages paid to ministers for services performed in the exercise of their ministry. The exemption does not apply to nonministerial church employees such as a secretary, organist, or custodian.

A minister-employee may have a *voluntary* withholding agreement with the employing church to cover income taxes (the amount may be set high enough to also cover the self-employment social security tax liability). An agreement to withhold income taxes from wages must be in writing. There is no required form for the agreement. It may be as simple as a letter from the minister to the church requesting that a specified amount be withheld as federal income taxes, or a minister may request voluntary withholding by submitting Form W-4 (Employee's Withholding Allowance Certificate) to the church and indicate an additional amount to be withheld in excess of the tax table amount.

If federal income taxes are withheld sufficient to cover both the minister's income and self-employment social security (SECA) taxes, it is very important that the amounts be reported as "federal income taxes withheld" when the church completes quarterly Form 941 and annual forms W-2 and W-3. FICA social security taxes are never withheld or remitted relating to qualified ministers.

An alternate procedure is acceptable whether a minister is considered an employee or self-employed for income tax purposes. For personal budgeting purposes, a minister may request the church to withhold amounts from compensation. Coinciding with the Form 1040-ES due dates (April 15, June 15, September 15, and January 15), the church pays the withheld amounts directly to the minister and then the minister uses the funds to make the appropriate estimated tax payments to the IRS.

The self-employed minister for income tax purposes reports and pays income taxes and social security taxes through the estimated tax procedure (Form 1040-ES). There is no provision for federal income tax withholding from payments made to ministers who are self-employed for income tax purposes, even on a voluntary basis.

Estimated Tax

Estimated tax is the method used to pay income and self-employment taxes for income that is not subject to withholding. Your estimated tax is your expected tax for the year minus your expected withholding and credits. Ministers with an adjusted gross income of over $75,000 may fall under special rules requiring larger estimated tax payments.

If you are filing a declaration of estimated tax, complete the quarterly Forms 1040-ES. If your 1997 estimated taxes are $500 or less, no declaration of estimated tax is required.

If your estimated tax payments for 1997 equal 90% of your 1996 tax liability, you will avoid underpayment penalties. An option is to make the 1997 estimated tax payments equal 100% of your 1996 federal and social security taxes (Form 1040, page 2, line 54). This method generally avoids underpayment penalties and is easier to calculate.

In estimating 1997 taxes, net earnings from self-employment should be reduced by 7.65% before calculating the self-employment tax of 15.3%. There also is an income tax deduction for one-half of your self-employment tax (Form 1040, page 1, line 25).

You pay one-fourth of your total estimated taxes in installments as follows:

For the Period	Due Date
Jan. 1 - Mar. 31	April 15
April 1 - May 31	June 15
June 1 - Aug. 31	September 15
Sept. 1 - Dec. 31	January 15

Estimated tax payments are counted as paid when the IRS receives them. Thus,

Three Ways To Pay Your Taxes

1

Estimated Taxes

The minister pays federal income taxes and social security taxes (SECA) directly to the IRS.

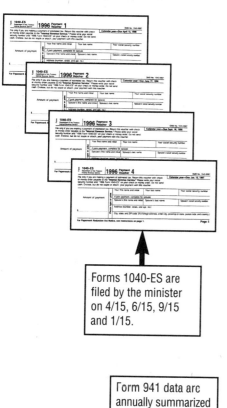

Forms 1040-ES are filed by the minister on 4/15, 6/15, 9/15 and 1/15.

2

Voluntary Withholding

Church withholds federal income tax and pays quarterly to the IRS. Additional federal income tax may be withheld to cover the minister's social security tax (SECA) liability.

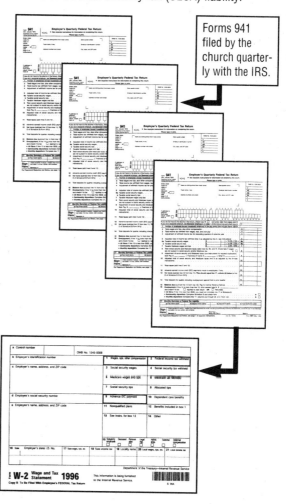

Forms 941 filed by the church quarterly with the IRS.

Form 941 data are annually summarized on Form W-2. The W-2 is provided to the minister and the IRS.

3

Payroll withholding from the minister's pay. The church does not remit the amounts withheld to the IRS. The amounts are paid directly to the minister on or before 4/15, 6/15, 9/15 and 1/15. The minister then files Form 1040 ES and remits the money to the IRS.

paying more later does not offset shortfalls from prior installments. Withheld tax is considered as paid evenly throughout the year. Therefore, increasing withholding late in a year offsets earlier underpayments.

Excess Social Security Withheld (FICA)

If you worked for two or more employers during 1996 and together they paid you more than $62,700 in wages, too much FICA tax may have been withheld from your wages. You can claim the extra amount as a credit to reduce your income tax when you file your return.

Earned Income Tax Credit

Many ministers qualify for the earned income tax credit (EITC). The program currently furnishes a basic benefit for families even when there are no dependent children. There are three supplemental benefits to adjust for families with two or more children, those with a newborn child, and those that incur certain health insurance costs for their children.

For 1996, the credit can be as much as $323 if you don't have a qualifying child; $2,152 if you have one qualifying child; $3,556 if you have more than one qualifying child. For 1996, "low income" generally means families with taxable and nontaxable earned income of less than $9,500 if there is no qualifying child, less than $25,078 if there is one qualifying child, and to those who earned less than $28,495 and have two or more children. A "qualifying child" generally includes any child of the individual who is under the age of 19 (or a full-time student under the age of 24).

The excluded portion of the minister's housing allowance and the fair rental value of church-provided housing must be included for purposes of calculating the EITC (see page 144 for an example). Also includable are 403(b) voluntary tax-sheltered annuity deferrals.

Claiming the credit

To claim the EITC, you must file a federal income tax return for the year, either Form 1040 or 1040A. A separate Schedule EIC must be completed if you have at least one qualifying child (if you do not have a qualifying child, the IRS will compute the credit, if any, without the completion of Schedule EIC.)

Extension of Time to File

Your 1996 return should be filed with the IRS service center and payment made by April 15, 1997, to avoid penalties and interest.

If you have obtained an extension of time to file your return, remember that your final payment is still due by April 15, with the extension application. *The extension of time to file is not an extension of your time to pay.*

Four-month extension

To receive a four-month extension of time, you should file Form 4868, Application for Automatic Extension of Time to File U.S. Individual Income Tax Return (see page 118). The form must be filed by April 15. You need not supply any reasons; the IRS will automatically grant the extension.

Two-month extension

If you have reached the end of the four-month automatic extension period and still need more time to file, you can request two additional months by filing Form 2688, Application for Additional Extension of Time to File (see page 119). Except for undue hardship, the IRS will not accept Form 2688 unless a Form 4868 has been filed.

Obtaining an extra two-month extension is *not* automatic. You must furnish a valid reason. If you have not yet received information from an outside party that is necessary for the completion of your return, this will generally be a valid reason. Other reasons that might be accepted by the IRS include illness in your family or destruction or loss of your records.

You may qualify to file Form 2350 for a special two-month extension of time to file in certain instances when you are out of the country.

Penalties

An elaborate system of penalties exists to make sure that tax returns are filed correctly and tax liabilities are paid on time. In addition, interest is charged on many penalties, including the late filing penalty, substantial understatement penalty, overvaluation penalty, negligence penalty, and fraud penalty.

- ✓ **Failure to pay penalty**. Even if the IRS grants an extension of time to file, if 90% of your tax is not paid on time, you will be subject to a penalty of one-half of 1% of the unpaid tax for each month or part of a month that the tax is not paid, to a maximum of 25% of the tax. You can avoid the penalty only if you can show that your failure to pay is due to reasonable cause and not willful neglect.

- ✓ **Penalty computed by the IRS**. If you do not want to figure your penalty and pay it when you file your tax return, you do not have to. The IRS will figure it for you and send you a bill. In certain situations you must complete Form 2210 and attach it to your return.

- ✓ **Form 2210**. If you want to figure your penalty, complete Part I and either Part II or Part III of Form 2210, Underpayment of Estimated Tax by Individuals and Fiduciaries.

You will not generally have to pay a penalty if any of the following situations applies to you:

- The total of your withholding and estimated tax payments was at least as much as your 1995 tax, you are not subject to the special rule limiting use of prior year's tax, and all required estimated tax payments were on time.

- The tax balance on your return is no more than 10% of your total 1996 tax, and all required estimated tax payments were on time.

- Your total 1996 tax minus withholding is less than $500.

- You did not owe tax for 1995.

Interest

If you have not paid the entire tax due by April 15, you must pay interest from then until the date you pay your tax liability. Receiving an automatic extension of time to file your tax return will not relieve you of the burden of interest.

State extensions

For states that have a state income tax, check the instruction forms that come with your return to determine how to file an extension. In some states, if you owe no additional tax, you need not file a separate state extension. Instead, the state will allow the same extensions that the IRS grants, and you just attach a copy of your federal extension to your state return for filing. Other states may require their own forms.

Extension of Time to Pay

Installment payments

The IRS may permit you to pay your taxes on the installment plan. When you file your tax return, include Form 9465 Installment Agreement Request (see page 120). Within a month, the IRS will notify you whether the installment payment plan has been approved. But the IRS requires you to start paying within a month. Moreover, you'll still owe the IRS the late-payment penalty plus interest including interest on the penalty. And you can't deduct either the penalty or the interest on your tax return. The IRS charges user fees of $43 for an installment agreement and $24 to restructure an agreement.

Six-month extension

Don't confuse the six-month extension with the four-month filing extension, which you can obtain automatically by submitting Form 4868. Even if you do get an extension to file your return by August 15 (by filing Form 4868), you must pay your taxes by April 15.

You may be able to put off paying your taxes for six months without a penalty by using Form 1127, Application for Extension of Time for Payment of Tax (see page 121).

Getting this extension isn't easy, though. You'll have to prove to the IRS that you don't have the money to pay the taxes, cannot borrow, and, if forced to pay up, you and your family will suffer "undue hardship." What's more, you will have to give the IRS a list of all your assets and liabilities.

Filing an Amended Tax Return

There is probably still time to revise your 1993 and 1994 and 1995 income tax returns by filing Form 1040X (see page 122). Review these tax returns to determine if you missed out on any tax savings. Or if you find you owe more money, you can pay before the IRS catches up with you and the interest due has increased.

Don't forget to amend your state return, too, especially if you owe additional tax. The IRS and the state tax authorities exchange information. If you file an amended federal return and forget to file one for the state, the state is likely to find out about the additional tax from the IRS.

Action Steps

- If you're afraid you won't be able to mail your return on time, just fill out Form 4868 and mail it to the IRS by midnight of April 15. If you owe income or social security tax, estimate the amount due and include your check with the extension.

- Try to file before the August 15 deadline. Obtaining an additional extension of time to file is relatively difficult.

- If you have been filing tax returns based on substantial data, do not be afraid to file an amended return.

- Carefully estimate your tax liability with a goal of owing very little tax or receiving a small refund.

- Pay your taxes through either Form 1040-ES or a voluntary withholding arrangement with your church.

- Include your social security taxes (SECA) in either the estimated tax payments or the withholding arrangement.

- To avoid underpayment penalties, pay in an amount equal to 100% of your previous year's tax liability.

1997 MINISTER'S TAX AND FINANCIAL GUIDE

1996 Form 4868  Department of the Treasury
Internal Revenue Service

General Instructions

Note: *Form 1040-T references are to a new form sent to certain individuals on a test basis.*

A Change To Note

We have combined Form 4868-V (payment voucher) and Form 4868 into one, smaller, detachable Form 4868. The form is at the bottom of this page.

Purpose of Form

Use Form 4868 to apply for 4 more months to file **Form 1040EZ, Form 1040A, Form 1040,** or **Form 1040-T.**

To get the extra time you **MUST:**
- Properly estimate your 1995 tax liability using the information available to you,
- Enter your tax liability on line 6a of Form 4868,
- Sign your Form 4868, **AND**
- File Form 4868 by the regular due date of your return.

If you cannot pay the entire balance due, see the instructions for line 6c.

You do not have to explain why you are asking for the extension. We will contact you only if your request is denied.

Do not file Form 4868 if you want the IRS to figure your tax or you are under a court order to file your return by the regular due date.

If you need an additional extension, see **Additional Time** on page 3.

Note: *An extension of time to file your 1995 calendar year income tax return also extends the time to file a gift or generation-skipping transfer (GST) tax return (Form 709 or 709-A) for 1995.*

Out of the Country

If you already had 2 extra months to file because you were a U.S. citizen or resident and were out of the country, use this form to obtain an additional 2 months to file. Write "Taxpayer Abroad" across the top of Form 4868. "Out of the country" means either **(a)** you live outside the United States and Puerto Rico **and** your main place of work is outside the United States and Puerto Rico, **or (b)** you are in military or naval service outside the United States and Puerto Rico.

When To File Form 4868

File Form 4868 by April 15, 1996. If you are filing a fiscal year return, file Form 4868 by the regular due date of your return.

If you had 2 extra months to file your return because you were out of the country, file Form 4868 by June 17, 1996, for a 1995 calendar year return.

For Paperwork Reduction Act Notice, see page 3. Cat. No. 13141W Form **4868** (1995)

▼ DETACH HERE ▼

Form **4868**
Department of the Treasury
Internal Revenue Service

Application for Automatic Extension of Time To File U.S. Individual Income Tax Return

OMB No. 1545-0188

1996

1 Your name(s) (see instructions)
Milton L. and Alessia S. Brown
Address (see instructions)
418 Trenton Street
City, town or post office, state, and ZIP code
Springfield, OH 45504

3 Your social security number 541 16 8194
4 Spouse's social security no. 238 49 7209

2a Amount due—
Add lines 6c, d, and e ▶ $ -0-
b Amount you are paying ▶ $ -0-

5 I request an automatic 4-month extension of time to August 15, 1996, to file my individual tax return for the calendar year 1995 or to _____, 19__, for the fiscal tax year ending _____, 19__.

6 **Individual Income Tax**—See instructions.
a Total tax liability for 1995 . . . . . $ 7,000
b Total payments for 1995 . . . . . $ 7,000
c Balance due. Subtract 6b from 6a . . $ -0-

Gift or GST Tax Return(s)—See instructions.
Check here **ONLY** if filing a gift or GST tax return Yourself ▶ ☐ Spouse ▶ ☐
d Amount of gift or GST tax **you** are paying $ _____
e Your spouse's gift/GST tax payment $ _____

Under penalties of perjury, I declare that I have examined this form, including accompanying schedules and statements, and to the best of my knowledge and belief, it is true, correct, and complete; and, if prepared by someone other than the taxpayer, that I am authorized to prepare this form.

▶ *Milton L. Brown* | 4/15/97 ▶ *Alessia S. Brown* | 4/15/97
   Your signature | Date   Spouse's signature, if filing jointly | Date

▶ _____
   Preparer's signature (other than taxpayer) | Date

Note: This form provides an extension of time to file, not an extension of time to pay (see page 115).

PAYING YOUR TAXES

Form 2688
Department of the Treasury
Internal Revenue Service

Application for Additional Extension of Time To File U.S. Individual Income Tax Return
▶ See instructions on back.
▶ You MUST complete all items that apply to you.

OMB No. 1545-0066
1996
Attachment Sequence No. 59

Please type or print.
File the original and one copy by the due date for filing your return.

Your first name and initial: Milton L. Last name: Brown
Your social security number: 541 16 8194

If a joint return, spouse's first name and initial: Alessia S. Last name: Brown
Spouse's social security number: 238 49 7209

Home address (number, street, and apt. no. or rural route). If you have a P.O. box, see the instructions.
418 Trenton Street
City, town or post office, state, and ZIP code
Springfield, OH 45504

1 I request an extension of time until 10/15, 19 97, to file Form 1040EZ, Form 1040A, Form 1040 or Form 1040-T for the calendar year 1995, or other tax year ending ...., 19......

2 Explain why you need an extension. All individuals filing this form must give an adequate explanation ▶ ....
Residence was damaged by tornadic winds in June 1997. Some of our 1996 tax records were destroyed. Additional time to file is needed to secure microfilm copies of bank statements and cancelled checks.

3 Have you filed Form 4868 to request an extension of time to file for this tax year? . . . . ☒ Yes ☐ No
If you checked "No," we will grant your extension only for undue hardship. Fully explain the hardship in item 2. Attach any information you have that helps explain the hardship.

If you expect to owe gift or generation-skipping transfer (GST) tax, complete line 4.

4 If you or your spouse plan to file a gift or GST tax return (Form 709 or 709-A) for 1995, generally } Yourself . ▶ ☐
due by April 15, 1996, see the instructions and check here . . . . } Spouse . . ▶ ☐

Signature and Verification
Under penalties of perjury, I declare that I have examined this form, including accompanying schedules and statements, and to the best of my knowledge and belief, it is true, correct, and complete; and, if prepared by someone other than the taxpayer, that I am authorized to prepare this form.

Signature of taxpayer ▶ *Milton L. Brown* Date ▶ 8/15/97
Signature of spouse ▶ *Alessia S. Brown* Date ▶ 8/15/97
(If filing jointly, BOTH must sign even if only one had income)
Signature of preparer other than taxpayer ▶ Date ▶

File original and one copy. The IRS will show below whether or not your application is approved and will return the copy.

Notice to Applicant—To Be Completed by the IRS

☐ We **HAVE** approved your application. Please attach this form to your return.
☐ We **HAVE NOT** approved your application. However, we have granted a 10-day grace period from the later of the date shown below or the due date of your return. This grace period is considered to be a valid extension of time for elections otherwise required to be made on a timely return. Please attach this form to your return.
☐ We **HAVE NOT** approved your application. After considering your reasons stated in item 2 above, we cannot grant your request for an extension of time to file. We are not granting a 10-day grace period.
☐ We cannot consider your application because it was filed after the due date of your return.
☐ We **HAVE NOT** approved your application. The maximum extension of time allowed by law is 6 months.
☐ Other ....

_____ Director
Date By _____

Please type or print
Name
Number and street (include suite, room, or apt. no.) or P.O. box number if mail is not delivered to street address
City, town or post office, state, and ZIP code

If you want the copy of this form returned to you at an address other than that shown above or to an agent acting for you, enter the name of the agent and/or the address to which the copy should be sent.

For Paperwork Reduction Act Notice, see back of form. Cat. No. 11958F Form **2688** (1995)

Note: Without a compelling reason for an additional extension, a request for further time will often be denied (see page 115).

Form **9465** (Rev. January 1996) Department of the Treasury Internal Revenue Service	**Installment Agreement Request** ▶ See instructions below and on back.	OMB No. 1545-1350

Note: *Do not file this form if you are currently making payments on an installment agreement. You must pay your other Federal tax liabilities in full or you will be in default on your agreement.*

If you can't pay the full amount you owe, you can ask to make monthly installment payments. If we approve your request, you will be charged a $43 fee. **Do not include the fee with this form.** We will deduct the fee from your first payment after we approve your request, unless you choose **Direct Debit** (see the line 13 instructions). We will usually let you know within 30 days after we receive your request whether it is approved or denied. But if this request is for tax due on a return you filed after March 31, it may take us longer than 30 days to reply.

To ask for an installment agreement, complete this form. Attach it to the front of your return when you file. If you have already filed your return or you are filing this form in response to a notice, see **How Do I File Form 9465?** on page 2. If you have any questions about this request, call 1-800-829-1040.

Caution: *A Notice of Federal Tax Lien may be filed to protect the government's interest until you pay in full.*

1	Your first name and initial Milton L.	Last name Brown	Your social security number 541 16 8194
	If a joint return, spouse's first name and initial Alessia S.	Last name Brown	Spouse's social security number 238 49 7209
	Your current address (number and street). If you have a P.O. box and no home delivery, show box number. 418 Trenton Street		Apt. number
	City, town or post office, state, and ZIP code. If a foreign address, show city, state or province, postal code, and full name of country. Springfield, OH 45504		

2 If this address is new since you filed your last tax return, check here . . . . ▶ ☐

3	(513) 831-8742		4	(513) 831-6873		9-5
	Your home phone number	Best time for us to call		Your work phone number	Ext.	Best time for us to call

5	Name of your bank or other financial institution:	6	Your employer's name:
	Springfield Credit Union		Magnolia Springs Church
	Address 489 High Drive		Address 4867 Douglas Road
	City, state, and ZIP code Springfield, OH 45504		City, state, and ZIP code Springfield, OH 45504

7	Enter the tax return for which you are making this request (for example, Form 1040). But if you are filing this form in response to a notice, don't complete lines 7 through 9. Instead, attach the bottom section of the notice to this form and go to line 10. . . . . ▶	Form 1040
8	Enter the tax year for which you are making this request (for example, 1995) . . . . ▶	1996
9	Enter the total amount you owe as shown on your tax return . . . . ▶	$ 8,642
10	Enter the amount of any payment you are making with your tax return (or notice). See instructions . ▶	$ 1,000
11	Enter the amount you can pay each month. **Make your payments as large as possible to limit interest and penalty charges.** The charges will continue until you pay in full . . . . ▶	$ 500
12	Enter the date you want to make your payment each month. Do not enter a date later than the 28th ▶	1st
13	If you would like to make your monthly payments using **Direct Debit** (automatic withdrawals from your bank account), check here.	☐

Your signature *Milton L. Brown*	Date 8/15/97	Spouse's signature. If a joint return, BOTH must sign. *Alessia S. Brown*	Date 8/15/97

Privacy Act and Paperwork Reduction Act Notice.—Our legal right to ask for the information on this form is Internal Revenue Code sections 6001, 6011, 6012(a), 6109, and 6159 and their regulations. We will use the information to process your request for an installment agreement. The reason we need your name and social security number is to secure proper identification. We require this information to gain access to the tax information in our files and properly respond to your request. If you do not enter the information, we may not be able to process your request. We may give this information to the Department of Justice as provided by law. We may also give it to cities, states, and the District of Columbia to carry out their tax laws.

Cat. No. 14842Y   Form **9465** (Rev. 1-96)

Note: This form must be filed with your tax return to request installment payment of your taxes (see page 116).

PAYING YOUR TAXES

Form **1127**
(Rev. 5-92)
Department of the Treasury
Internal Revenue Service

APPLICATION FOR EXTENSION OF TIME FOR PAYMENT OF TAX

(Please read conditions on back before completing this form)

Please Type or Print

Taxpayer's Name (include Spouse if this is for a joint return)
Milton L. and Alessia S. Brown

Present Address
418 Trenton Street

City, Town or Post Office, State, and Zip Code
Springfield, OH 45504

Social Security Number or Employer Identification Number
541-16-8194

Spouse's Social Security Number if this is for a Joint Return
238-49-7209

District Director of Internal Revenue at __Cincinnati, Ohio__
(Enter City and State where IRS Office is located)

I request an extension from __April 15__, 19__97__, to __December 31__, 19__97__
(Enter Due Date of Return)

to pay tax of $ __5,000__ for the year ended __December 31__, 19__97__.

This extension is necessary because *(If more space is needed, please attach a separate sheet):*
Both taxpayers have been unemployed for the past 90 days. Savings have been depleted to pay living expenses.

I can not borrow to pay the tax because: our credit rating is so bad that we are unable to borrow money.

To show the need for the extension, I am attaching: (1) a statement of my assets and liabilities at the end of last month (showing book and market values of assets and whether securities are listed or unlisted); and (2) an itemized list of money I received and spent for 3 months before the date the tax is due.

I propose to secure this liability as follows:
We have no security to offer.

Under penalties of perjury, I declare that I have examined this application, including any accompanying schedules and statements, and to the best of my knowledge and belief it is true, correct, and complete.

Milton L. Brown   Alessia S Brown   4/15/97
SIGNATURE (BOTH SIGNATURES IF THIS IS FOR A JOINT RETURN)   (DATE)

The District Director will let you know whether the extension is approved or denied and will tell you the form of bond, if necessary. However, the Director cannot consider an application if it is filed after the due date of the return. A list of approved surety companies will be sent to you upon request.

(The following will be filled in by the IRS.)

This application is ☐ approved   for the following reasons:
                    ☐ denied

Interest _____   Date of assessment _____   Identifying no. _____
Penalty _____   _____   _____
                                  (SIGNATURE)   (DATE)

(over)   Form **1127** (Rev. 5-92)

Note: This form must be filed by April 15 to request a six-month extension to pay your income tax (see page 117).

1997 MINISTER'S TAX AND FINANCIAL GUIDE

Form **1040X** (Rev. October 1995)
Department of the Treasury—Internal Revenue Service
Amended U.S. Individual Income Tax Return
▶ See separate instructions.
OMB No. 1545-0091

This return is for calendar year ▶ 19 95 , OR fiscal year ended ▶ , 19 .

Your first name and initial: Milton L.	Last name: Brown
Your social security number: 541 16 8194	
If a joint return, spouse's first name and initial: Alessia S.	Last name: Brown
Spouse's social security number: 238 49 7209	
Home address (number and street): 418 Trenton Street	Apt. no.
Telephone number (optional): ( )	
City, town or post office, state, and ZIP code: Springfield, OH 45504	

A If the name or address shown above is different from that shown on the original return, check here . . . . ▶ ☐

B Has original return been changed or audited by the IRS or have you been notified that it will be? . . . ☐ Yes ☒ No
If notified that it will be, identify the IRS office ▶

C If you are amending your return to include any item (loss, credit, deduction, other tax benefit, or income) relating to a tax shelter required to be registered, attach **Form 8271**, Investor Reporting of Tax Shelter Registration Number, and check here . . . . ▶ ☐

D Filing status claimed. **Note:** *You cannot change from joint to separate returns after the due date has passed.*
On original return ▶ ☐ Single ☒ Married filing joint return ☐ Married filing separate return ☐ Head of household ☐ Qualifying widow(er)
On this return ▶ ☐ Single ☒ Married filing joint return ☐ Married filing separate return ☐ Head of household ☐ Qualifying widow(er)

Income and Deductions (see instructions)
USE PART II ON PAGE 2 TO EXPLAIN ANY CHANGES

		A. As originally reported or as previously adjusted (see instructions)	B. Net change—Increase or (Decrease)—explain on page 2	C. Correct amount
1	Adjusted gross income (see instructions)	32,000	(3,000)	29,000
2	Itemized deductions or standard deduction	7,100	300	7,400
3	Subtract line 2 from line 1	24,900	(3,300)	21,600
4	Exemptions. If changing, fill in Parts I and II on page 2	9,400		9,400
5	Taxable income. Subtract line 4 from line 3	15,500	(3,300)	12,200

Tax Liability

6	Tax (see instructions). Method used in col. C Table	2,329	(495)	1,834
7	Credits (see instructions)			
8	Subtract line 7 from line 6. Enter the result but not less than zero			
9	Other taxes (see instructions)	5,500		5,500
10	Total tax. Add lines 8 and 9	7,829	495	7,334

Payments

11	Federal income tax withheld and excess social security, Medicare, and RRTA taxes withheld. If changing, see instructions	8,000		8,000
12	Estimated tax payments			
13	Earned income credit			
14	Credits for Federal tax paid on fuels, regulated investment company, etc.			
15	Amount paid with Form 4868, Form 2688, or Form 2350 (applications for extension of time to file)			
16	Amount of tax paid with original return plus additional tax paid after it was filed			
17	Total payments. Add lines 11 through 16 in column C			8,000

Refund or Amount You Owe

18	Overpayment, if any, as shown on original return or as previously adjusted by the IRS	18	171
19	Subtract line 18 from line 17 (see instructions)	19	7,829
20	**AMOUNT YOU OWE.** If line 10, column C, is more than line 19, enter the difference and see instructions	20	
21	If line 10, column C, is less than line 19, enter the difference	21	495
22	Amount of line 21 you want **REFUNDED TO YOU**	22	495
23	Amount of line 21 you want **APPLIED TO YOUR 19** **ESTIMATED TAX**	23	

Sign Here
Keep a copy of this return for your records.

Under penalties of perjury, I declare that I have filed an original return and that I have examined this amended return, including accompanying schedules and statements, and to the best of my knowledge and belief, this amended return is true, correct, and complete. Declaration of preparer (other than taxpayer) is based on all information of which the preparer has any knowledge.

Milton L. Brown 1/15/97   *Alessia S. Brown* 1/15/97
Your signature Date   Spouse's signature. If a joint return, BOTH must sign. Date

Paid Preparer's Use Only
Preparer's signature ▶   Date   Check if self-employed ☐   Preparer's social security no.
Firm's name (or yours if self-employed) and address ▶   EIN   ZIP code

Cat. No. 11360L   Form **1040X** (Rev. 10-95)

Note: Amended returns must be filed within three years of the return due date plus approved extensions (see page 117).

Sample Returns

The three examples on the following pages have been carefully designed to illustrate a number of different tax principles discussed in this book. Most ministers file as employees for income tax purposes. If you have an accountable expense plan, example No. 1 relates to your tax filing. Example No. 2 is for minister-employees who do not have an accountable expense plan.

Based on recent tax court decisions, very few ministers qualify to file as self-employed for income purposes. However, since many ministers continue to use this approach, the third example is provided for them.

The key principles illustrated in the examples are as follows:

Example No. 1 (pages 125-134)

A. Church provides the minister Form W-2 and the minister files as an employee for income tax purposes.

B. The minister has entered into a voluntary withholding arrangement with the church to withhold federal income tax (social security should never be withheld from a qualified minister).

C. The minister owns his own home and the church has designated a housing allowance.

D. The church reimburses moving expenses in 1996 to the minister for a move that occurred in 1996.

E. The church used an accountable reimbursement plan to reimburse 100% of the minister's church-related expenses.

F. Schedule C-EZ is used for income from ministerial honoraria.

G. Because of the salary level of the minister, Schedule B (long form) on Schedule SE is used.

Example No. 2 (pages 135-147)

A. Church provides the minister Form W-2 and the minister files as an employee for income tax purposes.

B. The minister pays federal taxes (income and social security) by quarterly filing Form 1040-ES.

C. The minister is renting a home and the church has designated a housing allowance.

D. The minister qualifies for the earned income credit and schedule EIC is completed.

E. The church provides the minister an expense allowance. This is a nonaccountable expense plan and the total allowance must be included as compensation on Form W-2.

F. The minister files Form 2106-EZ because expenses are not reimbursed under an accountable expense plan.

G. The minister's expenses are allocated on Form 2106 between taxable and tax-free income (housing allowance) based on IRS Publication 517 and recent tax court decisions. There is no requirement to allocate the expenses on Schedule SE.

H. Schedule C-EZ is used for income from ministerial honoraria.

I. Because of the salary level of the minister, Schedule A (short form) on Schedule SE is used, although using Schedule B (long form) would also have been acceptable.

Example No. 3 (pages 148-157)

A. The church treats the minister as self-employed for income tax purposes and provides Form 1099-MISC. The minister reports all ministerial income on Schedule C (Schedule C-EZ cannot be used because income and expenses exceed the limits for this form).

B. The minister is not eligible for a voluntary income tax withholding agreement (only minister-employees qualify for this). The minister could have paid federal taxes (income and social security) by filing quarterly Form 1040-ES. However, since the minister's spouse was employed, she increased her federal income tax withholding sufficiently to cover his income and social security tax liability.

C. The minister lives in a church-provided parsonage and the church has designated a housing allowance to cover expenses incurred by the minister. **Key point:** Virtually every minister should have a housing allowance, even ministers living in church-provided parsonages.

D. The church reimburses the minister's moving expenses in 1996 for a move made in 1996. Since the church treats him as self-employed for income tax purposes, the moving expenses reimbursed are included on Form 1099-MISC. The expenses are deductible by the minister on page one, Form 1040, but are not deductible in computing social security (SECA). The minister must file Form 3903 and the church must provide the minister with Form 4782.

E. The church provides the minister with an expense allowance. This is a nonaccountable expense plan and the minister must include the total allowance as income on Schedule C.

F. Expenses are not allocated on Schedule C between taxable and tax-free (fair rental value of parsonage) income because there is no apparent requirement to do so.

G. The health insurance premiums paid for the minister by the church are taxable income (included on Form 1099-MISC). This is a tax-free benefit only available to employees.

Example No. 1

Minister considered to be an employee for income tax purposes with an accountable business expense plan.

The Browns live in a home they are personally purchasing. Pastor Brown has entered into a voluntary withholding agreement with the church and $14,000 of federal income taxes are withheld.

Income, Benefits, and Reimbursements:

Church salary	$38,000
Cash housing allowance/ properly designated (see page 132)	16,500
Christmas and other special occasion gifts paid by the church based on designated member-gifts to the church	750
Honoraria for performing weddings, funerals, and baptisms	650
Honorarium for speaking as an evangelist at another church	1,000
Dividend income:	
Capital gain distributions	150
Ordinary	954
Interest income:	
Taxable	675
Tax-exempt	1,200
Reimbursement of self-employment tax	9,000
Reimbursement of moving expenses	4,100

Business Expenses, Itemized Deductions, and IRA Contributions:

100% of church-related expenses paid personally ($7,593) were reimbursed by the church under an accountable expense plan, based on timely substantiation of the expenses.

Potential itemized deductions:		
Doctors, dentists, and drugs		$1,500
State and local income taxes:		
1995 taxes paid in 1996		800
Withheld from salary		1,200
Real estate taxes on home		1,000
Home mortgage interest		5,000
Cash contributions		5,000
IRA contributions:		
Melvin L. Brown		$2,000
Alessia S. Brown		250
Housing data:		
Designation		$16,500
Actual expenses		16,250
Fair rental value		14,500

EXAMPLE NO. 1 - MINISTER-EMPLOYEE FOR INCOME TAX PURPOSES (ACCOUNTABLE PLAN)

Form 1040 Department of the Treasury—Internal Revenue Service
U.S. Individual Income Tax Return 1996 (99) IRS Use Only—Do not write or staple in this space.

For the year Jan. 1–Dec. 31, 1996, or other tax year beginning , 1996, ending , 19   OMB No. 1545-0074

Label (See instructions.)

Your first name and initial: Melvin L. Last name: Brown
Your social security number: 541 16 8194

If a joint return, spouse's first name and initial: Alessia S. Last name: Brown
Spouse's social security number: 238 49 7209

Home address (number and street): 418 Trenton Street

City, town or post office, state, and ZIP code: Springfield, OH 45504

Presidential Election Campaign (See page 11.)
Do you want $3 to go to this fund? Yes: X
If a joint return, does your spouse want $3 to go to this fund? Yes: X

Filing Status — Check only one box.
2 [X] Married filing joint return (even if only one had income)

Exemptions
6a [X] Yourself.
6b [X] Spouse
No. of boxes checked on lines 6a and 6b: **2**
Add numbers entered on lines above: **2**

(Proof as of July 1996 — Subject to change)

Income
Attach Copy B of your Forms W-2, W-2G, and 1099-R here.
If you did not get a W-2, see the line 7 instructions.
Please send any payment separately with Form 1040-V. See the line 62a instructions.

7	Wages, salaries, tips, etc. Attach Form(s) W-2	47,750
8a	Taxable interest. Attach Schedule B if over $400	675
8b	Tax-exempt interest. DON'T include on line 8a	
9	Dividend income. Attach Schedule B if over $400	954
10	Taxable refunds, credits, or offsets of state and local income taxes	
11	Alimony received	
12	Business income or (loss). Attach Schedule C or C-EZ	1,650
13	Capital gain or (loss). If required, attach Schedule D *Capital Gain Dist.*	150
14	Other gains or (losses). Attach Form 4797	
15a	Total IRA distributions 15b Taxable amount	
16a	Total pensions and annuities 16b Taxable amount	
17	Rental real estate, royalties, partnerships, S corporations, trusts, etc. Attach Schedule E	
18	Farm income or (loss). Attach Schedule F	
19	Unemployment compensation	
20a	Social security benefits 20b Taxable amount	
21	Other income. List type and amount — *Excess housing allowance*	2,000
22	Add the amounts in the far right column for lines 7 through 21. This is your **total income**	53,179

Adjusted Gross Income
If line 31 is under $28,495 (under $9,500 if a child didn't live with you), see the line 54 instructions.

23a	Your IRA deduction	2,000
23b	Spouse's IRA deduction	250
24	Moving expenses. Attach Form 3903 or 3903-F	
25	One-half of self-employment tax. Attach Schedule SE	4,640
26	Self-employed health insurance deduction	
27	Keogh & self-employed SEP plans. If SEP, check ▶ ☐	
28	Penalty on early withdrawal of savings	
29	Alimony paid. Recipient's SSN ▶	
30	Add lines 23a through 29	6,890
31	Subtract line 30 from line 22. This is your **adjusted gross income**	46,289

For Privacy Act and Paperwork Reduction Act Notice, see page 7. Cat. No. 11320B Form **1040** (1996)

Line 21 - See page 132 for calculation of the excess housing allowance.
Line 23 - See page 54 for IRA information.
Line 25 - See page 105 for material on the self-employment tax deduction.

EXAMPLE NO. 1 - MINISTER-EMPLOYEE FOR INCOME TAX PURPOSES (ACCOUNTABLE PLAN)

Form 1040 (1996) — Page 2

Tax Computation
- 32. Amount from line 31 (adjusted gross income) — **46,289**
- 33a. Check if: ☐ You were 65 or older, ☐ Blind; ☐ Spouse was 65 or older, ☐ Blind. Add the number of boxes checked above and enter the total here ▶ 33a
- b. If you are married filing separately and your spouse itemizes deductions or you are a dual-status alien, see instructions and check here ▶ 33b ☐
- 34. Enter the larger of your: Itemized deductions from Schedule A, line 28, OR Standard deduction shown below for your filing status. But see the instructions if you checked any box on line 33a or b or someone can claim you as a dependent.
  - Single—$4,000
  - Married filing jointly or Qualifying widow(er)—$6,700
  - Head of household—$5,900
  - Married filing separately—$3,350
  - 34 — **13,000**
- 35. Subtract line 34 from line 32 — **33,289**
- 36. If line 32 is $88,475 or less, multiply $2,550 by the total number of exemptions claimed on line 6d. If line 32 is over $88,475, see the worksheet in the inst. for the amount to enter — **5,100**
- 37. Taxable income. Subtract line 36 from line 35. If line 36 is more than line 35, enter -0- — **28,189**
- 38. Tax. See instructions. Check if total includes any tax from a ☐ Form(s) 8814 b ☐ Form 4970 c ☐ Form 4972 ▶ — **4,226**

Credits
- 39. Credit for child and dependent care expenses. Attach Form 2441
- 40. Credit for the elderly or the disabled. Attach Schedule R
- 41. Foreign tax credit. Attach Form 1116
- 42. Other. Check if from a ☐ Form 3800 b ☐ Form 8396 c ☐ Form 8801 d ☐ Form (specify)
- 43. Add lines 39 through 42
- 44. Subtract line 43 from line 38. If line 43 is more than line 38, enter -0- ▶ — **4,226**

Other Taxes
- 45. Self-employment tax. Attach Schedule SE — **9,279**
- 46. Alternative minimum tax. Attach Form 6251
- 47. Social security and Medicare tax on tip income not reported to employer. Attach Form 4137
- 48. Tax on qualified retirement plans, including IRAs. If required, attach Form 5329
- 49. Advance earned income credit payments from Form W-2
- 50. Household employment taxes. Attach Schedule H
- 51. Add lines 44 through 50. This is your total tax ▶ — **13,505**

Payments
- 52. Federal income tax withheld from Form(s) W-2 and 1099 — **14,000**
- 53. 1996 estimated tax payments and amount applied from 1995 return
- 54. Earned income credit. Attach Schedule EIC if you have a qualifying child. Nontaxable earned income: amount ▶ _____ and type ▶ _____
- 55. Amount paid with Form 4868 (extension request)
- 56. Excess social security and RRTA tax withheld (see inst.)
- 57. Other payments. Check if from a ☐ Form 2439 b ☐ Form 4136
- 58. Add lines 52 through 57. These are your total payments ▶ — **14,000**

Refund
- 59. If line 58 is more than line 51, subtract line 51 from line 58. This is the amount you OVERPAID — **495**
- 60a. Amount of line 59 you want REFUNDED TO YOU ▶ — **495**
- b. Routing number _____ c. Type: ☐ Checking ☐ Savings
- d. Account number _____
- 61. Amount of line 59 you want APPLIED TO YOUR 1997 ESTIMATED TAX ▶ 61

Amount You Owe
- 62a. If line 51 is more than line 58, subtract line 58 from line 51. This is the AMOUNT YOU OWE. For details on how to pay and use Form 1040-V, see instructions
- b. Are you paying the amount on line 62a in full with Form 1040-V? ▶ ☐ Yes ☐ No
- 63. Estimated tax penalty. Also include on line 62a

Sign Here
- Your signature: *Melvin L. Brown* — Date: 4/15/97 — Your occupation: Minister
- Spouse's signature: *Alessia S. Brown* — Date: 4/15/97 — Spouse's occupation: Housewife

Paid Preparer's Use Only
- Preparer's signature / Date / Check if self-employed ☐ / Preparer's social security no.
- Firm's name (or yours if self-employed) and address / EIN / ZIP code

Line 55 - The minister had income tax withheld under a voluntary withholding agreement with the church. Notice that income tax was withheld relating to both the income and social security tax liability.

EXAMPLE NO. 1 - MINISTER-EMPLOYEE FOR INCOME TAX PURPOSES (ACCOUNTABLE PLAN)

Schedule A—Itemized Deductions

SCHEDULES A&B (Form 1040)
Department of the Treasury
Internal Revenue Service (99)
(Schedule B is on back)
▶ Attach to Form 1040. ▶ See Instructions for Schedules A and B (Form 1040).

OMB No. 1545-0074
1996
Attachment Sequence No. 07

Name(s) shown on Form 1040: Melvin L. and Alessia S. Brown
Your social security number: 541 16 8194

(Proof as of July 1996 — Subject to change)

Medical and Dental Expenses	1	Medical and dental expenses (see page A-1)	1,500	
	2	Enter amount from Form 1040, line 32. 46,289		
	3	Multiply line 2 above by 7.5% (.075)	3,472	
	4	Subtract line 3 from line 1. If line 3 is more than line 1, enter -0-		0
Taxes You Paid (See page A-1.)	5	State and local income taxes	2,000	
	6	Real estate taxes (see page A-2)	1,000	
	7	Personal property taxes		
	8	Other taxes. List type and amount ▶		
	9	Add lines 5 through 8		3,000
Interest You Paid (See page A-2.) Note: Personal interest is not deductible.	10	Home mortgage interest and points reported to you on Form 1098	5,000	
	11	Home mortgage interest not reported to you on Form 1098. If paid to the person from whom you bought the home, see page A-3 and show that person's name, identifying no. and address ▶		
	12	Points not reported to you on Form 1098. See page A-3 for special rules		
	13	Investment interest. If required, attach Form 4952. (See page A-3.)		
	14	Add lines 10 through 13		5,000
Gifts to Charity If you made a gift and got a benefit for it, see page A-3.	15	Gifts by cash or check. If you made any gift of $250 or more, see page A-3	5,000	
	16	Other than by cash or check. If any gift of $250 or more, see page A-3. If over $500, you MUST attach Form 8283		
	17	Carryover from prior year		
	18	Add lines 15 through 17		5,000
Casualty and Theft Losses	19	Casualty or theft loss(es). Attach Form 4684. (See page A-4.)		
Job Expenses and Most Other Miscellaneous Deductions (See page A-5 for expenses to deduct here.)	20	Unreimbursed employee expenses—job travel, union dues, job education, etc. If required, you MUST attach Form 2106 or 2106-EZ. (See page A-5.) ▶		
	21	Tax preparation fees		
	22	Other expenses—investment, safe deposit box, etc. List type and amount ▶		
	23	Add lines 20 through 22		
	24	Enter amount from Form 1040, line 32.		
	25	Multiply line 24 above by 2% (.02)		
	26	Subtract line 25 from line 23. If line 25 is more than line 23, enter -0-		
Other Miscellaneous Deductions	27	Other—from list on page A-5. List type and amount ▶		
Total Itemized Deductions	28	Is Form 1040, line 32, over $117,950 (over $58,975 if married filing separately)? **NO.** Your deduction is not limited. Add the amounts in the far right column for lines 4 through 27. Also, enter on Form 1040, line 34, the **larger** of this amount or your standard deduction. **YES.** Your deduction may be limited. See page A-5 for the amount to enter. ▶		13,000

For Paperwork Reduction Act Notice, see Form 1040 instructions. Cat. No. 11330X Schedule A (Form 1040) 1996

Line 6 and 9a - The real estate taxes and home mortgage interest are deducted on this form plus excluded from income on line 7, Form 1040, page 1 as a housing allowance.

Line 20 - There are no unreimbursed employee expenses to deduct since the church reimbursed all the professional expenses under an accountable expense reimbursement plan.

EXAMPLE NO. 1 - MINISTER-EMPLOYEE FOR INCOME TAX PURPOSES (ACCOUNTABLE PLAN)

Schedules A&B (Form 1040) 1996 — OMB No. 1545-0074 — Page 2

Name(s) shown on Form 1040. Do not enter name and social security number if shown on other side.
Melvin L. and Alessia S. Brown

Your social security number: 541 16 8194

Schedule B—Interest and Dividend Income

Attachment Sequence No. 08

Part I — Interest Income (See page B-1.)

Note: If you had over $400 in taxable interest income, you must also complete Part III.

1. List name of payer. If any interest is from a seller-financed mortgage and the buyer used the property as a personal residence, see page B-1 and list this interest first. Also, show that buyer's social security number and address ▶

Payer	Amount
Franklin Corporation	675

Note: If you received a Form 1099-INT, Form 1099-OID, or substitute statement from a brokerage firm, list the firm's name as the payer and enter the total interest shown on that form.

2. Add the amounts on line 1 .... **2** 675
3. Excludable interest on series EE U.S. savings bonds issued after 1989 from Form 8815, line 14. You MUST attach Form 8815 to Form 1040 ..... **3**
4. Subtract line 3 from line 2. Enter the result here and on Form 1040, line 8a ▶ **4** 675

Proof as of July 1996 (subject to change)

Part II — Dividend Income (See page B-1.)

Note: If you had over $400 in gross dividends and/or other distributions on stock, you must also complete Part III.

5. List name of payer. Include gross dividends and/or other distributions on stock here. Any capital gain distributions and nontaxable distributions will be deducted on lines 7 and 8.

Payer	Amount
Vanguard	1,104

Note: If you received a Form 1099-DIV or substitute statement from a brokerage firm, list the firm's name as the payer and enter the total dividends shown on that form.

6. Add the amounts on line 5 .... **6** 1,104
7. Capital gain distributions. Enter here and on Schedule D* . **7** 150
8. Nontaxable distributions. (See the inst. for Form 1040, line 9.) **8**
9. Add lines 7 and 8 .... **9** 150
10. Subtract line 9 from line 6. Enter the result here and on Form 1040, line 9 ▶ **10** 954

*If you do not need Schedule D to report any other gains or losses, see the instructions for Form 1040, line 13.

Part III — Foreign Accounts and Trusts (See page B-2.)

If you had over $400 of interest or dividends **or** had a foreign account or were a grantor of, or a transferor to, a foreign trust, you must complete this part.

	Yes	No
11a At any time during 1996, did you have an interest in or a signature or other authority over a financial account in a foreign country, such as a bank account, securities account, or other financial account? See page B-2 for exceptions and filing requirements for Form TD F 90-22.1		X
b If "Yes," enter the name of the foreign country ▶		
12 Were you the grantor of, or transferor to, a foreign trust that existed during 1996, whether or not you have any beneficial interest in it? If "Yes," you may have to file Form 3520, 3520-A, or 926 .		X

For Paperwork Reduction Act Notice, see Form 1040 instructions. Schedule B (Form 1040) 1996

EXAMPLE NO. 1 - MINISTER-EMPLOYEE FOR INCOME TAX PURPOSES (ACCOUNTABLE PLAN)

SCHEDULE C-EZ (Form 1040)
Department of the Treasury
Internal Revenue Service

Net Profit From Business
(Sole Proprietorship)
▶ Partnerships, joint ventures, etc., must file Form 1065.
▶ Attach to Form 1040 or Form 1041. ▶ See instructions on back.

OMB No. 1545-0074
1996
Attachment Sequence No. **09A**

Name of proprietor: Melvin L. Brown
Social security number (SSN): 541 16 8194

Part I General Information

You May Use This Schedule Only If You:
- Had business expenses of $2,500 or less.
- Use the cash method of accounting.
- Did not have an inventory at any time during the year.
- Did not have a net loss from your business.
- Had only one business as a sole proprietor.

And You:
- Had no employees during the year.
- Are not required to file Form 4562, Depreciation and Amortization, for this business. See the instructions for Schedule C, line 13, on page C-3 to find out if you must file.
- Do not deduct expenses for business use of your home.
- Do not have prior year unallowed passive activity losses from this business.

Proof as of July 1996 (subject to change)

A Principal business or profession, including product or service: Minister
B Enter principal business code (see page C-6) ▶ 8771
C Business name. If no separate business name, leave blank.
D Employer ID number (EIN), if any
E Business address (including suite or room no.). Address not required if same as on Form 1040, page 1.
City, town or post office, state, and ZIP code

Part II Figure Your Net Profit

1. **Gross receipts.**
   Caution: If this income was reported to you on Form W-2 and the "Statutory employee" box on that form was checked, see **Statutory Employees** in the instructions for Schedule C, line 1, on page C-2 and check here ▶ ☐ **1** 1,650

2. **Total expenses.** If more than $2,500, you **must** use Schedule C. See instructions **2**

3. **Net profit.** Subtract line 2 from line 1. If less than zero, you **must** use Schedule C. Enter on **Form 1040, line 12,** and ALSO on **Schedule SE, line 2.** (Statutory employees **do not** report this amount on Schedule SE, line 2. Estates and trusts, enter on Form 1041, line 3.) **3** 1,650

Part III Information on Your Vehicle. Complete this part **ONLY** if you are claiming car or truck expenses on line 2.

4. When did you place your vehicle in service for business purposes? (month, day, year) ▶ ..... / ..... / .....

5. Of the total number of miles you drove your vehicle during 1996, enter the number of miles you used your vehicle for:
   a Business .... **b** Commuting .... **c** Other ....

6. Do you (or your spouse) have another vehicle available for personal use? .... ☐ Yes ☐ No

7. Was your vehicle available for use during off-duty hours? .... ☐ Yes ☐ No

8a. Do you have evidence to support your deduction? .... ☐ Yes ☐ No
  b. If "Yes," is the evidence written? .... ☐ Yes ☐ No

For Paperwork Reduction Act Notice, see Form 1040 instructions.   Cat. No. 14374D   Schedule C-EZ (Form 1040) 1996

Gross receipts:

Honoraria (weddings, etc.)	$650
Speaking honorarium	1,000
	$1,650

Note: Most ministers considered to be employees for income tax purposes (with that income reported on line 7, Form 1040, page 1) also have honoraria and fee income and related expenses that are reportable on Schedule C (C-EZ).

EXAMPLE NO. 1 - MINISTER-EMPLOYEE FOR INCOME TAX PURPOSES (ACCOUNTABLE PLAN)

Schedule SE (Form 1040) 1996 — Attachment Sequence No. 17 — Page 2

Name of person with **self-employment** income (as shown on Form 1040): Melvin L. Brown
Social security number of person with **self-employment** income ▶ 541 16 8194

Section B—Long Schedule SE

Part I Self-Employment Tax

Note: *If your only income subject to self-employment tax is* **church employee income,** *skip lines 1 through 4b. Enter -0- on line 4c and go to line 5a. Income from services you performed as a minister or a member of a religious order* **is not** *church employee income. See page SE-1.*

A   If you are a minister, member of a religious order, or Christian Science practitioner **and** you filed Form 4361, but you had $400 or more of **other** net earnings from self-employment, check here and continue with Part I . . . . . ▶ ☐

1	Net farm profit or (loss) from Schedule F, line 36, and farm partnerships, Schedule K-1 (Form 1065), line 15a. **Note:** *Skip this line if you use the farm optional method. See page SE-3*	1
2	Net profit or (loss) from Schedule C, line 31; Schedule C-EZ, line 3; and Schedule K-1 (Form 1065), line 15a (other than farming). Ministers and members of religious orders see page SE-1 for amounts to report on this line. See page SE-2 for other income to report. **Note:** *Skip this line if you use the nonfarm optional method. See page SE-3*	2	65,900
3	Combine lines 1 and 2	3	65,900
4a	If line 3 is more than zero, multiply line 3 by 92.35% (.9235). Otherwise, enter amount from line 3	4a	60,859
b	If you elected one or both of the optional methods, enter the total of lines 15 and 17 here	4b	
c	Combine lines 4a and 4b. If less than $400, **do not** file this schedule; you do not owe self-employment tax. **Exception.** If less than $400 and you had **church employee income,** enter -0- and continue ▶	4c	60,859
5a	Enter your **church employee income** from Form W-2. **Caution:** *See page SE-1 for definition of church employee income* . 5a		
b	Multiply line 5a by 92.35% (.9235). If less than $100, enter -0-	5b	
6	**Net earnings from self-employment.** Add lines 4c and 5b	6	60,859
7	Maximum amount of combined wages and self-employment earnings subject to social security tax or the 6.2% portion of the 7.65% railroad retirement (tier 1) tax for 1996	7	62,700 00
8a	Total social security wages and tips (total of boxes 3 and 7 on Form(s) W-2) and railroad retirement (tier 1) compensation . . . 8a		
b	Unreported tips subject to social security tax (from Form 4137, line 9) 8b		
c	Add lines 8a and 8b	8c	
9	Subtract line 8c from line 7. If zero or less, enter -0- here and on line 10 and go to line 11 ▶	9	62,700
10	Multiply the **smaller** of line 6 or line 9 by 12.4% (.124)	10	7,514
11	Multiply line 6 by 2.9% (.029)	11	1,765
12	**Self-employment tax.** Add lines 10 and 11. Enter here and on **Form 1040, line 45**	12	9,279
13	**Deduction for one-half of self-employment tax.** Multiply line 12 by 50% (.5). Enter the result here and on **Form 1040, line 25** 13 4,640		

Part II Optional Methods To Figure Net Earnings (See page SE-3.)

Farm Optional Method. You may use this method **only** if:
- Your gross farm income[1] was not more than $2,400, **or**
- Your gross farm income[1] was more than $2,400 and your net farm profits[2] were less than $1,733.

14	Maximum income for optional methods	14	1,600 00
15	Enter the **smaller** of: two-thirds (⅔) of gross farm income[1] (not less than zero) **or** $1,600. Also, include this amount on line 4b above	15	

Nonfarm Optional Method. You may use this method **only** if:
- Your net nonfarm profits[3] were less than $1,733 and also less than 72.189% of your gross nonfarm income,[4] **and**
- You had net earnings from self-employment of at least $400 in 2 of the prior 3 years.

Caution: *You may use this method no more than five times.*

16	Subtract line 15 from line 14	16	
17	Enter the **smaller** of: two-thirds (⅔) of gross nonfarm income[4] (not less than zero) **or** the amount on line 16. Also, include this amount on line 4b above	17	

[1] From Schedule F, line 11, and Schedule K-1 (Form 1065), line 15b.
[2] From Schedule F, line 36, and Schedule K-1 (Form 1065), line 15a.
[3] From Schedule C, line 31; Schedule C-EZ, line 3; and Schedule K-1 (Form 1065), line 15a.
[4] From Schedule C, line 7; Schedule C-EZ, line 1; and Schedule K-1 (Form 1065), line 15c.

Line 2 - See the worksheet on page 133 for the calculation of this amount.
Line 4 - This line results in the deduction of about one-half of the self-employment tax liability.
Note: A minister may use Section A-Short Schedule unless he or she received nonministerial wages (subject to FICA) and the total of these wages and net ministerial self-employment earnings (W-2 and Schedule C [C-EZ] -related) is more than $62,700.

EXAMPLE NO. 1 - MINISTER-EMPLOYEE FOR INCOME TAX PURPOSES (ACCOUNTABLE PLAN)

Housing Allowance Worksheet
Minister Living in Home
Minister Owns or Is Buying

Minister's Name: __Melvin L. Brown__

For the period __January 1__, 199_6_ to __December 31__, 199_6_

Date designation approved __December 20__, 199_5_

Allowable Housing Expenses *(expenses paid by minister from current income)*

	Estimated Expenses	Actual
Down payment on purchase of housing	$	$
Housing loan principal and interest payments	9,500	9,500
Real estate commission, escrow fees		
Real property taxes	900	1,000
Personal property taxes on contents		
Homeowner's insurance	500	550
Personal property insurance on contents	150	200
Umbrella liability insurance	100	
Structural maintenance and repair		550
Landscaping, gardening, and pest control		200
Furnishings *(purchase, repair, replacement)*		400
Decoration and redecoration		
Utilities *(gas, electricity, water)* and trash collection	3,500	3,500
Local telephone expense *(base charge)*	150	150
Homeowner's association dues/condominium fees	200	200
Subtotal	15,000	
10% allowance for unexpected expenses	1,500	
TOTAL	$ 16,500	$ 16,250 (A)

Fair rental value of home furnished
plus utilities $ 14,500 (B)

Properly designated housing allowance $ 16,500 (C)

Note: The amount excludable from income for federal income tax purposes is the *lowest* of A, B, or C.

Note: The fair rental value is less than the designated allowance or the actual housing expenses. The $2,000 difference between the designation and the fair rental value is reported as additional income on Form 1040, line 21.

EXAMPLE NO. 1 - MINISTER-EMPLOYEE FOR INCOME TAX PURPOSES (ACCOUNTABLE PLAN)

Self-Employment Social Security Tax Worksheet

Inclusions:

Salary paid by church as reflected on Form W-2	$ 47,750
Net profit or loss as reflected on Schedule C or C-EZ (includes speaking honoraria, offerings you receive for marriages, baptisms, funerals, and other fees)	1,650
Housing allowance excluded from salary on Form W-2 or from income on Schedule C (C-EZ)	16,500
Fair rental value of parsonage provided (including paid utilities)	_____
Nonaccountable business expense reimbursements (if not included on Form W-2, Schedule C, or C-EZ)	_____
Reimbursement of self-employment taxes (if not included on Form W-2, Schedule C, or C-EZ)	_____
Value of meals provided to you, your spouse, and your dependents whether or not provided for your employer's convenience (these amounts may have been excluded from gross income)	_____
Total inclusions	65,900

Deductions:

Unreimbursed ministerial business and professional expenses (included on Form W-2) or reimbursed expenses paid under a nonaccountable plan (included on Form W-2)
  A. Deductible on Schedule A before the 2% of AGI limitation whether or not you itemized[1] or _____
  B. Not deductible on Form 2106/2106 EZ or Schedule C/C-EZ because expenses were allocated to taxable/nontaxable income. _____

Total deductions _____

Net earnings from self-employment (to Schedule SE) $ 65,900

[1] The 50% unreimbursed meal and entertainment expense limitation applies to amounts subject to social security tax. In other words, if some of your meal and entertainment expenses were subjected to the 50% limit, the remainder cannot be deducted here.

Note 1: Your net earnings from self-employment are not affected by the foreign earned income exclusion or the foreign housing exclusion or deduction if you are a U.S. citizen or resident alien who is serving abroad and living in a foreign country.

Note 2: Amounts received as pension payments or annuity payments related to a church-sponsored tax-sheltered annuity by a retired minister are generally considered to be excluded from the social security calculation.

Note: Net earnings from self-employment are entered on Schedule SE, line 2 (see page 131). While the W-2 portion of the self-employment income could be shown on Schedule SE, line 5a, the example shows the simpler approach of transferring the total self-employment income to line 2.

EXAMPLE NO. 1 - MINISTER-EMPLOYEE FOR INCOME TAX PURPOSES (ACCOUNTABLE PLAN)

a Control number		OMB No. 1545-0008		
b Employer's identification number 38-9418217			1 Wages, tips, other compensation 47750.00	2 Federal income tax withheld 14000.00
c Employer's name, address, and ZIP code Magnolia Springs Church 4865 Douglas Road Springfield, OH 45504			3 Social security wages	4 Social security tax withheld
			5 Medicare wages and tips	6 Medicare tax withheld
			7 Social security tips	8 Allocated tips
d Employee's social security number 541-16-8194			9 Advance EIC payment	10 Dependent care benefits
e Employee's name, address, and ZIP code Melvin L. Brown 418 Trenton Street Springfield, OH 45504			11 Nonqualified plans	12 Benefits included in box 1
			13 See Instrs. for box 13	14 Other
			15 Statutory employee ☐ Deceased ☐ Pension plan ☐ Legal rep. ☐ Hshld. emp. ☐ Subtotal ☐ Deferred compensation ☐	
16 State OH	17 Employer's state I.D. No. 627893	17 State wages, tips, etc. 47750.00	18 State income tax 1200.00	19 Locality name	20 Local wages, tips, etc.	21 Local income tax

Department of the Treasury—Internal Revenue Service

Form **W-2** Wage and Tax Statement **1996**
Copy B To Be Filed With Employee's FEDERAL Tax Return

This information is being furnished to the Internal Revenue Service.

5 WA

Explanation of compensation reported on Form W-2, box 1:
    Salary $38,000
    Special occasion gifts   750
    Reimbursement of self-employment tax   9,000
                                                                        $47,750

Note: Pastor Brown was reimbursed $4,100 for moving expenses that he could have deducted on Form 1040, page 1, line 24 if the expenses had not been reimbursed.
    Pastor Brown received reimbursements of $7,593 under an accountable expense reimbursement plan. The reimbursements are not included on Form W-2 or deductible on Form 1040. There is no requirement to add either of the reimbursements to income taxable for social security purposes on Schedule SE.

EXAMPLE NO. 2 - MINISTER-EMPLOYEE FOR INCOME TAX PURPOSES (NONACCOUNTABLE PLAN)

Example No. 2

Minister considered to be an employee for income tax purposes with a nonaccountable business expense plan.

The Halls live in an apartment they rent personally. Pastor Hall files Form 1040-ES to pay income and social security (SECA) taxes and paid $575 each quarter.

Income, Benefits, and Reimbursements:

Church salary	$8,500
Cash housing allowance/properly designated (see page 145)	7,040
Christmas and other special occasion gifts paid by the church based on designated member-gifts to the church	600
Honoraria for performing weddings, funerals, and baptisms	700
Reimbursement of self-employment tax	2,500
Business expense allowance (no accounting provided to church)	3,700

Business Expenses, Itemized Deductions, and IRA Contributions:

Business use of personally owned auto: 12,988 miles

Church-related expenses paid personally:
Seminar expenses:
Airfare	$533	(1)
Meals	233	(1)
Lodging	167	(1)
Subscriptions	200	(1)
Supplies	850	(1)
Entertainment expenses	1,207	(1)

Travel expense related to honoraria:
Lodging	$100	(1)
Supplies	50	(1)

Potential itemized deductions:
Doctors, dentists, and drugs	$1,200
State and local income taxes	750
Personal property taxes	300
Cash contributions	2,000

IRA contributions:
Donald R. Hall	$2,000
Jackie B. Hall	250

Housing data:
Designation	$7,040
Actual expenses	6,485

(1) 40% of these expenses are unallowable (see page 142).

EXAMPLE NO. 2 - MINISTER-EMPLOYEE FOR INCOME TAX PURPOSES (NONACCOUNTABLE PLAN)

Form 1040 Department of the Treasury—Internal Revenue Service
U.S. Individual Income Tax Return **1996** (99) IRS Use Only—Do not write or staple in this space.
For the year Jan. 1–Dec. 31, 1996, or other tax year beginning , 1996, ending , 19 OMB No. 1545-0074

Label (See instructions.)
Use the IRS label. Otherwise, please print or type.

Your first name and initial: Donald L. Last name: Hall
Your social security number: 482 11 6043

If a joint return, spouse's first name and initial: Jackie B. Last name: Hall
Spouse's social security number: 720 94 1327

Home address (number and street). If you have a P.O. box, see page 11.: 604 Linden Avenue Apt. no.
City, town or post office, state, and ZIP code. If you have a foreign address, see page 11.: Wabash, IN 46992

For help finding line instructions, see pages 2 and 3 in the booklet.

Presidential Election Campaign (See page 11.)
Do you want $3 to go to this fund? . . . . Yes: X No:
If a joint return, does your spouse want $3 to go to this fund? . . . . . . Yes: X No:
Note: Checking "Yes" will not change your tax or reduce your refund.

Filing Status
Check only one box.
1. ☐ Single
2. ☒ Married filing joint return (even if only one had income)
3. ☐ Married filing separate return. Enter spouse's social security no. above and full name here. ▶
4. ☐ Head of household (with qualifying person). (See instructions.) If the qualifying person is a child but not your dependent, enter this child's name here. ▶
5. ☐ Qualifying widow(er) with dependent child (year spouse died ▶ 19). (See instructions.)

Exemptions
6a ☒ Yourself. If your parent (or someone else) can claim you as a dependent on his or her tax return, **do not** check box 6a . . . .
b ☒ Spouse . . . .
No. of boxes checked on lines 6a and 6b: **2**

c Dependents:
(1) First name / Last name: David K. Hall
(2) Dependent's social security number. If born in Dec. 1996, see inst.: 942 12 4916
(3) Dependent's relationship to you: son
(4) No. of months lived in your home in 1996: 12

No. of your children on line 6c who:
• lived with you: **1**
• didn't live with you due to divorce or separation (see instructions)
Dependents on 6c not entered above

If more than six dependents, see the line 6c instructions.

d Total number of exemptions claimed . . . . Add numbers entered on lines above ▶ **3**

Income

Attach Copy B of your Forms W-2, W-2G, and 1099-R here.

If you did not get a W-2, see the line 7 instructions.

Please send any payment separately with Form 1040-V. See the line 62a instructions.

7	Wages, salaries, tips, etc. Attach Form(s) W-2	15,300
8a	Taxable interest. Attach Schedule B if over $400	
8b	Tax-exempt interest. DON'T include on line 8a	
9	Dividend income. Attach Schedule B if over $400	
10	Taxable refunds, credits, or offsets of state and local income taxes (see instructions)	
11	Alimony received	
12	Business income or (loss). Attach Schedule C or C-EZ	610
13	Capital gain or (loss). If required, attach Schedule D	
14	Other gains or (losses). Attach Form 4797	
15a	Total IRA distributions 15a / b Taxable amount (see inst.) 15b	
16a	Total pensions and annuities 16a / b Taxable amount (see inst.) 16b	
17	Rental real estate, royalties, partnerships, S corporations, trusts, etc. Attach Schedule E	
18	Farm income or (loss). Attach Schedule F	
19	Unemployment compensation	
20a	Social security benefits 20a / b Taxable amount (see inst.) 20b	
21	Other income. List type and amount—see instructions Excess housing allowance	555
22	Add the amounts in the far right column for lines 7 through 21. This is your **total income** ▶	16,465

Adjusted Gross Income

If line 31 is under $28,495 (under $9,500 if a child didn't live with you), see the line 54 instructions.

23a	Your IRA deduction (see instructions)	2,000	
23b	Spouse's IRA deduction (see instructions)	250	
24	Moving expenses. Attach Form 3903 or 3903-F		
25	One-half of self-employment tax. Attach Schedule SE	1,162	
26	Self-employed health insurance deduction (see inst.)		
27	Keogh & self-employed SEP plans. If SEP, check ▶ ☐		
28	Penalty on early withdrawal of savings		
29	Alimony paid. Recipient's SSN ▶		
30	Add lines 23a through 29		3,412
31	Subtract line 30 from line 22. This is your **adjusted gross income** ▶		13,053

For Privacy Act and Paperwork Reduction Act Notice, see page 7.   Cat. No. 11320B   Form **1040** (1996)

Line 21 - See page 144 for the calculation of the excess housing allowance.
Line 23 - See page 54 for IRA information.
Line 25 - See page 105 for material on the self-employment tax deduction.

EXAMPLE NO. 2 - MINISTER-EMPLOYEE FOR INCOME TAX PURPOSES (NONACCOUNTABLE PLAN)

Form 1040 (1996) Page 2

Tax Computation

32 Amount from line 31 (adjusted gross income) ... **32** 13,053
33a Check if: ☐ You were 65 or older, ☐ Blind; ☐ Spouse was 65 or older, ☐ Blind.
   Add the number of boxes checked above and enter the total here ... ▶ 33a
 b If you are married filing separately and your spouse itemizes deductions or you are a dual-status alien, see instructions and check here ... ▶ 33b ☐
34 Enter the larger of your:
   • Itemized deductions from Schedule A, line 28, OR
   • Standard deduction shown below for your filing status. But see the instructions if you checked any box on line 33a or b or someone can claim you as a dependent.
     • Single—$4,000   • Married filing jointly or Qualifying widow(er)—$6,700
     • Head of household—$5,900   • Married filing separately—$3,350
   34 6,909
35 Subtract line 34 from line 32 ... **35** 6,144
36 If line 32 is $88,475 or less, multiply $2,550 by the total number of exemptions claimed on line 6d. If line 32 is over $88,475, see the worksheet in the inst. for the amount to enter . **36** 7,650
37 **Taxable income.** Subtract line 36 from line 35. If line 36 is more than line 35, enter -0- ... **37** -0-

If you want the IRS to figure your tax, see the line 37 instructions.

38 Tax. See instructions. Check if total includes any tax from a ☐ Form(s) 8814
   b ☐ Form 4970   c ☐ Form 4972 ... ▶ **38** -0-

Credits

39 Credit for child and dependent care expenses. Attach Form 2441   **39**
40 Credit for the elderly or the disabled. Attach Schedule R .   **40**
41 Foreign tax credit. Attach Form 1116 ...   **41**
42 Other. Check if from a ☐ Form 3800   b ☐ Form 8396
   c ☐ Form 8801   d ☐ Form (specify)   **42**
43 Add lines 39 through 42 ... **43**
44 Subtract line 43 from line 38. If line 43 is more than line 38, enter -0- ... **44**

Other Taxes

45 Self-employment tax. Attach Schedule SE ... **45** 2,325
46 Alternative minimum tax. Attach Form 6251 ... **46**
47 Social security and Medicare tax on tip income not reported to employer. Attach Form 4137 **47**
48 Tax on qualified retirement plans, including IRAs. If required, attach Form 5329 **48**
49 Advance earned income credit payments from Form W-2 ... **49**
50 Household employment taxes. Attach Schedule H ... **50**
51 Add lines 44 through 50. This is your **total tax** ... ▶ **51** 2,325

Payments

52 Federal income tax withheld from Forms W-2 and 1099 ... **52**
53 1996 estimated tax payments and amount applied from 1995 return . **53** 2,300
54 Earned income credit. Attach Schedule EIC if you have a qualifying child. Nontaxable earned income: amount ▶ 7,040
   and type ▶ Housing allowance   **54** 323

Attach Forms W-2, W-2G, and 1099-R on the front.

55 Amount paid with Form 4868 (extension request) ... **55**
56 Excess social security and RRTA tax withheld (see inst.) ... **56**
57 Other payments. Check if from a ☐ Form 2439   b ☐ Form 4136 **57**
58 Add lines 52 through 57. These are your **total payments** ... ▶ **58** 2,623

Refund

59 If line 58 is more than line 51, subtract line 51 from line 58. This is the amount you **OVERPAID** **59** 298
60a Amount of line 59 you want **REFUNDED TO YOU** ... ▶ **60a** 298

Send it right to your bank! See inst. and fill in 60b, c, and d.

 b Routing number ☐☐☐☐☐☐☐☐☐   c Type: ☐ Checking   ☐ Savings
 d Account number ☐☐☐☐☐☐☐☐☐☐☐☐☐☐☐☐☐
61 Amount of line 59 you want **APPLIED TO YOUR 1997 ESTIMATED TAX** ▶ **61**

Amount You Owe

62a If line 51 is more than line 58, subtract line 58 from line 51. This is the **AMOUNT YOU OWE**.
   For details on how to pay and use Form 1040-V, see instructions ... ▶ **62a**
 b Are you paying the amount on line 62a **in full** with Form 1040-V? ▶ ☐ Yes   ☐ No
63 Estimated tax penalty. Also include on line 62a ... **63**

Sign Here

Under penalties of perjury, I declare that I have examined this return and accompanying schedules and statements, and to the best of my knowledge and belief, they are true, correct, and complete. Declaration of preparer (other than taxpayer) is based on all information of which preparer has any knowledge.

Keep a copy of this return for your records.

Your signature ▶ Donald L. Hall   Date 4/15/97   Your occupation Minister
Spouse's signature. If a joint return, BOTH must sign. Jackie B. Hall   Date 4/15/97   Spouse's occupation Housewife

Paid Preparer's Use Only

Preparer's signature ▶   Date   Check if self-employed ☐   Preparer's social security no.
Firm's name (or yours if self-employed) and address ▶   EIN
   ZIP code

(Draft as of 1996 — subject to change)

Line 56 - The minister pays federal taxes (income and social security) by quarterly filing Form 1040-ES.

137

EXAMPLE NO. 2 - MINISTER-EMPLOYEE FOR INCOME TAX PURPOSES (NONACCOUNTABLE PLAN)

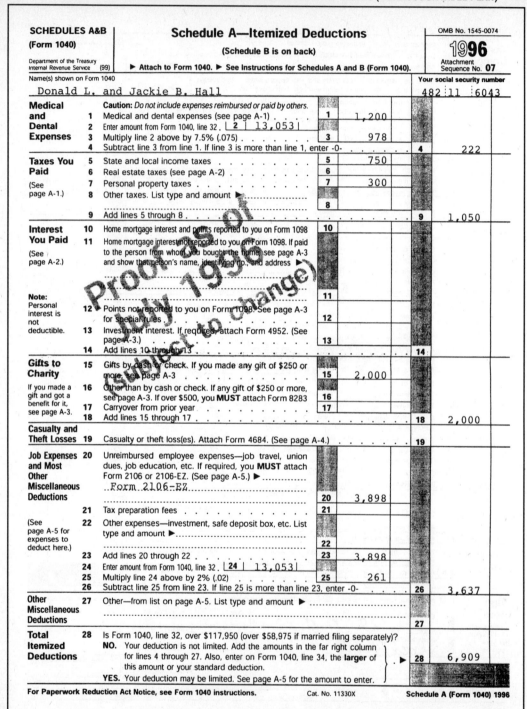

Line 20 - Because the minister did not have an accountable expense reimbursement plan, the unreimbursed expenses appear on this line. One of the disadvantages of this approach is the 2% deduction (line 25), which costs the minister $261 of deductions.

EXAMPLE NO. 2 - MINISTER-EMPLOYEE FOR INCOME TAX PURPOSES (NONACCOUNTABLE PLAN)

SCHEDULE C-EZ (Form 1040)
Department of the Treasury
Internal Revenue Service

Net Profit From Business
(Sole Proprietorship)
▶ Partnerships, joint ventures, etc., must file Form 1065.
▶ Attach to Form 1040 or Form 1041. ▶ See instructions on back.

OMB No. 1545-0074
1996
Attachment Sequence No. **09A**

Name of proprietor: Donald L. Hall
Social security number (SSN): 482 : 11 : 6043

Part I — General Information

You May Use This Schedule Only If You:
- Had business expenses of $2,500 or less.
- Use the cash method of accounting.
- Did not have an inventory at any time during the year.
- Did not have a net loss from your business.
- Had only one business as a sole proprietor.

And You:
- Had no employees during the year.
- Are not required to file Form 4562, Depreciation and Amortization, for this business. See the instructions for Schedule C, line 13, on page C-3 to find out if you must file.
- Do not deduct expenses for business use of your home.
- Do not have prior year unallowed passive activity losses from this business.

A Principal business or profession, including product or service: Minister
B Enter principal business code (see page C-6) ▶ 8771
C Business name. If no separate business name, leave blank.
D Employer ID number (EIN), if any
E Business address (including suite or room no.). Address not required if same as on Form 1040, page 1.
   City, town or post office, state, and ZIP code

(Proof as of July 1996 (Subject to change))

Part II — Figure Your Net Profit

1 **Gross receipts.** **Caution:** If this income was reported to you on Form W-2 and the "Statutory employee" box on that form was checked, see **Statutory Employees** in the instructions for Schedule C, line 1, on page C-2 and check here . . . . ▶ ☐ **1** | 700

2 **Total expenses.** If more than $2,500, you **must** use Schedule C. See instructions . . . . . **2** | 90

3 **Net profit.** Subtract line 2 from line 1. If less than zero, you **must** use Schedule C. Enter on **Form 1040, line 12**, and ALSO on **Schedule SE, line 2.** (Statutory employees **do not** report this amount on Schedule SE, line 2. Estates and trusts, enter on Form 1041, line 3.) . . . . . **3** | 610

Part III — Information on Your Vehicle. Complete this part ONLY if you are claiming car or truck expenses on line 2.

4 When did you place your vehicle in service for business purposes? (month, day, year) ▶ ...../...../.....

5 Of the total number of miles you drove your vehicle during 1996, enter the number of miles you used your vehicle for:

   a Business ....   b Commuting ....   c Other ....

6 Do you (or your spouse) have another vehicle available for personal use? . . . . ☐ Yes ☐ No

7 Was your vehicle available for use during off-duty hours? . . . . ☐ Yes ☐ No

8a Do you have evidence to support your deduction? . . . . ☐ Yes ☐ No

 b If "Yes," is the evidence written? . . . . ☐ Yes ☐ No

For Paperwork Reduction Act Notice, see Form 1040 instructions.   Cat. No. 14374D   Schedule C-EZ (Form 1040) 1996

Line 2 - Expenses of $150 have been reduced by 40% as allocable to tax-free income (see calculation on page 142).

Note: Most ministers who consider themselves employees for income tax purposes (with that income reported on line 7, Form 1040, page 1) also have honoraria and fee income and related expenses that are reportable on Schedule C (C-EZ).

EXAMPLE NO. 2 - MINISTER-EMPLOYEE FOR INCOME TAX PURPOSES (NONACCOUNTABLE PLAN)

SCHEDULE SE (Form 1040) Department of the Treasury Internal Revenue Service (99)	Self-Employment Tax ▶ See Instructions for Schedule SE (Form 1040). ▶ Attach to Form 1040.	OMB No. 1545-0074 **1996** Attachment Sequence No. **17**
Name of person with **self-employment** income (as shown on Form 1040) Donald L. Hall		Social security number of person with **self-employment** income ▶ 482 : 11 : 6043

Who Must File Schedule SE

You must file Schedule SE if:
- You had net earnings from self-employment from **other than** church employee income (line 4 of Short Schedule SE or line 4c of Long Schedule SE) of $400 or more, **OR**
- You had church employee income of $108.28 or more. Income from services you performed as a minister or a member of a religious order **is not** church employee income. See page SE-1.

Note: *Even if you had a loss or a small amount of income from self-employment, it may be to your benefit to file Schedule SE and use either "optional method" in Part II of Long Schedule SE. See page SE-3.*

Exception. If your only self-employment income was from earnings as a minister, member of a religious order, or Christian Science practitioner **and** you filed Form 4361 and received IRS approval not to be taxed on those earnings, **do not** file Schedule SE. Instead, write "Exempt–Form 4361" on Form 1040, line 45.

May I Use Short Schedule SE or MUST I Use Long Schedule SE?

[Flowchart]

YOU MAY USE SHORT SCHEDULE SE BELOW | YOU MUST USE LONG SCHEDULE SE ON THE BACK

Section A—Short Schedule SE. Caution: *Read above to see if you can use Short Schedule SE.*

1	Net farm profit or (loss) from Schedule F, line 36, and farm partnerships, Schedule K-1 (Form 1065), line 15a	1	
2	Net profit or (loss) from Schedule C, line 31; Schedule C-EZ, line 3; and Schedule K-1 (Form 1065), line 15a (other than farming). Ministers and members of religious orders see page SE-1 for amounts to report on this line. See page SE-2 for other income to report	2	16,454
3	Combine lines 1 and 2	3	16,454
4	**Net earnings from self-employment.** Multiply line 3 by 92.35% (.9235). If less than $400, **do not** file this schedule; you do not owe self-employment tax . . . . ▶	4	15,195
5	**Self-employment tax.** If the amount on line 4 is: • $62,700 or less, multiply line 4 by 15.3% (.153). Enter the result here and on **Form 1040, line 45.** • More than $62,700, multiply line 4 by 2.9% (.029). Then, add $7,774.80 to the result. Enter the total here and on **Form 1040, line 45.**	5	2,325
6	**Deduction for one-half of self-employment tax.** Multiply line 5 by 50% (.5). Enter the result here and on **Form 1040, line 25**	6	1,162

For Paperwork Reduction Act Notice, see Form 1040 instructions.   Cat. No. 11358Z   Schedule SE (Form 1040) 1996

Line 2 - See the schedule on page 146 for the calculation of this amount.
Line 4 - This line results in the deduction of about one-half of the self-employment tax liability.
Note: A minister may use Section A-Short Schedule unless he received nonministerial wages (subject to FICA) and the total of these wages and net ministerial self-employment earnings (W-2 and Schedule C-related) is more than $62,700.

EXAMPLE NO. 2 - MINISTER-EMPLOYEE FOR INCOME TAX PURPOSES (NONACCOUNTABLE PLAN)

Form **2106-EZ**	**Unreimbursed Employee Business Expenses**	OMB No. 1545-1441
Department of the Treasury Internal Revenue Service (99)	▶ See instructions on back. ▶ Attach to Form 1040 or Form 1040-T.	**1996** Attachment Sequence No. **54A**
Your name Donald L. Hall	Social security number 482 11 6043	Occupation in which expenses were incurred Minister

Part I **General Information**

You May Use This Form ONLY if All of the Following Apply:
- You are an employee deducting expenses attributable to your job.
- You **do not** get reimbursed by your employer for any expenses (amounts your employer included in box 1 of your Form W-2 are not considered reimbursements).
- If you are claiming vehicle expense,
  a You own your vehicle, and
  b You are using the standard mileage rate for 1995 **and** also used it for the year you first placed the vehicle in service.

Part II **Figure Your Expenses**

1	Vehicle expense using the standard mileage rate. Complete Part III and multiply line 8a by 30¢ (.30)	1	2,416
2	Parking fees, tolls, and transportation, including train, bus, etc., that **did not** involve overnight travel	2	
3	Travel expense while away from home overnight, including lodging, airplane, car rental, etc. **Do not** include meals and entertainment	3	420
4	Business expenses not included on lines 1 through 3. **Do not** include meals and entertainment .	4	630
5	Meals and entertainment expenses: $ _____864_____ x 50% (.50)	5	432
6	**Total expenses.** Add lines 1 through 5. Enter here and **on line 20 of Schedule A (Form 1040), or Form 1040-T, Section B, line n.** (Qualified performing artists and individuals with disabilities, see the instructions for special rules on where to enter this amount.)	6	3,898

Part III **Information on Your Vehicle.** Complete this part **ONLY** if you are claiming vehicle expense on line 1.

7 When did you place your vehicle in service for business purposes? (month, day, year) ▶ 6 / 1 / 95.

8 Of the total number of miles you drove your vehicle during 1995, enter the number of miles you used your vehicle for:

  a Business 12,988   b Commuting 562   c Other 2,487

(12,988 x 60% allowable = 7,793 x 31 cents per mile 2,416 (line 1)

9 Do you (or your spouse) have another vehicle available for personal use? . . . . ☒ Yes ☐ No

10 Was your vehicle available for use during off-duty hours? . . . . ☒ Yes ☐ No

11a Do you have evidence to support your deduction? . . . . ☒ Yes ☐ No

  b If "Yes," is the evidence written? . . . . ☒ Yes ☐ No

For Paperwork Reduction Act Notice, see back of form.   Cat. No. 20604Q   Form **2106-EZ** (1996)

Lines 1, 3, 4, 5 - See allocations on page 142.
Line 6 - The total expenses on this line are carried forward to Form 1040, Schedule A, line 20.

Computation of Unallowed Part of Business Expenses

		Taxable	Tax-Free	Total
Salary as a minister		$8,500		$8,500
Housing allowance:				
Designated	$7,040			
Less expenses	6,485			
Excess	$555	555	$6,485	7,040
Schedule C gross income from ministry		700		700
Ministerial income		$9,755	$6,485	$16,240
		60%	40%	100%

Note: Each expense line on Schedule C-EZ (page 139) and Form 2106-EZ (page 141) has been reduced by 40% because the expenses are allocable to tax-free income. Expenses reflected on Form 2106-EZ were allocated as follows:

		60% Deductible	40% Not Deductible
Vehicle expense (31 cents per mile)		$2,416	$1,610
Travel expense:			
Airfare		320	213
Lodging		100	67
Business expenses:			
Subscriptions		120	80
Supplies		510	340
Meals and entertainment expense:			
Meals	$233		
Entertainment	1,207		
	$1,440 (1)	432	288
		$3,898	$2,598

(1) 50% disallowed by meals and entertainment rules before allocating for taxable and tax-free income.

EXAMPLE NO. 2 - MINISTER-EMPLOYEE FOR INCOME TAX PURPOSES (NONACCOUNTABLE PLAN)

SCHEDULE EIC (Form 1040A or 1040) Department of the Treasury Internal Revenue Service (99)	Earned Income Credit (Qualifying Child Information) ▶ Attach to Form 1040A or 1040. ▶ See instructions on back.	OMB No. 1545-0074 **1996** Attachment Sequence No. **43**
Name(s) shown on return: First Donald L. and Jackie B.	Last Hall	Your social security number 482-11-6043

Before You Begin . . .

- See the instructions for Form 1040A, line 29c, or Form 1040, line 54, to find out if you can take this credit.
- If you can take the credit, fill in the worksheet in those instructions to figure your credit. **But if you want the IRS to figure it for you, see instructions on back.**

Then, you **must** complete and attach Schedule EIC only if you have a qualifying child (see boxes on back).

Information About Your Qualifying Child or Children

If you have more than two qualifying children, you only have to list two to get the maximum credit.

Caution: If you don't attach Schedule EIC and fill in all the lines that apply, it will take us longer to process your return and issue your refund.

		(a) Child 1	(b) Child 2
1	Child's name	First name: David K. Last name: Hall	First name: Last name:
2	Child's year of birth	19 91	19
3	If the child was born **before 1978** AND—		
a	was **under age 24** at the end of 1996 **and** a student, check the "Yes" box, **OR** . . .	☐ Yes	☐ Yes
b	was permanently and totally disabled (see back), check the "Yes" box	☐ Yes	☐ Yes
4	Enter the child's social security number. If born in December 1996, see instructions on back	942-12-8431	
5	Child's relationship to you (for example, son, grandchild, etc.) . .	Son	
6	Number of months child lived with you in the United States in 1996 . .	12 months	months

TIP: Do you want the earned income credit added to your take-home pay in 1997? To see if you qualify, get **Form W-5** from your employer or by calling the IRS at 1-800-TAX-FORM (1-800-829-3676).

For Paperwork Reduction Act Notice, see Form 1040A or 1040 instructions.   Cat. No. 13339M   Schedule EIC (Form 1040A or 1040) 1996

Note: If you are eligible for the Earned Income Credit, you must file page 1 of Schedule EIC if you have a qualifying child. Compute your credit on the worksheet on page 28 in the IRS instruction booklet (see page 144).

There could have been a much larger Earned Income Credit if Pastor Hall's business expenses had been reimbursed and a lower salary prospectively established. The expenses claimed on Form 2106-EZ do not offset earned income for the EIC calculation.

EXAMPLE NO. 2 - MINISTER-EMPLOYEE FOR INCOME TAX PURPOSES (NONACCOUNTABLE PLAN)

Earned Income Credit Worksheet—Line 57
(keep for your records)

> **Caution:** If you were a household employee who didn't receive a Form W-2 because your employer paid you less than $1,000 in 1995 **or** you were a minister or member of a religious order, see **Special Rules** on page 29 before completing this worksheet. Also, see **Special Rules** if Form 1040, line 7, includes any amount paid to an inmate in a penal institution.

1. Enter the amount from Form 1040, line 7 . . . . 1. _15,300_
2. If you received a taxable scholarship or fellowship grant that wasn't reported on a W-2 form, enter that amount here . . 2. _____
3. Subtract line 2 from line 1 . . . . 3. _15,300_
4. Enter any **nontaxable earned income** (see this page). Types of nontaxable earned income include contributions to a 401(k) plan, and military housing and subsistence. These should be shown in box 13 of your W-2 form . . . . 4. _7,040_
5. If you were self-employed **or** used Schedule C or C-EZ as a statutory employee, enter the amount from the worksheet on page 29 . . . . 5. _58_
6. Add lines 3, 4, and 5 . . . . 6. _22,398_
7. Look up the amount on **line 6** above in the **EIC Table** on pages **30–31** to find your credit. Enter the credit here . . . . 7. _323_

   If line 7 is zero, **stop.** You **cannot** take the credit. Enter "No" next to Form 1040, line 57.

8. Enter the amount from Form 1040, line 31 . . . . 8. _13,053_
9. Is line 8 less than—
   - $5,150 if you don't have a qualifying child?
   - $11,300 if you have at least one qualifying child?
   - ☐ **YES.** Go to line 10 now.
   - ☒ **NO.** Look up the amount on **line 8** above in the **EIC Table** on pages **30–31** to find your credit. Enter the credit here . . 9. _1,809_
10. **Earned income credit.**
    - If you checked "YES" on line 9, enter the amount from line 7.
    - If you checked "NO" on line 9, enter the **smaller** of line 7 or line 9 . . . . 10. _323_

    Next: Take the amount from line 10 above and enter it on Form 1040, line 57.

    AND

    If you had any nontaxable earned income (see line 4 above), enter the amount and type of that income in the spaces provided on line 57.

    AND

    Complete **Schedule EIC** and attach it to your return ONLY if you have a qualifying child.

    Note: If you owe the alternative minimum tax (Form 1040, line 48), subtract it from the amount on line 10 above. Then, enter the result (if more than zero) on Form 1040, line 57. Also, replace the amount on line 10 above with the amount entered on Form 1040, line 57.

Note: This worksheet is found on page 28 in the IRS instruction booklet. Complete this worksheet whether or not you have a qualifying child.

EXAMPLE NO. 2 - MINISTER-EMPLOYEE FOR INCOME TAX PURPOSES (NONACCOUNTABLE PLAN)

Housing Allowance Worksheet
Minister Living in Home
Minister Is Renting

Minister's Name: __Donald R. Hall__

For the period __January 1__, 199_6_ to __December 31__, 199_6_

Date designation approved __December 20__, 199_5_

Allowable Housing Expenses *(expenses paid by minister from current income)*

	Estimated Expenses	Actual
Housing rental payments	$ 4,600	$ 5,000
Personal property insurance on minister-owned contents	200	180
Personal property taxes on contents	100	125
Umbrella liability		
Structural maintenance and repair		
Landscaping, gardening, and pest control		
Furnishings *(purchase, repair, replacement)*	240	
Decoration and redecoration		
Utilities *(gas, electricity, water)* and trash collection	1,060	1,000
Local telephone expense *(base charge)*	200	180
Mobile home space rental		
Subtotal	6,400	
10% allowance for unexpected expenses	640	
TOTAL	$ 7,040	$ 6,485 (A)
Properly designated housing allowance.		$ 7,040 (B)

Note: The amount excludable from income for federal income tax purposes is the *lower* of A or B.

Note: Because actual housing expenses are less than the designated allowance, the housing exclusion is limited to $6,485. The $555 difference between the designation and the exclusion is reported as excess housing allowance on Form 1040, line 21 (see page 136).

EXAMPLE NO. 2 - MINISTER-EMPLOYEE FOR INCOME TAX PURPOSES (NONACCOUNTABLE PLAN)

Self-Employment Social Security Tax Worksheet

Inclusions:

Salary paid by church as reflected on Form W-2	$ 15,300
Net profit or loss as reflected on Schedule C or C-EZ (includes speaking honoraria, offerings you receive for marriages, baptisms, funerals, and other fees)	610
Housing allowance excluded from salary on Form W-2 or from income on Schedule C (C-EZ)	7,040
Fair rental value of parsonage provided (including paid utilities)	
Nonaccountable business expense reimbursements (if not included on Form W-2, Schedule C, or C-EZ)	
Reimbursement of self-employment taxes (if not included on Form W-2, Schedule C, or C-EZ)	
Value of meals provided to you, your spouse, and your dependents whether or not provided for your employer's convenience (these amounts may have been excluded from gross income)	
Total inclusions	22,950

Deductions:

Unreimbursed ministerial business and professional expenses (included on Form W-2) or reimbursed expenses paid under a nonaccountable plan (included on Form W-2)

A. Deductible on Schedule A before the 2% of AGI limitation whether or not you itemized[1] or (see page 142)	3,898
B. Not deductible on Form 2106/2106 EZ or Schedule C/C-EZ because expenses were allocated to taxable/nontaxable income. (see page 142)	2,598
Total deductions	6,496
Net earnings from self-employment (to Schedule SE)	$ 16,454

[1]The 50% unreimbursed meal and entertainment expense limitation applies to amounts subject to social security tax. In other words, if some of your meal and entertainment expenses were subjected to the 50% limit, the remainder cannot be deducted here.

Note 1: Your net earnings from self-employment are not affected by the foreign earned income exclusion or the foreign housing exclusion or deduction if you are a U.S. citizen or resident alien who is serving abroad and living in a foreign country.

Note 2: Amounts received as pension payments or annuity payments related to a church-sponsored tax-sheltered annuity by a retired minister are generally considered to be excluded from the social security calculation.

Note: Net earnings from self-employment are entered on Schedule SE, line 2 (see page 140).

EXAMPLE NO. 2 - MINISTER-EMPLOYEE FOR INCOME TAX PURPOSES (NONACCOUNTABLE PLAN)

a Control number		OMB No. 1545-0008		
b Employer's identification number 35-7921873		1 Wages, tips, other compensation 15300.00	2 Federal income tax withheld	
c Employer's name, address, and ZIP code Lancaster Community Church 1425 Spencer Avenue Wabash, IN 46992		3 Social security wages	4 Social security tax withheld	
		5 Medicare wages and tips	6 Medicare tax withheld	
		7 Social security tips	8 Allocated tips	
d Employee's social security number 482-11-6043		9 Advance EIC payment	10 Dependent care benefits	
e Employee's name, address, and ZIP code Donald R. Hall 604 Linden Avenue Wabash, IN 46992		11 Nonqualified plans	12 Benefits included in box 1	
		13 See Instrs. for box 13	14 Other	

Form **W-2** Wage and Tax Statement **1996**
Copy B To Be Filed With Employee's FEDERAL Tax Return

This information is being furnished to the Internal Revenue Service.

Department of the Treasury—Internal Revenue Service

Explanation of compensation reported on Form W-2, box 1:

Salary	$8,500
Special occasion gifts	600
Reimbursement of self-employment tax	2,500
Expense allowance under nonaccountable plan	3,700
	$15,300

Form **1040-ES** Department of the Treasury Internal Revenue Service **1996** Payment Voucher **1**

OMB No. 1545-0087

File only if you are making a payment of estimated tax. Return this voucher with check or money order payable to the "**Internal Revenue Service.**" Please write your social security number and "1996 Form 1040-ES" on your check or money order. Do not send cash. Enclose, but do not staple or attach, your payment with this voucher.

Calendar year—Due April 15, 1996

Amount of payment
$ 575

Your first name and initial	Your last name	Your social security number
Donald R.	Hall	482-11-6043
Spouse's first name and initial	Spouse's last name	Spouse's social security number
Jackie B.	Hall	720-94-1327
Address (number, street, and apt. no.) 604 Linden Avenue		
City, state, and ZIP code. (If a foreign address, enter city, province or state, postal code, and country.) Wabash, IN 46992		

For Paperwork Reduction Act Notice, see instructions on page 1.

Note: This is an example of one of the quarterly estimate forms. The taxpayer filed the other three estimates on a timely basis.

EXAMPLE NO. 3 - MINISTER AS SELF-EMPLOYED FOR INCOME TAX PURPOSES

Example No. 3

Minister considered to be self-employed for income tax purposes.

The Sterlings live in a parsonage provided by the church. Since Pastor Sterling is considered to be self-employed for income tax purposes, he is not eligible for voluntary withholding. Mrs. Sterling is employed and increased her federal income tax withholding sufficiently to cover his income and social security tax liability.

Income, Benefits, and Reimbursements:

Church salary	$8,500
Cash housing allowance/ properly designated (see page 155)	2,000
Christmas and other special occasion gifts paid by the church based on designated member-gifts to the church	1,200
Honoraria for performing weddings, funerals, and baptisms	500
Reimbursement of self-employment tax	3,500
Reimbursement of moving expenses	3,600
Health insurance paid by the church	3,700
Business expense allowance (no accounting provided to church)	4,300
Gross wages/Mrs. Sterling	11,000

Business Expenses, Itemized Deductions, and Keogh Contributions:

Business use of personally owned auto: 13,812 miles

Church-related expenses were paid personally (business expense payments by the church are a nonaccountable expense plan):

Seminar expenses:	
Airfare	$500
Meals	140
Lodging	200
Subscriptions	350
Supplies	880
Entertainment expenses	1,340
Potential itemized deductions:	
Doctors, dentists, and drugs	$875
State and local income taxes	500
Personal property taxes	200
Cash contributions	2,000
Keogh plan contributions	2,500
Housing data:	
Designation	$2,000
Actual expenses	1,480
Fair rental value of furnishings	2,100

EXAMPLE NO. 3 - MINISTER AS SELF-EMPLOYED FOR INCOME TAX PURPOSES

Form 1040 — Department of the Treasury—Internal Revenue Service
U.S. Individual Income Tax Return 1996 (99) IRS Use Only—Do not write or staple in this space.

For the year Jan. 1–Dec. 31, 1996, or other tax year beginning , 1996, ending , 19 OMB No. 1545-0074

Label (See instructions.)
Use the IRS label. Otherwise, please print or type.

Your first name and initial: Michael A.
Last name: Sterling
Your social security number: 517 28 6451

If a joint return, spouse's first name and initial: Laurie N.
Last name: Sterling
Spouse's social security number: 402 51 3082

Home address (number and street). If you have a P.O. box, see page 11.: 15550 Cleveland Avenue
Apt. no.

City, town or post office, state, and ZIP code. If you have a foreign address, see page 11.: Traverse City, MI 49615

For help finding line instructions, see pages 2 and 3 in the booklet.

Presidential Election Campaign (See page 11.)
Do you want $3 to go to this fund? — Yes: X — Note: Checking "Yes" will not change your tax or reduce your refund.
If a joint return, does your spouse want $3 to go to this fund? — Yes: X

Filing Status
Check only one box.
1. Single
2. [X] Married filing joint return (even if only one had income)
3. Married filing separate return. Enter spouse's social security no. above and full name here. ▶
4. Head of household (with qualifying person). (See instructions.) If the qualifying person is a child but not your dependent, enter this child's name here. ▶
5. Qualifying widow(er) with dependent child (year spouse died ▶ 19). (See instructions.)

Exemptions
6a [X] Yourself. If your parent (or someone else) can claim you as a dependent on his or her tax return, **do not** check box 6a
b [X] Spouse
c Dependents:
(1) First name / Last name: Julie M. Sterling
(2) Dependent's social security number. If born in Dec. 1996, see inst.: 481 22 6419
(3) Dependent's relationship to you: Daughter
(4) No. of months lived in your home in 1996: 7

No. of boxes checked on lines 6a and 6b: 2
No. of your children on line 6c who:
• lived with you: 1
• didn't live with you due to divorce or separation (see instructions)
Dependents on 6c not entered above
Add numbers entered on lines above ▶ 3

d Total number of exemptions claimed

(Stamp: Proof as of July 1996 (subject to change))

Income
Attach Copy B of your Forms W-2, W-2G, and 1099-R here.
If you did not get a W-2, see the line 7 instructions.
Please send any payment separately with Form 1040-V. See the line 62a instructions.

7 Wages, salaries, tips, etc. Attach Form(s) W-2 ..... 7 11,000
8a Taxable interest. Attach Schedule B if over $400 ..... 8a
b Tax-exempt interest. DON'T include on line 8a | 8b |
9 Dividend income. Attach Schedule B if over $400 9
10 Taxable refunds, credits, or offsets of state and local income taxes (see instructions) 10
11 Alimony received 11
12 Business income or (loss). Attach Schedule C or C-EZ 12 18,348
13 Capital gain or (loss). If required, attach Schedule D 13
14 Other gains or (losses). Attach Form 4797 14
15a Total IRA distributions .. | 15a | b Taxable amount (see inst.) 15b
16a Total pensions and annuities | 16a | b Taxable amount (see inst.) 16b
17 Rental real estate, royalties, partnerships, S corporations, trusts. Attach Schedule E 17
18 Farm income or (loss). Attach Schedule F 18
19 Unemployment compensation 19
20a Social security benefits | 20a | b Taxable amount (see inst.) 20b
21 Other income. List type and amount—see instructions
   Excess housing allowance 21 520
22 Add the amounts in the far right column for lines 7 through 21. This is your **total income** ▶ 22 29,868

Adjusted Gross Income
If line 31 is under $28,495 (under $9,500 if a child didn't live with you), see the line 54 instructions.

23a Your IRA deduction (see instructions) 23a
b Spouse's IRA deduction (see instructions) 23b
24 Moving expenses. Attach Form 3903 or 3903-F 24 3,600
25 One-half of self-employment tax. Attach Schedule SE 25 1,967
26 Self-employed health insurance deduction (see inst.) 26 1,110
27 Keogh & self-employed SEP plans. If SEP, check ▶ ☐ 27 2,500
28 Penalty on early withdrawal of savings 28
29 Alimony paid. Recipient's SSN ▶ 29
30 Add lines 23a through 29 ..... 30 9,177
31 Subtract line 30 from line 22. This is your **adjusted gross income** ▶ 31 20,691

For Privacy Act and Paperwork Reduction Act Notice, see page 7. Cat. No. 11320B Form **1040** (1996)

Line 21 - See page 155 for the calculation of the excess housing allowance.
Line 24 - See page 57 for an explanation of the moving expense deduction.
Line 25 - See page 105 for material on the self-employment tax deduction.
Line 27 - See page 54 for explanation of the Keogh deduction.

EXAMPLE NO. 3 - MINISTER AS SELF-EMPLOYED FOR INCOME TAX PURPOSES

Form 1040 (1996) — Page 2

Tax Computation

- 32. Amount from line 31 (adjusted gross income) — **20,691**
- 33a. Check if: ☐ You were 65 or older, ☐ Blind; ☐ Spouse was 65 or older, ☐ Blind. Add the number of boxes checked above and enter the total here ▶ 33a
- 33b. If you are married filing separately and your spouse itemizes deductions or you are a dual-status alien, see instructions and check here ▶ 33b ☐
- 34. Enter the larger of your: Itemized deductions from Schedule A, line 28, OR Standard deduction shown below for your filing status. But see the instructions if you checked any box on line 33a or b or someone can claim you as a dependent.
  - Single—$4,000 • Married filing jointly or Qualifying widow(er)—$6,700
  - Head of household—$5,900 • Married filing separately—$3,350 — **6,700**
- 35. Subtract line 34 from line 32 — **13,991**
- 36. If line 32 is $88,475 or less, multiply $2,550 by the total number of exemptions claimed on line 6d. If line 32 is over $88,475, see the worksheet in the inst. for the amount to enter — **7,650**
- 37. **Taxable income.** Subtract line 36 from line 35. If line 36 is more than line 35, enter -0- — **6,341**
- 38. **Tax.** See instructions. Check if total includes any tax from a ☐ Form(s) 8814 b ☐ Form 4970 c ☐ Form 4972 ▶ — **949**

Credits

- 39. Credit for child and dependent care expenses. Attach Form 2441 — 39
- 40. Credit for the elderly or the disabled. Attach Schedule R — 40
- 41. Foreign tax credit. Attach Form 1116 — 41
- 42. Other. Check if from a ☐ Form 3800 b ☐ Form 8396 c ☐ Form 8801 d ☐ Form (specify) — 42
- 43. Add lines 39 through 42 — 43
- 44. Subtract line 43 from line 38. If line 43 is more than line 38, enter -0- ▶ **949**

Other Taxes

- 45. Self-employment tax. Attach Schedule SE — **3,935**
- 46. Alternative minimum tax. Attach Form 6251 — 46
- 47. Social security and Medicare tax on tip income not reported to employer. Attach Form 4137 — 47
- 48. Tax on qualified retirement plans, including IRAs. If required, attach Form 5329 — 48
- 49. Advance earned income credit payments from Form W-2 — 49
- 50. Household employment taxes. Attach Schedule H — 50
- 51. Add lines 44 through 50. This is your **total tax** ▶ **4,884**

Payments

- 52. Federal income tax withheld from Form(s) W-2 and 1099 — **5,000**
- 53. 1996 estimated tax payments and amount applied from 1995 return — 53
- 54. Earned income credit. Attach Schedule EIC if you have a qualifying child. Nontaxable earned income: amount ▶ and type ▶ — 54
- 55. Amount paid with Form 4868 (extension request) — 55
- 56. Excess social security and RRTA tax withheld — 56
- 57. Other payments. Check if from a ☐ Form 2439 b ☐ Form 4136 — 57
- 58. Add lines 52 through 57. These are your **total payments** ▶ **5,000**

Refund

- 59. If line 58 is more than line 51, subtract line 51 from line 58. This is the amount you **OVERPAID** — **116**
- 60a. Amount of line 59 you want **REFUNDED TO YOU** ▶ **116**
- b. Routing number _____ c. Type: ☐ Checking ☐ Savings
- d. Account number _____
- 61. Amount of line 59 you want **APPLIED TO YOUR 1997 ESTIMATED TAX** ▶ 61

Amount You Owe

- 62a. If line 51 is more than line 58, subtract line 58 from line 51. This is the **AMOUNT YOU OWE.** For details on how to pay and use Form 1040-V, see instructions — 62a
- b. Are you paying the amount on line 62a in full with Form 1040-V? ▶ ☐ Yes ☐ No
- 63. Estimated tax penalty. Also include on line 62a — 63

Sign Here

Your signature: *Michael A. Sterling* Date: 4/15/97 Your occupation: Minister
Spouse's signature: *Laurie N. Sterling* Date: 4/15/97 Spouse's occupation: Secretary

Paid Preparer's Use Only

Preparer's signature ▶ Date Check if self-employed ☐ Preparer's social security no.
Firm's name (or yours if self-employed) and address EIN ZIP code

(Stamped across form: "Not as of Nov 1996 (subject to change)")

EXAMPLE NO. 3 - MINISTER AS SELF-EMPLOYED FOR INCOME TAX PURPOSES

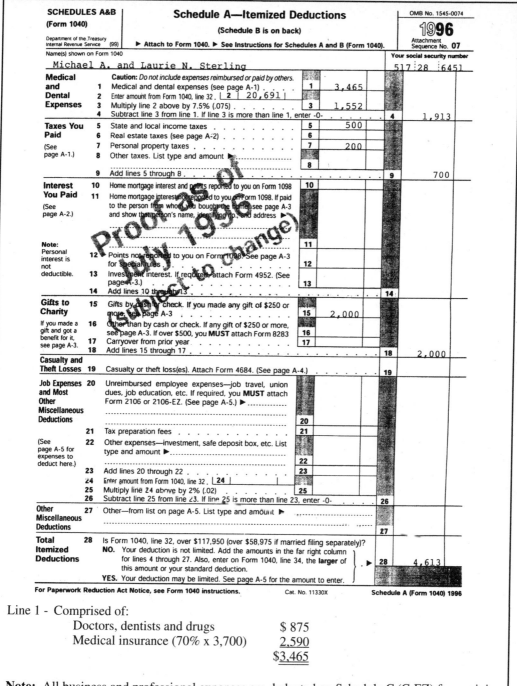

Line 1 - Comprised of:
    Doctors, dentists and drugs $ 875
    Medical insurance (70% x 3,700)   2,590
                                            $3,465

Note: All business and professional expenses are deducted on Schedule C (C-EZ) for a minister who is considered to be self-employed for income tax purposes. These expenses are not deducted on line 20.

The standard deduction was claimed on Form 1040, line 34, since it exceeded itemized deductions.

EXAMPLE NO. 3 - MINISTER AS SELF-EMPLOYED FOR INCOME TAX PURPOSES

SCHEDULE C (Form 1040)
Profit or Loss From Business (Sole Proprietorship)
▶ Partnerships, joint ventures, etc., must file Form 1065.
▶ Attach to Form 1040 or Form 1041. ▶ See Instructions for Schedule C (Form 1040).

OMB No. 1545-0074
1996
Attachment Sequence No. 09

Name of proprietor: Michael A. Sterling
Social security number (SSN): 517 : 28 : 6451

A. Principal business or profession, including product or service (see page C-1): Minister
B. Enter principal business code (see page C-6) ▶

C. Business name. If no separate business name, leave blank.
D. Employer ID number (EIN), if any

E. Business address (including suite or room no.) ▶
   City, town or post office, state, and ZIP code

F. Accounting method: (1) ☒ Cash   (2) ☐ Accrual   (3) ☐ Other (specify) ▶
G. Did you "materially participate" in the operation of this business during 1996? If "No," see page C-2 for limit on losses. ☒ Yes ☐ No
H. If you started or acquired this business during 1996, check here ☐

Part I Income

1 Gross receipts or sales. Caution: If this income was reported to you on Form W-2 and the "Statutory employee" box on that form was checked, see page C-2 and check here ▶ ☐	1	25,300
2 Returns and allowances	2	
3 Subtract line 2 from line 1	3	25,300
4 Cost of goods sold (from line 42 on page 2)	4	
5 Gross profit. Subtract line 4 from line 3	5	25,300
6 Other income, including Federal and state gasoline or fuel tax credit or refund (see page C-2)	6	
7 Gross income. Add lines 5 and 6 ▶	7	25,300

Part II Expenses. Enter expenses for business use of your home only on line 30.

8 Advertising	8		19 Pension and profit-sharing plans	19	
9 Bad debts from sales or services (see page C-3)	9		20 Rent or lease (see page C-4): a Vehicles, machinery and equipment	20a	
10 Car and truck expenses (see page C-3)	10		b Other business property	20b	
11 Commissions and fees	11		21 Repairs and maintenance	21	
12 Depletion	12		22 Supplies (not included in Part III)	22	880
13 Depreciation and section 179 expense deduction (not included in Part III) (see page C-3)	13		23 Taxes and licenses	23	
			24 Travel, meals, and entertainment:		
14 Employee benefit programs (other than on line 19)	14		a Travel	24a	700
15 Insurance (other than health)	15		b Meals and entertainment	1,480	
16 Interest:			c Enter 50% of line 24b subject to limitations (see page C-4)	740	
a Mortgage (paid to banks, etc.)	16a				
b Other	16b		d Subtract line 24c from line 24b	24d	740
17 Legal and professional services	17		25 Utilities	25	
18 Office expense	18	350	26 Wages (less employment credits)	26	
			27 Other expenses (from line 48 on page 2)	27	6,952
28 Total expenses before expenses for business use of home. Add lines 8 through 27 in columns ▶				28	18,348

29 Tentative profit (loss). Subtract line 28 from line 7 .... | 29 | |
30 Expenses for business use of your home. Attach Form 8829 .... | 30 | |
31 Net profit or (loss). Subtract line 30 from line 29.
• If a profit, enter on Form 1040, line 12, and ALSO on Schedule SE, line 2 (statutory employees, see page C-5). Estates and trusts, enter on Form 1041, line 3.
• If a loss, you MUST go on to line 32. | 31 | 18,348 |

32 If you have a loss, check the box that describes your investment in this activity (see page C-5).
• If you checked 32a, enter the loss on Form 1040, line 12, and ALSO on Schedule SE, line 2 (statutory employees, see page C-5). Estates and trusts, enter on Form 1041, line 3.
• If you checked 32b, you MUST attach Form 6198.
32a ☐ All investment is at risk.
32b ☐ Some investment is not at risk.

For Paperwork Reduction Act Notice, see Form 1040 Instructions.   Cat. No. 11334P   Schedule C (Form 1040) 1996

Schedule C (Form 1040) 1996   Page 2

Part III Cost of Goods Sold (see page C-5)

33 Method(s) used to value closing inventory: a ☐ Cost   b ☐ Lower of cost or market   c ☐ Other (attach explanation)
34 Was there any change in determining quantities, costs, or valuations between opening and closing inventory? If "Yes," attach explanation ☐ Yes ☐ No

35 Inventory at beginning of year. If different from last year's closing inventory, attach explanation	35	
36 Purchases less cost of items withdrawn for personal use	36	
37 Cost of labor. Do not include salary paid to yourself	37	
38 Materials and supplies	38	
39 Other costs	39	
40 Add lines 35 through 39	40	
41 Inventory at end of year	41	
42 Cost of goods sold. Subtract line 41 from line 40. Enter the result here and on page 1, line 4	42	

Part IV Information on Your Vehicle. Complete this part ONLY if you are claiming car or truck expenses on line 10 and are not required to file Form 4562 for this business. See the instructions for line 13 on page C-3 to find out if you must file.

43 When did you place your vehicle in service for business purposes? (month, day, year) ▶ 9/1/95
44 Of the total number of miles you drove your vehicle during 1996, enter the number of miles you used your vehicle for:
   a Business 13,812   b Commuting _____   c Other 4,579
45 Do you (or your spouse) have another vehicle available for personal use? .... ☒ Yes ☐ No
46 Was your vehicle available for use during off-duty hours? .... ☒ Yes ☐ No
47a Do you have evidence to support your deduction? .... ☒ Yes ☐ No
   b If "Yes," is the evidence written? .... ☒ Yes ☐ No

Part V Other Expenses. List below business expenses not included on lines 8-26 or line 30.

48 Total other expenses. Enter here and on page 1, line 27	48	

Part 1, line 1 - Consists of $24,800 from Form 1099-MISC plus $500 of honoraria.

EXAMPLE NO. 3 - MINISTER AS SELF-EMPLOYED FOR INCOME TAX PURPOSES

SCHEDULE SE (Form 1040) Department of the Treasury Internal Revenue Service (99)	Self-Employment Tax ▶ See Instructions for Schedule SE (Form 1040). ▶ Attach to Form 1040.	OMB No. 1545-0074 **1996** Attachment Sequence No. **17**
Name of person with **self-employment** income (as shown on Form 1040) Michael A. Sterling	Social security number of person with **self-employment** income ▶	517 : 28 : 6451

Who Must File Schedule SE

You must file Schedule SE if:
- You had net earnings from self-employment from **other than** church employee income (line 4 of Short Schedule SE or line 4c of Long Schedule SE) of $400 or more, **OR**
- You had church employee income of $108.28 or more. Income from services you performed as a minister or a member of a religious order **is not** church employee income. See page SE-1.

Note: Even if you had a loss or a small amount of income from self-employment, it may be to your benefit to file Schedule SE and use either "optional method" in Part II of Long Schedule SE. See page SE-3.

Exception. If your only self-employment income was from earnings as a minister, member of a religious order, or Christian Science practitioner **and** you filed Form 4361 and received IRS approval not to be taxed on those earnings, **do not** file Schedule SE. Instead, write "Exempt–Form 4361" on Form 1040, line 45.

May I Use Short Schedule SE or MUST I Use Long Schedule SE?

```
                    DID YOU RECEIVE WAGES OR TIPS IN 1996?
                    /                                    \
                   No                                    Yes
                    |                                     |
  Are you a minister, member of a religious order,    Was the total of your wages and tips subject to social security
  or Christian Science practitioner who received     or railroad retirement tax plus your net earnings from      → Yes
  IRS approval not to be taxed on earnings from  Yes self-employment more than $62,700?
  these sources, but you owe self-employment
  tax on other earnings?                                 |
                    |                                    No
                   No                                     |
                    |                               Did you receive tips subject to social security or Medicare tax → Yes
  Are you using one of the optional methods to      that you did not report to your employer?
  figure your net earnings (see page SE-3)?    Yes
                    |                                    No
                   No                                     |
                    |
  Did you receive church employee income
  reported on Form W-2 of $108.28 or more?      Yes
                    |
                   No
                    ↓
  YOU MAY USE SHORT SCHEDULE SE BELOW          YOU MUST USE LONG SCHEDULE SE ON THE BACK
```

Section A—Short Schedule SE. Caution: *Read above to see if you can use Short Schedule SE.*

1	Net farm profit or (loss) from Schedule F, line 36, and farm partnerships, Schedule K-1 (Form 1065), line 15a	**1**
2	Net profit or (loss) from Schedule C, line 31; Schedule C-EZ, line 3; and Schedule K-1 (Form 1065), line 15a (other than farming). Ministers and members of religious orders see page SE-1 for amounts to report on this line. See page SE-2 for other income to report	**2** 27,848
3	Combine lines 1 and 2	**3** 27,848
4	**Net earnings from self-employment.** Multiply line 3 by 92.35% (.9235). If less than $400, **do not** file this schedule; you do not owe self-employment tax . . . . ▶	**4** 25,718
5	**Self-employment tax.** If the amount on line 4 is: • $62,700 or less, multiply line 4 by 15.3% (.153). Enter the result here and on **Form 1040, line 45.** • More than $62,700, multiply line 4 by 2.9% (.029). Then, add $7,774.80 to the result. Enter the total here and on **Form 1040, line 45.**	**5** 3,935
6	**Deduction for one-half of self-employment tax.** Multiply line 5 by 50% (.5). Enter the result here and on **Form 1040, line 25** . . .	**6** 1,967

For Paperwork Reduction Act Notice, see Form 1040 instructions.   Cat. No. 11358Z   Schedule SE (Form 1040) 1996

Line 2 - See the schedule on page 156 for the calculation of this amount.
Line 4 - This line results in the deduction of about one-half of the self-employment tax liability.
Note: A minister may use Section A-Short Schedule unless he received nonministerial wages (subject to FICA) and the total of these wages and net ministerial self-employment earnings (Schedule C-related) are more than $62,700.

EXAMPLE NO. 3 - MINISTER AS SELF-EMPLOYED FOR INCOME TAX PURPOSES

Form **3903**
Department of the Treasury
Internal Revenue Service

Moving Expenses
▶ Attach to Form 1040.
▶ See instructions on back.

OMB No. 1545-0062
1996
Attachment Sequence No. **62**

Name(s) shown on Form 1040: Michael A. and Laurie N. Sterling
Your social security number: 517 28 6451

Caution: *If you are a member of the armed forces, see the instructions before completing this form.*

1. Enter the number of miles from your **old home** to your **new workplace** . . **1** 285 miles
2. Enter the number of miles from your **old home** to your **old workplace** . . **2** 10 miles
3. Subtract line 2 from line 1. Enter the result but not less than zero . . . . **3** 275 miles

Is line 3 at least 50 miles?

Yes ▶ Go to line 4. Also, see **Time Test** in the instructions.

No ▶ You **cannot** deduct your moving expenses. Do not complete the rest of this form.

4. Transportation and storage of household goods and personal effects **4** 3,360
5. Travel and lodging expenses of moving from your old home to your new home. **Do not** include meals **5** 240
6. Add lines 4 and 5 . . . . **6** 3,600
7. Enter the total amount your employer paid for your move (including the value of services furnished in kind) that is **not** included in the wages box (box 1) of your W-2 form. This amount should be identified with code **P** in box 13 of your W-2 form. **7**

Is line 6 more than line 7?

Yes ▶ Go to line 8.

No ▶ You **cannot** deduct your moving expenses. If line 6 is less than line 7, subtract line 6 from line 7 and include the result in income on Form 1040, line 7.

8. Subtract line 7 from line 6. Enter the result here and on Form 1040, line 24. This is your **moving expense deduction** **8** 3,600

For Paperwork Reduction Act Notice, see back of form.   Cat. No. 12490K   Form **3903** (1995)

Note: This form must include moving expenses of a minister filing as self-employed for income tax purposes whether or not the expenses are reimbursed by the church. The church properly includes the reimbursed moving expenses on Form 1099-MISC (see page 157).

EXAMPLE NO. 3 - MINISTER AS SELF-EMPLOYED FOR INCOME TAX PURPOSES

Housing Allowance Worksheet
Minister Living in a Parsonage
Owned by or Rented by the Church

Minister's Name: __Michael A. Sterling__

For the period __January 1__, 199_6_ to __December 31__, 199_6_

Date designation approved __December 20__, 199_5_

Allowable Housing Expenses *(expenses paid by minister from current income)*

	Estimated Expenses	Actual
Utilities *(gas, electricity, water)* and trash collection	$ _____	$ _____
Local telephone expense *(base charge)*	273	260
Decoration and redecoration	_____	_____
Structural maintenance and repair	_____	_____
Landscaping, gardening, and pest control	_____	_____
Furnishings *(purchase, repair, replacement)*	1,255	925
Personal property insurance on minister-owned contents	_____	_____
Personal property taxes on contents	190	200
Umbrella liability insurance	100	95
Subtotal	1,818	
10% allowance for unexpected expenses	182	
TOTAL	$ 2,000	$ 1,480 (A)

Fair rental value of furnishings owned by the minister $ 2,100 (B)
Properly designated housing allowance $ 2,000 (C)

Note: The amount excludable from income for federal income tax purposes is the *lowest* of A, B, or C.

Note: Since actual housing expenses are less than the designated allowance, the housing exclusion is limited to $1,480. The $520 difference between the designation and the exclusion is reported by the minister as an excess housing allowance on line 21, Form 1040 (see page 149).

EXAMPLE NO. 3 - MINISTER AS SELF-EMPLOYED FOR INCOME TAX PURPOSES

Self-Employment Social Security Tax Worksheet

Inclusions:

Salary paid by church as reflected on Form W-2 $ _____

Net profit or loss as reflected on Schedule C or C-EZ
(includes speaking honoraria, offerings you receive
for marriages, baptisms, funerals, and other fees)   _18,348_

Housing allowance excluded from salary on Form W-2 or from
income on Schedule C (C-EZ)   _2,000_

Fair rental value of parsonage provided (including paid utilities)   _7,500_

Nonaccountable business expense reimbursements
(if not included on Form W-2, Schedule C, or C-EZ)   _____

Reimbursement of self-employment taxes (if not
included on Form W-2, Schedule C, or C-EZ)   _____

Value of meals provided to you, your spouse, and your dependents
whether or not provided for your employer's convenience (these
amounts may have been excluded from gross income)   _____

Total inclusions   _27,848_

Deductions:

Unreimbursed ministerial business and professional expenses
(included on Form W-2) or reimbursed expenses paid under
a nonaccountable plan (included on Form W-2)
    A. Deductible on Schedule A before the 2% of AGI limitation
        whether or not you itemized[1] or
    B. Not deductible on Form 2106/2106 EZ or
        Schedule C/C-EZ because expenses were
        allocated to taxable/nontaxable income.   _____

Total deductions   _____

Net earnings from self-employment (to Schedule SE) $ _27,848_

[1] The 50% unreimbursed meal and entertainment expense limitation applies to amounts subject to social security tax. In other words, if some of your meal and entertainment expenses were subjected to the 50% limit, the remainder cannot be deducted here.

Note 1:   Your net earnings from self-employment are not affected by the foreign earned income exclusion or the foreign housing exclusion or deduction if you are a U.S. citizen or resident alien who is serving abroad and living in a foreign country.

Note 2:   Amounts received as pension payments or annuity payments related to a church-sponsored tax-sheltered annuity by a retired minister are generally considered to be excluded from the social security calculation.

Note: Net earnings from self-employment are entered on Schedule SE, line 2 (see page 153).

EXAMPLE NO. 3 - MINISTER AS SELF-EMPLOYED FOR INCOME TAX PURPOSES

☐ CORRECTED (if checked)

PAYER'S name, street address, city, state, and ZIP code
Little Valley Church
2670 North Hull Road
Traverse City, MI 49615

1 Rents $
2 Royalties $
3 Other income $

OMB No. 1545-0115

1996

Form **1099-MISC**

Miscellaneous Income

PAYER'S Federal identification number	RECIPIENT'S identification number
35-2946039	517-28-6451

RECIPIENT'S name
Michael A. Sterling

Street address (including apt. no.)
15550 Cleveland Avenue

City, state, and ZIP code
Traverse City, MI 49615

Account number (optional)

4 Federal income tax withheld $
5 Fishing boat proceeds $
6 Medical and health care payments $
7 Nonemployee compensation $ 24,800.00
8 Substitute payments in lieu of dividends or interest $
9 Payer made direct sales of $5,000 or more of consumer products to a buyer (recipient) for resale ▶ ☐
10 Crop insurance proceeds $
11 State income tax withheld $
12 State/Payer's state number

Copy B For Recipient

This is important tax information and is being furnished to the Internal Revenue Service. If you are required to file a return, a negligence penalty or other sanction may be imposed on you if this income is taxable and the IRS determines that it has not been reported.

Form **1099-MISC**   (Keep for your records.)   Department of the Treasury - Internal Revenue Service

Explanation of nonemployee compensation reported on Form 1099-MISC:

Salary	$8,500
Special occasion gifts	1,200
Reimbursement of self-employment tax	3,500
Reimbursement of moving expenses	3,600
Health insurance paid by the church	3,700
Business expense allowance	4,300
	$24,800

---

a Control number

OMB No. 1545-0008

b Employer's identification number
48-9418366

c Employer's name, address, and ZIP code
L. A. Browning, Inc.
800 Central Avenue
Traverse City, MI 49615

d Employee's social security number
402-51-3082

e Employee's name, address, and ZIP code
Laurie N. Sterling
15550 Cleveland Avenue
Traverse City, MI 49615

1 Wages, tips, other compensation 11000.00
2 Federal income tax withheld 5000.00
3 Social security wages 11000.00
4 Social security tax withheld 682.00
5 Medicare wages and tips 11000.00
6 Medicare tax withheld 159.50
7 Social security tips
8 Allocated tips
9 Advance EIC payment
10 Dependent care benefits
11 Nonqualified plans
12 Benefits included in box 1
13 See Instrs. for box 13
14 Other

15 Statutory employee ☐ Deceased ☐ Pension plan ☐ Legal rep. ☐ Hshld. emp. ☐ Subtotal ☐ Deferred compensation ☐

16 State | **Employer's state I.D. No.** | **17 State wages, tips, etc.** | **18 State income tax** | **19 Locality name** | **20 Local wages, tips, etc.** | **21 Local income tax**

Department of the Treasury—Internal Revenue Service

Form **W-2 Wage and Tax Statement 1996**
Copy B To Be Filed With Employee's FEDERAL Tax Return

This information is being furnished to the Internal Revenue Service.

5 WA

Note: This W-2 relates to the employment of Mrs. Sterling.

Citations

Internal Revenue Code (Code): The Code is the "tax law" as enacted and amended by Congress and is the highest authority in all tax matters.

Federal Tax Regulations (Reg.): These are regulations published by the Department of the Treasury (it oversees the IRS) that seek to explain the sometimes vague language of the Internal Revenue Code. The Regulations give definitions, examples, and more plain-language explanations.

Treasury Decisions (T.D.): These are instructions and interpretations issued by the IRS Commissioner with the approval of the Treasury Secretary.

Private letter rulings (Ltr. Rul.): A private letter ruling is issued by the IRS at the request of a taxpayer. It's requested for the purpose of getting the IRS's opinion on a specific transaction or issue facing a taxpayer. Although it can't be used as precedent by anyone else, it usually reflects the IRS's current attitude toward a particular tax matter.

Revenue rulings (Rev. Rul.): A revenue ruling is issued by the IRS and is similar to a letter ruling, but it's not directed to a specific taxpayer. It is designed to give the public the IRS's opinion concerning how the tax law applies to some type of transaction, giving examples and explanations. It also gives the tax consequences of specific transactions.

Revenue procedures (Rev. Proc.): A revenue procedure is similar to a revenue ruling, but it gives more general guidelines and procedural information. It usually does not give tax consequences of specific transactions.

Technical Advice Memoranda (T.A.M.): These consist of written counsel or guidance furnished by the IRS National Office on the interpretation and proper application of the tax law to a specific set of facts.

Court cases: Taxpayer disputes with the IRS may end up in court if a taxpayer is issued an unfavorable ruling by the IRS and is hit with back taxes. There are two routes to take if the taxpayer wants to take the IRS to court. The taxpayer can elect not to pay the back taxes and petition the Tax Court to find that the proposed back tax assessment is incorrect. Or, the taxpayer can pay the disputed amount and sue the IRS for a refund in a district court. A taxpayer can appeal an adverse court decision in an appellate court, and if unsuccessful, can take it to the U.S. Supreme Court.

The IRS is bound by decisions of the Supreme Court for all taxpayers. It is bound by the decisions of the other courts only for the particular taxpayer involved and only for the years involved in the litigation.

CITATIONS

Chapter 1, Taxes for Ministers

- **Administrative and teaching positions**

  Treas. Reg. 31.3401(a)(9)-1(b) (3)-(5)

  Treas. Reg. 31.3121(b)(8)-1(c)(2)-(3)

  Treas. Reg. 1. 1402(c)-5(b)(2)

  Ltr. Rul. 9608027

  Ltr. Rul. 9144047

  Ltr. Rul. 9126048

  Ltr. Rul. 9052001

  T.A.M. 9033002

  Ltr. Rul. 8930038

  Ltr. Rul. 8922077

  Ltr. Rul. 8826043

  Rev. Rul. 84-13

  Flowers v. Commissioner,
  82-1 USTC para. 9114 (N.D. Tex. 1981)

  Boyer v. Commissioner,
  69 T.C.M. 521 (1977)

  Rev. Rul. 72-606

  Rev. Rul. 70-549

  Rev. Rul. 59-50

  Rev. Rul. 58-550

  Rev. Rul. 57-129

- **Commissioned ministers**

  Ltr. Rul. 9221025

- **Employees v. self-employed for income tax purposes**

  Treas. Reg. 31.3401(c)-1(b)-(c)

  Weber v. Commissioner,
  103 T.C.M. 19 (1994), Affirmed
  4th Cir., 94-2609 (1995)

  Shelley v. Commissioner,
  T.C.M. 432 (1994)

  Ltr. Rul. 9414022

  Cosby v. Commissioner,
  T.C.M. Sum. Op. 1987-141

  Rev. Rul. 87-41

  Rev. Proc. 85-18

  Rev. Rul. 80-110

- **Exempt from FICA**

  Code Sec. 3121(b)(8)(A)

- **Exempt from income tax withholding**

  Code Sec. 3121(b)(8)

  Code Sec. 3401(a)(9)

  Treas. Reg. 31.3401(a)(8)-1

- **Qualifications of religious orders**

  Rev. Proc. 91-20

- **Qualifying tests for ministerial status**

  Treas. Reg. 1.1402(c)-5

  Reeder v. Commissioner,
  T.C.M. 287 (1993)

  Ltr. Rul. 9221025

  Eade v. U.S., Dist. Court, Western Dist.,
  VA, Roanoke Division (1991)

  Knight v. Commissioner,
  92 T.C.M. 12 (1989)

  T.A.M. 8915001

Wingo v. Commissioner,
89 T.C.M. 922 (1987)

Ltr. Rul. 8825025

Rev. Rul. 80-59

Silverman v. Commissioner,
57 T.C.M. 727 (1972)

Lawrence v. Commissioner,
50 T.C.M. 494 (1968)

Salkov v. Commissioner,
46 T.C.M. 190 (1966)

Rev. Rul. 59-270

- **Subject to income tax**

    Murdock v. Pennsylvania,
    319 U.S. 105 (1943)

- **Voluntary withholding of income tax for ministers**

    Treas. Reg. 31.3402(p)-1

    Treas. Reg. 31.4302(i)-1(a)

    Rev. Rul. 68-507

- **Withholding of income tax for nonministerial employees**

    Bethel Baptist Church v. U.S., 822 F.2d 1334 (3rd Cir. 1987)

    Eighth Street Baptist Church, Inc. v. U. S., 295 F. Supp. 1400 (D. Kan. 1969)

Chapter 2, Compensation and Financial Planning

- **Avoiding recharacterization of income**

    Ltr. Rul. 9325023

Chapter 3, The Pay Package

- **Deferred compensation**

    Code Sec. 457

    Rev. Proc. 92-64

- ***De Minimis* fringes**

    Code Sec. 132(e)(1)

- **Dependent care**

    Code Sec. 129

- **Disability payments**

    Code Sec. 104(a)(3)

    Reg. 1.104-1(d)

    Ltr. Rul. 9103014

    Ltr. Rul. 9103043

    Ltr. Rul. 9105032

- **Educational assistance**

    Code Sec. 127

- **Employer-paid vehicle fuel**

    Notice 91-41

- **Group-term life insurance**

    Code Sec. 3401(a)(14)

- **Highly compensated employees**

    Code Sec. 414(q)
    Treas. Reg. 1.132-8(f)(1)

- **Key employees**

    Code Sec. 416(i)(1)

- **Loans to employees**

Code Sec. 7872(c)(1)(B)

Code Sec. 7872(c)(3)(A)

Code Sec. 7872 (f)(10)

- **Meals and lodging**

  Code Sec. 119(a)

  Kalms v. Commissioner,
  T.C.M. 394 (1992)

  Ltr. Rul. 9129037

  Goldsboro Christian School, Inc. v. Commissioner, 436 F. Supp. 1314 (D.D.C. 1978), Affirmed 103 S. Ct. 2017 (1983)

  Ltr. Rul. 8213005

  Bob Jones University v. Commissioner, 670 F.2d 167 Ct. Cl. (1982)

  Rev. Rul. 77-80

- **Medical expense reimbursement plans**

  Code Sec. 105

  Ltr. Rul. 9112022

  Ltr. Rul. 9101023

- **Medical insurance premiums paid by the employer**

  Code Sec. 106(a)

  Code Sec. 4980B

  Treas. Reg. 1.106-1

  Rev. Rul. 70-179

  Rev. Rul. 58-90

- **Medical insurance premiums paid by employee/reimbursed by church**

  Ltr. Rul. 9022060

  Rev. Rul. 85-44

  Rev. Rul. 75-241

  Rev. Rul. 61-146

- **Medical plans, self-insured**

  Code Sec. 105(h)

- **Moving expenses**

  Code Sec. 132(g)

  Code Sec. 217

- **Nontaxable fringe benefits**

  Code Sec. 132

- **Pension plans**

  Code Sec. 83

  Code Sec. 401(a)

  Code Sec. 414(e)

- **Property transfers**

  Treas. Reg. 1.61-2(d)(2)

  Potito v. Commissioner,
  534 F.2d 49 (5th Cir. 1976)

- **Reasonable compensation**

  Truth Tabernacle, Inc. v. Commissioner, T.C.M. (1989)-451

  Heritage Village Church and Missionary Fellowship, Inc. 92 B.R. 1000 (D.S.C. 1988)

- **Reimbursement payments excludable from recipient's income**

  Ltr. Rul. 9112022

- **Retirement gifts**

    Code Sec. 102(c)

    Commissioner v. Duberstein,
    363 U.S. 278, 285 (1960)

    Perkins v. Commissioner,
    34 T.C.M. 117 (1960)

    Stanton v. U.S.,
    163 F.2d 727 (2nd Cir. 1959)

    Rev. Rul. 55-422

    Abernathy v. Commissioner,
    211 F.2d 651 (D.C. Cir. 1954)

    Kavanagh v. Hershman,
    210 F.2d 654 (6th Cir. 1954)

    Mutch v. Commissioner,
    209 F.2d 390 (3rd Cir. 1954)

    Schall v. Commissioner,
    174 F.2d 893 (5th Cir. 1949)

    Rev. Rul. 55-422

- **Social security reimbursements**

    Rev. Rul. 68-507

- **Special occasion gifts**

    Goodwin v. U.S.
    94-2 U.S.T.C (S.D. Iowa 1994)
    Affirmed 8th Cir. Ct. of Appeals

    Banks v. Commissioner,
    T.C.M. 641 (1991)

- **Tax-sheltered annuities**

    Code Sec. 403(b)

    Code Sec. 415

    Code Sec. 1402(a)

    Code Sec. 3121(a)(5)(D)

    Rev. Rul. 78-6

    Rev. Rul. 68-395

    Azad v. Commissioner,
    388 F.2d 74 (8th Cir. 1968)

    Rev. Rul. 66-274

- **Tuition and fee reductions**

    Code Sec. 117(d)

    Rasmussen v. Commissioner,
    T.C. 7264-92 (1994)

Chapter 4, Home Sweet Home

- **Allowed without documentation**

    Kizer v. Commissioner,
    T.C.M. 582 (1992)

- **Designation of housing allowance**

    Treas. Reg. 1.107-1(b)

    Mobley v. Commissioner,
    T.C.M. 457 (1994)

    Kiser v. Commissioner,
    T.C.M. 584 (1992)

    Warnke v. Commissioner,
    641 F. Supp. 1083 (D.C. Ky. 1986)

    Swaggart v. Commissioner,
    48 T.C.M. 759 (1984)

    Holland v. Commissioner,
    47 T.C.M. 494 (1983)

    Libman v. Commissioner,
    44 T.C.M. 370 (1982)

    Hoelz v. Commissioner,
    42 T.C.M. 1037 (1981)

CITATIONS

Boyd v. Commissioner,
42 T.C.M. 1136 (1981)

Rev. Rul. 75-22

Rev. Rul. 62-117

Eden v. Commissioner,
41 T.C.M. 605 (1961)

- **Determination of housing exclusion amount**

Rasmussen v. Commissioner,
T.C. 7264-92 (1994)

Ltr. Rul. 8937025

Swaggart v. Commissioner,
48 T.C.M. 759 (1984)

Rev. Rul. 78-448

- **Double deduction of interest and taxes**

Code Sec. 265(6)

Rev. Rul. 87-32

- **Exclusion of the housing allowance**

Code Sec. 107

- **Fair rental value test**

Ltr. Rul. 8825025

Rev. Rul. 71-280

- **Housing allowance for minister-counselor**

Ltr. Rul. 9231053

- **Housing allowance for prison chaplain**

Ltr. Rul. 9052001

- **Housing allowances for retired clergy**

Rev. Proc. 92-3

Rev. Rul. 75-22

- **Including interest on home equity loan**

Ltr. Rul. 9115051

- **Minister who owns home outright cannot exclude parsonage allowance**

Ltr. Rul. 9115051

- **Minister performing routine services**

Rev. Rul. 57-129

- **Reasonability of housing allowance**

Heritage Village Church and Missionary Fellowship, Inc.
92 B.R. 1000 (D.S.C. 1988)

Chapter 5, Business Expenses

- **Accountable expense reimbursement plans**

Treas. Reg. 1.62-2

Treas. Reg. 1.274-5(e)

Ltr. Rul. 9317003

Ltr. Rul. 9325023

- **Accounting for business and professional expenses by independent contractors**

Treas. Reg. 1.274-5(g)

- **Allocation of unreimbursed business expenses**

McFarland v. Commissioner,
T.C.M. 440 (1992)

Dalan v. Commissioner,
T.C.M. 106 (1988)

Deason v. Commissioner,
41 T.C.M. 465 (1964)

- **Auto expense substantiation**

  Parker v. Commissioner,
  T.C.M. 15 (1993)

- **Club dues**

  T.D. 8601

- **Computer expenses**

  Bryant v. Commissioner,
  T.C. 597 (1993)

- **Contributions treated as business expenses**

  Forbes v. Commissioner,
  T.C. Sum. Op. 167 (1992)

- **Deductibility of spouse's travel**

  Code Sec. 1.162-2(c)

  Stockton v. Commissioner,
  36 T.C.M. 114 (1977)

  U.S. v. Disney, 413 F.2d 783 (9th Cir. 1969)

- **Educational expenses**

  Ltr. Rul. 9431024

  Burt v. Commissioner,
  40 T.C.M. 1164 (1980)

  Glasgow v. Commissioner,
  31 T.C.M. 310 (1972)

- **Home-office expenses**

  Code Sec. 280A

  Rev. Rul. 94-24

  Rev. Rul. 94-47

- **Other business and professional expense deductions**

  Treas. Reg. 1.1402(a)-11(a)

  Bass v. Commissioner,
  T.C.M. 536 (1983)

  Rev. Rul. 80-110

  Rev. Rul. 79-78

- **Personal computer expenses**

  Code Sec. 280F

  Rev. Rul. 86-129

- **Substantiation of business expenses**

  Code Sec. 274(d)

  Rev. Proc. 92-71

- **Travel/Away From Home**

  Rev. Rul. 83-82

  Rev. Rul. 75-432

- **Travel/Commuting**

  Treas. Reg. 1.262-1(b)(5)

  Rev. Rul. 94-47

  Rev. Rul. 90-23

  Walker v. Commissioner,
  101 T.C.M. 537 (1993)

  Soliman v. Commissioner,
  94 T.C.M. 20 (1990), Supreme Court (1993)

  Hamblen v. Commissioner,
  78 T.C.M. 53 (1981)

- **Travel/Mileage Rates**

  Rev. Proc. 94-73

  Rev. Proc. 94-77

CITATIONS

- **Unreimbursed business expenses**

    Gravett v. Commissioner,
    T.C.M. 156 (1994)

Chapter 6, Social Security Tax

- **Age not a limitation**

    Levine v. Commissioner,
    T.C.M. 469 (1992)

- **Nullifying the exemption**

    Rev. Rul. 70-197

- **Opting out of social security**

    Code Sec. 1402(e)

    Treas. Reg. 1.1402(e)-3A

    Eade v. U.S., Dist Court, Western Dist. VA, Roanoke Div. (1991)

    T.A.M. 8741002

    Balinger v. Commissioner,
    728 F.2d 1287 (10th Cir. 1984)

    Treadway v. Commissioner,
    47 T.C.M. 1375 (1984)

    Olsen v. Commissioner,
    709 F.2d 278 (4th Cir. 1983)

    Holland v. Commissioner,
    47 T.C.M. 494 (1983)

    Paschall v. Commissioner,
    46 T.C.M. 1197 (1983)

    Hess v. Commissioner,
    40 T.C.M. 415 (1980)

    Rev. Rul. 77-78

    Rev. Rul. 75-189

- **Second ordination/social security exemption**

    Hall v. Commissioner, T.C.M. 360 (1993), 10th Cir. (July 19, 1994)

- **Social security coverage for ministers**

    Code Sec. 1402(c)(2) and (4)

    Code Sec. 3121(b)(8)(A)

    Code Sec. 3401(a)(9)

    Rev. Rul. 80-110

    Rev. Rul. 79-78

    Silvey v. Commissioner,
    35 T.C.M. 1812 (1976)

- **Taxability of fair rental value of church-owned parsonage for social security purposes**

    Treas. Reg. 1.1402(a)-11(a)

    Flowers v. Commissioner,
    T.C.M. 542 (1991)

    Bass v. Commissioner,
    T.C.M. 536 (1983)

Chapter 7, Paying Your Taxes

- **Housing allowance included for earned income credit**

    Treas. Reg. 1.43-2(c)(2)(ii)

    Jones v. Commissioner,
    T.C.M. 358 (1993)

Index

A

Accountable plan, *31, 40-41, 48, 83-85*
Administrative positions, *24-25*
Adoption expenses, *11*
Agency of a religious organization, *2-3, 24-25*
Allocation of business expenses, *99-100, 142*
Allowances, *47-48, 85-86*
Amended returns, *117, 122*
Annuities, tax-sheltered, *31, 46, 61*
Assignment by a church, *25-26*
Automobiles,
    Actual expense method, *91-93*
    Allowances, *47-48, 85-86*
    Church-provided, *93*
    Commuting, *5, 93-94*
    Deductions, *90-95*
    Depreciation, *92-93*
    Documenting expenses, *95*
    Interest Expense, *97*
    Leasing, *93*
    Luxury, *92-93*
    Mileage rate method, *90-91*
    Reporting business expenses, *95*
Awards, *47*

B

Birthday gifts, *53*
Bonuses, *47, 85-86*
Books, *47, 98-99*
Business and professional expenses,
    Accounting for, *83-86*
    Allocation of, *99-100, 142*
    Allowances, *47-48, 85-86*
    Automobile, *90-95*
    Cellular phones, *61, 98*
    Clothing, *48, 96*
    Club dues, *5-6, 50, 53*
    Computers, *48, 98*
    Contributions, *95-96*
    Conventions, *49*
    Depreciation, *92-93*
    Dues and memberships, *50, 53*
    Educational expenses, *6, 50-51, 96*
    Entertainment expenses, *52, 96-97*
    Gifts, *95*
    Interest, auto, *97*
    Moving expenses, *57, 97-98*
    Office-in-the-home, *53-54, 97*
    Personal computers, *48, 98*

Recordkeeping requirements, *86-87*
Reimbursements, *47-48*
Section 179 deductions, *8, 98-99*
Subscriptions and books, *61, 98*
Telephone expenses, *61, 98-99*
Travel expenses, *61-62, 87-90*

C

Cafeteria plans, *52*
Canada Pension Plan, *110*
Cellular telephones, *61, 98-99*
Charitable contributions, *95-96*
Child care, *49-50*
Christmas gifts, *53*
Citations, *158-65*
Clothing, *48, 96*
Club dues, *50*
Commissioned ministers, *21*
Common law rules, *26-30*
Commuting expenses, *93-94*
Compensation,
    Packages, *35-38*
    Reasonable, *34-35*
    Recharacterization, *38-39*
    Worksheet, *36*
Computers, *48, 98*
Continuing education, *50-51, 96*
Contributions as business expenses, *95-96*
Conventions, *49*

D

Debt, *43*
Deferred compensation, *49*
Deferred income limits, *46*
Denominational pension plans, *40, 58*
Denominational service, *24-26*
Dependent care, *49-50*
Depreciation, *4, 92-93*
Disability,
    Insurance, *50*
    Pay, *60*
Discretionary fund, *50*
Discrimination of benefits, *46-47*
Documenting expenses, *86-87*
"Double deduction" of interest and taxes, *16, 77*
Dues and memberships, *50, 53*

E

Earned income tax credit, *5, 15, 114, 143-4*
Educational expenses, *50-51, 96*

INDEX

Educational assistance programs, *8, 51*
Employee vs. self-employed, *1, 31-32*
Entertainment expenses, *52, 96-97*
Equipment write-off, *8, 98-99*
Estimated taxes, *112-14*
Evangelists,
    Housing allowance, *78*
    Qualifications, *21-22*
Exemption from social security tax, *106-9*
Expense allowances, *47-48, 85-86*
Expense reimbursement, *47-48*
Extension of time to file, *114-16, 118, 119*

F

Fair rental value of parsonage, *75-76*
Federal Insurance Contributions Act
    (FICA), *101-2, 114*
First-year write-off of business expense, *98*
Flexible spending arrangements, *52*
Forgiveness of debt, *55-56*
Form 1040X, *117, 122*
Form W-2, *134, 147*
Form 1040, *126-7, 136-37, 149-150*
Form 1040-ES, *112-4, 147*
Form 1099-MISC, *157*
Form 1127, *117, 121*
Form 2106, *87*
Form 2106-EZ, *141*
Form 2210, *115-16*
Form 2350, *115*
Form 2688, *115, 119*
Form 3903, *154*
Form 4361, *106-9*
Form 4868, *115, 118*
Form 9465, *116, 120*
179 expenses, *8, 98-99*
401(k) plans, *8, 52*
403(b) plans, *7, 31, 61*
Frequent flyer awards, *52*
Fringe benefits, *39-40, 47-63*
Furlough travel, *89*
Furnishings,
    Excludable as housing expense, *78-79*
    Fair rental value, *70, 79*
    Included in housing allowance limitation, *69*

G

Gift/personal, *52*
Gift/special occasion, *53*
Greens fees, *59*
Group-term life insurance, *30, 54-55*

H

Health club memberships, *50*
Health insurance, *12, 31, 53*
Health insurance deduction, *9*
Highly compensated employees, *47*
Holy Land trips, *88-89*
Home equity loans, *76*
Home office, *53-54, 97*
Housing allowance,
    Accounting for the allowance, *75-76*
    Advance designation, *71*
    Allowable expenses, *80-82*
    Amending the designation, *72, 73-74*
    Cost to the church, *77*
    Denominational, *74*
    Designating the allowance, *71-73*
    Eligibility, *20-26*
    Evangelists, *21-22, 78*
    Excess, *14*
    Fair rental value, *75-76*
    In general, *54*
    Limits on the designation, *72-73*
    Limits on the exclusion, *69-70, 75-76*
    Multiple ministers of one church, *74*
    Ordained, commissioned, or
        licensed ministers, *21*
    Parsonage owned or rented by
        church, *69-70, 80*
    Parsonage owned or rented by
        minister, *70, 81, 82*
    Payment of, *77*
    Percentage of salary, *74*
    Reporting, *72, 74-75*
    Retired ministers, *77-78*
    Second mortgages, *76*
    Worksheets, *80-82, 132, 145, 155*

I

Income, reporting, *31-32*
Income tax status of ministers, *26-30*
Individual retirement accounts (IRA), *9, 11, 54*
Insurance,
    Disability, *60*
    Health, *31, 53*
    Life, *31, 54-55*
    Long-term care, *56*
    Medical, *31, 53-54*
Integral agencies of a church, *2-3, 24-25*
Interest,
    Auto, *97*

Mortgage, *16, 20, 76, 77*
International travel, *88*
IRA, *54*
Itemized deductions,
    Contributions, *95-96*
    Mortgage interest, *16, 20, 76, 77*
    Real Estate Taxes, *16, 20, 77*

K

Keogh plans, *31, 54*

L

Leased car, *93*
Licensed ministers, *21*
Life insurance, *31, 54-55*
Loan-grants, *55*
Loans to clergy, *55-56*
Long-term care insurance, *10, 56*
Love offerings, *53*
Luxury auto, *92-93*

M

Meals and entertainment, *97*
Meals, church-provided, *56*
Medical insurance, *31, 53-54*
Medical expense reimbursement plan, *11-12, 56*
Medical Savings Accounts, *11*
Memberships, *50*
Mileage rate,
    Business, *4, 90-91*
    Charitable, *4*
    Medical, *4*
Minimal fringe benefits, *57*
Minister,
    Administrative and teaching positions, *24-25*
    Assignment, *25-26*
    Denominational service, *24-26*
    Eligibility for treatment as, *20-26*
    Employee, *31-32*
    Income tax status, *26-30*
    Licensed or commissioned, *21*
    Nonqualifying, *26-27*
    Self-employed, *31-32*
    Serving local churches, *20-21*
    Social security tax status, *27*
Missionary,
    Furlough travel, *89*
    Qualifications, *21-22*
    Social security tax, *61*
Moving expenses, *57, 97-98*

N

Nonaccountable plan, *47-48, 85-86*
Nondiscrimination rules, *46-47*
Nonqualified deferred compensation plans, *49*
Nonqualifying clergy, *26-27*
Nursing home insurance, *56*

O

Office-in-the-home, *53-54, 97*

P

Parking, *58*
Parsonage allowance *(See housing allowance)*
Payroll deductions, *58, 63*
Penalties,
    Failure to pay, *115-16*
Pension plans,
    General, *58*
    Denominational, *40, 58*
Per diem, *89-90*
Percentage housing allowance, *74*
Personal computers, *48, 98*
Personal exemptions, *5*
Personal gifts, *52*
Pre-employment expense reimbursements, *58*
Property,
    Purchased from church, *59*
    Transferred to minister, *59*

R

Rabbi trust, *59*
Rates,
    Income tax, *5*
    Social security, tax, *103*
Real estate taxes, *16, 20, 77*
Reasonable compensation, *34-35*
Recharacterization of income, *38-39, 85-86*
Recordkeeping requirements, *86-87*
Recreational expenses, *59*
Reimbursements,
    General, *47-48*
    Social security, *60-61, 102*
Religious orders, *22-24*
Rental value, *75-76*
Renting home, *70, 82*
Retired ministers' housing allowance, *6, 77-78*
Retirement gifts, *59*
Retirement plans,
    Deferred compensation plans, *49*

INDEX

Denominational plans, *40, 58*
Housing allowances, *77-78*
IRAs, *54*
Keogh plans, *31, 54*
Retirement gifts, *59*
Rabbi trust, *59*
SEPs, *60*
Tax-sheltered annuities, Section 403(b) plans, *31, 46, 61*

S

Salary, *59*
Salary reduction arrangements, *31, 56-57, 61*
Schedule A, *128, 138, 151*
Schedule B, *129*
Schedule C, *152*
Schedule C-EZ, *3, 130, 139*
Schedule EIC, *114, 143*
Schedule SE, *131, 140, 153*
Scholarship fund, *60*
SECA, *101-10*
Second mortgages, *76*
Section 179 deductions, *8, 98-99*
Self-employed vs. employee, *31-32*
Self-employment earnings, *102-5*
Self-employment tax deductions, *105*
Self-funded medical plan, *56*
Seminars, *48-49*
SEPs, *60*
Severance pay, *60*
Sick pay, *60*
SIMPLE plans, *6*
Simplified Employee Pension (SEP) Plans, *60*
Social security,
    Benefits, *3*
    Both spouses are ministers, *103, 105*
    Canada Pension Plan, *110*
    Computation of tax, *102-3*
    Deductions, *105*
    Exemption of ministers, *106-9*
    Form 4361, *106-9*
    Nullifying exemption, *108*
    Opting out of, *106-9*
    Reimbursement, *60-61, 102*
    Second ordination, *108*
    Services in which exemption applies, *20-25*
    Status of ministers, *25-26*
    Tax rates, *103*
    Voluntary withholding agreement, *105-6*

Working after retirement, *109-10*
Special occasion gifts, *53*
Spouse, minister, *103, 105*
Spousal or children travel, *2, 89*
Standard mileage rate,
    Business, *4, 90-91*
Subscriptions, *61, 98*
Substantiation,
    Business and professional expenses, *86-87*

T

Tax withholding, *111-12*
Taxes, real estate, *16, 77*
Tax-sheltered annuities, *7, 31, 46, 61*
Teaching positions, *24-25*
Telephone, *61, 98, 99*
TIAA-CREF, *77*
Tithes, *95-96*
Travel expenses,
    Furlough, *89*
    General, *2, 61-62, 87-88*
    Holy Land, *88-89*
    International, *88*
    Per diem allowance, *89-90*
    Spousal or children, *2, 89*
Trust, rabbi, *59*
Tuition reductions, *62*

U

Underpayment penalty, *115-16*
Unreimbursed business and professional expenses, *83-86*

V

Vacation pay, *62*
Vehicle,
    Nonpersonal, *62-63*
    Personal use of church-owned, *62*
Vestments, *96*
Voluntary withholding, *20, 31, 105-6, 111-12*

W

Wage continuation, *63*
Withholding,
    Exemption of ministers, *20, 111-12*
    In general, *63*
    Social security taxes, *105-6*
    Voluntary, *20, 31, 105-6, 111-12*
Workers' Compensation, *63*

Important Tax Dates for 1997

January 1 — Be sure you have an up-to-date housing allowance resolution in effect.

January 15 — Due date for your final payment of 1996 estimated tax, unless you file your return by January 31.

February 1 — If you file your 1996 income tax return by this date, the deadline for final payment of your 1996 estimated tax is extended to this date. Form W-2 and 1099 information statements are due by today from employers, banks, and brokers.

April 15 — Form 1040 for 1996 income tax and self-employment tax is due with payment of tax. An extension request must be filed today if you need extra time.

IRA and SEP contributions can be made through today for 1996.
The first installment on your 1997 estimated tax is due.

June 15 — Second installment of 1997 estimated tax is due.

August 16 — If you received an automatic 4-month extension of the April 15 deadline, your tax return is due today; or you can file for an additional extension.

September 15 — Time to pay the third installment on your 1997 estimated tax.

October 15 — If you were granted a second extension, your income tax return is due today—final deadline.

Start your year-end tax planning.

December 15 — Attend to year-end transactions so they will be finished in time to report as 1997 transactions.

December 31 — Keogh plans must be established by today for 1997.